The Teenager's Guide to the Real World

The Teenager's Guide to the Real World

Marshall Brain

BYG Publishing, Inc.

The Teenager's Guide to the Real World

by Marshall Brain

Published by:

BYG Publishing, Inc.
P.O. Box 40492
Raleigh, NC 27629 U.S.A.
http://www.bygpub.com
(888) 294-7820

FIRST EDITION

10 9 8 7 6

Publisher's Cataloging-in-Publication Data
(Provided by Quality Books, Inc.)

Brain, Marshall.
      The teenager's guide to the real world / Marshall Brain.
      p. cm.
      Includes bibliographical references and index.
      Preassigned LCCN: 97-93314
      ISBN 0-9657430-3-9
      1.   Teenagers—Life skills guides. I. Title
      HQ796.B73 1997   646.7'00835
                           QBI97-40444

Contents

Preface

I have to start by confessing to you that I was a pretty miserable teenager. I can remember thinking, "What the heck is going on here?" quite a bit. I can remember feeling like an idiot a great deal of the time. I can painfully remember "not fitting in" and how bad that felt. I can remember being totally petrified by girls and dating and everything about it. I can remember knowing that I was doing the "right" thing, while most other people at school were doing the "wrong" thing. Yet they were having a lot more fun, and I was sitting home alone. I can remember feeling like most people hated me. I simply could not understand how the world works.

Let me give you some examples:

- I can remember falling madly in love with a girl in the ninth grade. This was from a distance, of course. There was no way I would ever have the nerve to actually go talk with her, much less tell her how I felt. I was petrified around girls. So when Valentine's Day came around I had an idea. I bought her a nice card, signed it and put it in her locker late one afternoon when the halls were deserted. God, I loved this girl! If only she knew, and if only she felt the same way. The next day between classes I opened my locker and out fell a sheet of paper that said in large emphatic letters, "DO NOT EVER COME NEAR ME OR MY LOCKER AGAIN!!!!" I was devastated.

- I can remember applying for jobs and being rejected. I can remember working in a bike shop for free one summer because I really wanted to have a job and I liked working on my bicycle. And I can remember wondering why the owner was always so uptight. Why was he so worried about money all the time? I just didn't get it. I was working for free and I was doing fine. Why should money be so important to him?

- I can remember thinking that my mother was an absolute idiot. About nearly everything. I simply could not understand why she would not listen to me. I can remember asking her for things and her saying, "No," and finding that incomprehensible. She would not give me money. She would not let me ride my bicycle at night. She would not let me take trips with my friends on weekends. And yet, I can remember asking a girl out, actually going out with her, having it go so badly that all I could do when I got home was curl up in bed in a fetal position while waves of embarrassment and agony washed over me and my mother came and rubbed my back. She didn't say a word. She was just there, and she made me feel like a person again.

- I can remember seeing cliques of people in high school and not understanding what was happening or what they were all about. Why couldn't everyone just like everyone else? Why were some people cool, even though they were doing the worst in school? Why did the football players get all the girls? Why would the pretty girls not talk to me, and why were the nice girls so different when they were in a group?

- I can remember a friend of mine trying to commit suicide. I can remember another friend of mine dying helplessly of leukemia. And I can remember wondering how one could want to die so badly and one could want to live so badly, yet neither of them got what they wanted.

- I can remember being rejected by the college I wanted to go to and how bad that made me feel.

- I can remember that when anyone—especially an adult—complimented me on anything, my response was, "Not really," or, "No, I'm not." For example, if a teacher said, "That was a great report you handed in. You are a good writer," my response would be, "Not really," or, "No, I'm not." It was not until I had published four books that I could first accept that I might be a good writer.

- I can remember how absolutely geeky I felt whenever I had to wear a suit.

- I can remember going to things like weddings, church meetings, adult parties, etc. and listening to the adults talking about things like money, the stock market, taxes, bosses, politics, the news, and so on and thinking, "My God, these people are boring. All they care about is money and gossip. I hope I am never an adult."

- I can remember getting pulled over for wearing Walkman headphones in Maryland. I can remember getting pulled over in a small town in Vermont for going three miles over the speed limit.

And I can remember asking, "Why are the police bugging me while hundreds of people are robbed and murdered every day?"

- I can remember taking classes like economics, psychology, accounting and history and thinking, "When will I ever use this stuff?" I can remember writing papers and doing math problems that I was sure were useless. Over and over and over again for no apparent reason.
- I can remember hating PE, hating my body, hating sports, hating locker rooms.

Perhaps you have felt some of these things yourself.

And yet I was a pretty OK guy. Although I felt like an idiot all during my teen years, I look back now and wonder why I felt that way. As an adult I have been successful. My sister and I, who were sworn enemies as teenagers, have a great relationship now. I am married to a kind and beautiful woman who would have melted me on the spot if I had seen her in high school. I have a loving mother who I now consider one of my best friends. *It turns out that nearly everything I felt as a teenager was wrong.*

Maybe you feel like I felt as a teenager. You don't fit in, people seem to hate you, no one understands you and you feel unhappy and alone much of the time. Yet when you look around everyone else seems happy, they have jobs and they are successful and you are thinking, "They are so happy and I am so miserable—there must be something wrong with me." Let me fill you in on one of the facts of life: The vast majority of people feel like that when they are teenagers. The handsome star quarterback who makes straight As and has all the girls hanging all over him—he *might* be happy. Most everyone else is confused much of the time. Ask almost any adult and they will tell you stories of mistakes and mortification as teens. Then you get older, things actually get better and you become an adult.

If someone had said to me at 16, "You feel horrible now, but in 20 years you will be a happy, normal, successful, married adult," I would have laughed in his face. There was just no way. The reason I would have laughed is because I could see no path from where I stood at 16 to any happy place. The world and everyone in it made no sense most of the time.

I really wish someone had taken the time to sit down with me when I was 16 and tell me how the world works and why all these crazy and incomprehensible things happened to me. Not in the way most adults did, with phrases like, "One day you will understand," "It will get better," or "You are a good person, really!" I needed someone to explain it to me in detail. For example, why do girls hate me? Why do people wear suits? Why are football players popular? Why do I feel so incompetent all the time? Why does the world seem so unfair? What are the rules to the game of life? That last one is a question I thought about a lot as a teenager, although it never would have occurred to me to put it into words. It really would have saved me a lot of time and trouble if there had been something I could have read that had all the rules. Why wasn't there a book that told me all of this stuff so that I could understand?

The book you are now holding is an answer to that question. I have written it to help teenagers in general, but really I am writing it to myself. This is the book that I wish someone had handed me when I was 16 so that I could understand what was going on around me. Think of it as the "Secret Handbook" that all successful adults carry with them. It explains the game of life. It shows you why adults do the things they do. It explains how the world works and how you will become an adult yourself.

The question I have now, and will always have, is this: Would I have listened to this book when I was 16? Could I have understood what it is saying? Would I have started to read Chapter 1, gotten to about the bottom of the second page, and said, "The author of this book is a Total Idiot!" and thrown the book away? I cannot answer that question. But I'd say there is about a 50% chance that might have happened.

I am going to ask you to be smarter than that. Even if you don't like it at first, or if it initially seems to be way off base, read this book from cover to cover. Circle the things that you think are unfair or ridiculous and go ask your parents or an adult friend for another point of view. Talk to your teachers. Talk to your friends. Show people the book and say, "Can you explain this to me?" Try out some of the suggestions. See what happens. After you have read this book once, put it down and return to it again a few months later and see if your opinions change. You might be surprised.

My goal in writing this book is to help you to see how the world works so that you don't feel so mystified, so that you can see that you are OK, so that you can understand what is going on around you, so that you can find your place in the world more quickly, and so that you can be more successful. If I can help you to do that, then I am glad. Drop me a note; I would love to hear from you.

Marshall Brain
c/o BYG Publishing, Inc.
P.O. Box 40492
Raleigh, NC 27629
info@bygpub.com

Acknowledgments

I would like to thank several people who helped me by reading an early copy of this book and providing extremely valuable comments, suggestions and insights: Kevin Webb, Rebecca Laughlin, Hollin Norwood, Jeremy Broughman, Katherine Maxwell, Sandy Brain, Shari Laughlin, Steven Brunsvold and Lloyd Westbrook. Their input dramatically improved this book by showing me other points of view, and I am deeply grateful to them for their time and effort.

I would also like to thank my wife, Leigh Ann, for the hundreds of hours she has put into the production of this book. I am glad we were able to do this together.

Like everyone else, I have a huge crowd of people who have taught me what I know today. These people include my parents, my parents' friends and acquaintances as I was growing up, teachers in school and college, my peers in school, advisors, business associates, neighbors and so on. It would be impossible for me to list them all, but I would be remiss if I did not say thank you to all of them here. I truly appreciate the time, effort and patience they have shown in teaching me the things that make me who I am today.

The Teenager's Guide to the Real World

CHAPTER 0

You Get to Design Your Life

How many times have you heard the question, "What do you want to be when you grow up?" As a teenager you tend to hear this question a lot, but you have probably heard it since you were five years old. It is often connected to questions like, "Where do you want to go to college?" and "What will be your major?" and "What are you good at?"

You may also be asking *yourself* the same questions. You may find that you are sitting around one day minding your own business when the question, "What am I going to do with my life?" flits through your brain. And that is a good thing. You are in a position of incredible power when you ask yourself questions like, "Who am I?" and "Who do I want to become?" You are the only person who can answer these questions. You, and only you, get to choose exactly who you will become in the future.

Think about that for a minute. The power of these questions lies in the fact that *you can choose to become anything you want!* Imagine becoming *anything*. Think about the freedom that gives you. The great thing about being a teenager is that you are a blank slate. You can pick almost any answer to the question, "Who do I want to become?" at this point in your life, and you are in a unique position to make it happen. You can, to a large extent, design your life completely from scratch. You get to make thousands of choices that will determine exactly who you will become as an adult. Choices like these:

- What will I choose for my career?
- How much money will I make, and why?
- Who will I marry?
- How many children will I have?
- How will I dress?
- Where will I live?
- What kind of car will I drive?
- Will I go to college; if so, which one will I attend?

3

- What will be my major in college?
- What will be my attitude toward life?
- What will be my values?
- Will I smoke? Will I take drugs?
- What sports do I want to play?
- And so on.

As you can see, the answers to all of these questions are wide open for any teenager. You could decide today, "By age 25 I will be an architect in Hawaii, and I will drive a red Corvette." And you could make that happen. There is absolutely nothing to stop you. You could decide on just about any course and make it happen in just the same way. At no other point in your life do you have the absolute freedom of choice that you have as a teenager. That is not to say that you cannot change your mind later. You can completely redesign your life from scratch at age 30 or 40 if you

> *You could decide today, "By age 25 I am going to be an architect in Hawaii, and I will drive a red Corvette." And you could make that happen.*

find that to be appropriate. It simply is a fact that as a teenager *all* of these questions are wide open and you get to select the initial answers for all of them from an infinite pool. *That is a lot of freedom.*

The average teenager often faces three significant problems in making all of these choices:

- *Most teenagers never realize that they have total control of their lives.* The questions "Who am I?" and "Who do I want to become?" never quite make it up into the average teenager's conscious mind, so life just sort of bumbles along letting things happen randomly. These teenagers miss a great opportunity because they miss the possibility of becoming *anything they want.* Your range of options is wide open as a teenager. Much of this book is devoted to helping you understand your options and showing you how to make the most of the freedom you have as a teenager.
- *Most teenagers do not understand the realities of the world into which they are about to enter.* American society is an exciting but tough environment. It requires quite a bit of knowledge to become successful in this environment. As a teenager you are fairly naïve about the real world (see Chapter 2). Most teenagers also live in a protected dream land created by their parents (see Chapter 1). That is probably hard for you to imagine, but it is definitely the case. It

is easy for you to make mistakes that can affect you negatively for the rest of your life. Therefore, the first part of this book shows you the fundamental facts of life that you must use as your base of reality. The rest of the book shows you what you need to know to succeed in American society and in life.

- *Most teenagers do not believe in themselves, nor do they believe that there is any way to improve their odds of success.* No matter what path you choose to follow in your life, you have to be confident and believe in yourself to succeed. You also need to learn key facts and techniques that will improve your odds of succeeding. One of the best ways to get started is to simply ask the people around you for their thoughts and ideas. Another is to experiment. Your time as a teenager is a great time for that sort of experimentation.

As a teenager you can explore a whole set of options to learn more about yourself and the world around you. You can pick something you really want to do well and you can go do it right now. You don't have to amorphously think, "Acting might be fun..." Instead say, "I am going to be an actor!" and then pursue it. You can audition for acting parts. You can find some friends and do plays together. You can write and film your own movies (see Chapter 6 for details). One of the great things about being a teenager is that you can pursue many things at once. You can also afford to fail, and you don't have to worry about it if you do. Head in a direction and see what you find there. That is one of the most important messages in this book.

Much of this book discusses concepts and techniques that you can use to become informed, confident and successful more quickly. You can

Why Does Being a Teenager Feel so Weird?

For many teenagers the teen years can be *extremely* uncomfortable. Here's one reason why. Imagine that you are a member of the Star Trek crew and you are beamed onto a alien planet. You do not know the language, the social customs, the "right" way to do things nor any of the side effects of your actions. You would expect a good bit of discomfort, especially if any mistakes you made in this alien culture might have life-long consequences. This is essentially where you are as a teenager. The alien planet is the adult world. You do not know the language, the customs, the right way to do things or the consequences. And even if you do know the "right" thing to do, it may make no sense to you.

One goal of this book is to help you understand the adult world so that you can function successfully in it as quickly as possible.

also use it to make better and more effective choices. The book is divided into seven sections that help you to understand the fundamental facts of life and the world around you. Sections in this book include:

- **Part 1**—The Hard Facts. These are the basic facts of life that you must understand before you can do anything else. Most of these are hard because they will force you to break down fundamental assumptions that you may have about yourself and your world right now. Start with them.
- **Part 2**—Facts About Jobs and Careers. You *will* have a job—that is a fact of life. By planning ahead you can get a job that is both high-paying and enjoyable.
- **Part 3**—Facts About Love and Marriage. You might have noticed that, as a teenager, your brain and body seem to be obsessed with members of the opposite sex. This section explains "the facts of life" and what they mean to you both now and in the future.
- **Part 4**—Facts About Your Attitude and Values. You are in total control of your attitude and your values. You can choose to be happy or sad, optimistic or pessimistic, shy or boisterous, honest or dishonest, or anything in between. The only person who has any control over your attitude and values is you. This section will show you some of the possibilities.
- **Part 5**—Facts About Success. There are a number of things you can do to help yourself become successful. This section explores some of the most important facts of life.
- **Part 6**—Facts About Money. Money is incredibly important in American society. You become homeless if you don't have enough. If you have more than you need, you can afford to do things that enrich your life or the lives of others. Money management can be fairly complicated, however, and it is easy to make mistakes. This section shows you the fundamental facts of money management so you learn the basic vocabulary and concepts.
- **Part 7**—Other Facts of Life. There is a wide variety of other things that will be useful to you as you work your way toward becoming a successful adult. This section lists a number of other important facts of life.

After reading these sections you will understand a great deal more about yourself and the world around you than you do right now. You will be able to explore and think about your choices with a new clarity and understanding. You will be able to plan a path to success. Have fun!

PART 1

The Hard Facts

This section contains the basic facts of life that you must accept and understand before you can move forward. Most of these facts are hard because they will force you to break down fundamental assumptions that you may have about yourself and the world right now. Start here.

CHAPTER 1

Money Really Matters

Have you ever wondered why so many adults spend so much time worrying about money? Why do millions of adults get up every morning and go to work for 8 or 10 hours a day? Why do adults spend so much time discussing taxes and prices and the cost of living? Why are news shows and newspapers so full of economic news? Why do married couples frequently fight about money? To understand adults, you have to understand money. Once you understand money, adults make a lot more sense.

For any normal adult living in America today money ranks right up there next to oxygen. Without money you cannot eat. You have no place to sleep. You cannot drive. You have no freedom. If you don't have money, you are forced to live in a homeless shelter or on the street. If you have ever been to a homeless shelter, you can understand why that is not an appetizing option. *It is this simple reality that causes adults to be so concerned about money.*

Most teenagers do not understand the importance of money. They also do not understand the amount of money that is required to live a normal life. This occurs for a very simple reason—parents provide teenagers with everything. Teenagers, therefore, live in a dream world. *The moment you exit this dream world and have to live life yourself, your opinions about money will change dramatically.* What I would like to do in this chapter is show you how much money it takes to live a normal life in America. Once you understand that, adults and everything about them begin to make a lot more sense.

Let's say that you were to get totally fed up with your parents. In a fit of passion you decide at age 16 to run away from home. You hop a freight train and you end up in Raleigh, North Carolina to begin your new life. Your goal is to live a normal life—not an extravagant life, just a normal life.

9

Note: All of the prices listed in this chapter are actual 1997 prices for Raleigh, NC. If you live in a larger city things will cost more. If you are reading this book and it happens to be 1999, you will find that the minimum wage is probably higher, but all the prices will have gone up proportionally. It all evens out, so these examples are just as valid.

So, you are standing on a street corner in Raleigh, NC. What is your first step? First, you need an apartment. You stop by a local convenience store and find a copy of the apartment locator magazine. Every major city in America has apartment locator magazines, and you can find racks of them at grocery stores, convenience stores and so on. Pick one up some time. What you quickly find is that any "nice" apartment costs about $600 for a one-bedroom unit. A "nice" apartment has a pool, probably a club house, well-kept buildings, nice landscaping and so on.

You realize that $600 a month is impossible. Where are you going to get $600 every month as a runaway? So you get a copy of the paper to look in the classified ads. What you find is that the cheapest apartment available is a "student" unit near the university. You go to take a look. It is really just half of the upstairs of an old house. It is a dump. No air conditioning, for example. Peeling paint. The carpeting is dirty and worn down. The toilet won't flush, but the man showing you the apartment says he will fix that. You can see all the pipes and they are all rusty. It is $350 a month. You also have to put down the last month's rent and a security deposit of $300. Just to move in you need $1,000. Then you need $350 per month, every month.

Now you need power for the apartment. You call the power company. They want $17 to turn on the power. Since you have no credit history, they also want a $200 security deposit. You ask the landlord for an estimate, and he says that the power bill will run about $250 per month in the winter because the apartment is heated with electric baseboard heaters, but it drops to $40 per month in the summer. The average is about $150 a month.

You would also like to have a phone and cable TV. Cable is $50 a month and $70 to install it. The phone is $40 to install, $100 for a deposit and about $25 per month if you make no long distance calls.

Now you need some furniture for the apartment. You need a sofa, a chair, a living room table, a shelf, a TV, a table for the TV, a kitchen table and chairs, pots and pans, silverware, plates, utensils, a bed, a dresser, a night stand, several lamps, several phones and so on. Forget luxuries like a stereo, computer, VCR, Nintendo, etc. You have no money for those. You also need sheets, towels and blankets. If you were going to go out and buy nice stuff, and buy it all new, this would all cost thousands of dollars. You look in the classified ads and manage to find used stuff that is pretty beat up but serviceable and it all costs about $1,000. You end up renting a truck to pick it all up; that costs $100 for two days. The sheets, towels and blankets you get cheap at K-Mart for $70. You also spend $100 on paper towels, toilet paper, cleaning supplies, soap, toothpaste, shampoo, toothbrush, garbage bags, aluminum foil and so on. All of this is "stuff," but it is kind of hard to make it past the first day without toilet paper.

Now you need a car. The average price for a new car in America is over $20,000 in 1997, and the cheapest new car you can buy is about $8,000, so that's out. You start looking for a used one.

Running Away from Home

When teenagers decide to "run away from home" they aren't thinking about the financial implications of what they are doing. They just want *out*. They aren't thinking, "Let's see, to live a minimal American life the cost of entry is $5,000, so I need to raise that money prior to departure and then..." Instead they take off, end up in a city, and immediately are destitute. They have no money, no food, and no place to stay. There is no way to get a job and no other way to make money. Someone eventually suggests or forces drugs or prostitution. And there it is.

You know what you want—a hot, red, two-seat sports car.

Unfortunately, you find that there are two kinds of used cars: nice ones and junkers. You can't afford the nice ones. The junkers look like crap and feel like they are going to fall apart any minute. You keep hunting until you find a 1986 Plymouth Horizon. It looks like hell because all the paint is peeling off and the seats are torn, but it seems to run well and the guy only wants $800. To buy it you need to transfer the title and get a license plate. The Department of Motor Vehicles wants $35 for the title, $25 for the plate, $24 in taxes and $2 to notarize everything. However, they won't give you the plate because you must have insurance and the car needs to be inspected. The inspection costs $25. The inspection station tells you that you must buy new tires, and they end up costing $250. The first insurance agent you call won't even talk to you because you are under 20. Neither will the second. Neither will the third. You eventually find an agent who will get you insurance, but it costs $1,800 per year. You have to pay the first $900 up front to activate the insurance.

Now you have a place to stay and a car. Certainly this is not a luxury situation. You are living in a dump with beat up furniture and a junky car. But you now have the essentials. So far it has cost you this much to get situated:

Apartment deposits	$ 1,000.00
Power installation	$ 217.00
Cable installation	$ 70.00
Phone installation	$ 140.00
Furniture	$ 1,000.00
Truck	$ 100.00
Supplies	$ 100.00
Linens	$ 70.00
Car	$ 800.00
Car fees	$ 96.00
Tires	$ 250.00
Inspection	$ 25.00
First insurance bill	$ 900.00
Total start-up costs	**$ 4,768.00**

When you ran away from home, you probably didn't happen to stick nearly $5,000 in your pocket. Where would you get that kind of money to begin with? What this shows you is the "cost of entry" into an American lifestyle is high. Very high. Keep in mind that the example presented here is the absolute bottom of the barrel. It gets no cheaper than this and it gets significantly more expensive for anything nicer.

Now that you are on your own you have monthly expenses. Some we talked about above. Several we have not discussed yet, like food, gasoline, car repairs, clothes, property taxes, etc. They are summarized below:

Rent	$ 350.00
Car insurance	$ 150.00
Car maintenance, average	$ 100.00
Power, average	$ 150.00
Cable	$ 50.00
Phone	$ 25.00
Food	$ 100.00
Clothing	$ 100.00
Health insurance	$ 200.00
Random	$ 75.00
Total Monthly Expenses	**$ 1,300.00**

The car maintenance category includes gasoline and regular maintenance like oil changes, new tires, repairs, etc. The random category handles all the random unexpected things that crop up without warning. Property taxes are a good example. Parking tickets. Drivers license renewal. Money you lose. Things like that.

Note that this monthly budget includes no luxuries or entertainment: no dinners out, movies, dates, videos, CDs, tapes, books, magazines, trips, vacations, air conditioning, cell phones, beer, cigarettes and so on. If you smoke, that simple fact alone can add up to $100 a month to your monthly expenses. Beer could add $50. Note again that this is a bottom of the barrel existence. You can double this number if you want to live in a nice place, drive a nice car, have some normal luxuries and so on.

At the same time you were forgetting to grab $5,000 as you walked out your parents' door, you probably also forgot to grab the $1,300 you need for this month. Or the $1,300 you need for next month. Or...

Therefore, you need a job.

So far we have ignored the income side of all of this. You should keep in mind that none of the above could have happened if you did not have a job first. You could not get an apartment without a job. Or a phone. Or power. Or car insurance. You must have the job first. Every single place you go to will ask for your job history and credit references. You have none. We have ignored that fact for the sake of the example. What you know is that you need $5,000 to get started and $1,300 per month to live your life.

Since you dropped out of high school to run away, you don't have a high school diploma. Therefore, the only place you can get a job is at a fast food place. It pays $5.00 an hour. You do some quick math. If you work 10 hours a day, 6 days a week, you can make $300 a week. Of course, no place will let you work more than 40 hours a week because of overtime restrictions. So you work at one restaurant 40 hours per week and another restaurant 20 hours per week. That earns you just about exactly $1,300 a month in a 31-day month. Just enough to squeeze by.

Who wants to work 10 hours a day, 6 days a week scrubbing toilets and flipping burgers? The problem is, what choice do you have? If you want to live in this trashy apartment, you have to make money. If you want to drive this trashy car, you have to make money. If you want to eat, you have to make money. *You have no choice.* With this job you can at least break even on monthly expenses. Maybe once you get situated for a month or two you can figure something else out.

Unfortunately, you have miscalculated. You have forgotten about taxes. When you get your first pay check you are stunned to find that the federal government has erased 15% of your check. The state of North Carolina has taken another 7%. The social security administration and Medicare has lifted 7.5%. Your monthly income actually looks like this:

Monthly pay	$ 1,300.00
Federal income tax (15%)	$ (195.00)
State income tax (7%)	$ (91.00)
Social Security (7.5%)	$ (97.50)
Monthly take-home pay	$ 916.50

You are nowhere close to breaking even. So what are you going to cut? Medical insurance is probably the first thing to go, but that is extremely, incredibly risky. Even the simplest illness can cost several hundred dollars by the time you cover the office visit to the doctor and the cost of prescription drugs; if you get in a car wreck you will be in debt for life. Now you have to cut another $200. So you cut cable. What else, exactly, are you going to cut? Food? Phone? Clothes? You can't move to a cheaper apartment. You can't get a cheaper car. You are already at the bottom.

So, you are working 10 hours a day, 6 days a week. You live in a dump with junky furniture and a trashy car. You have no health insurance, no cable TV, no phone, no clothes, and you are eating what you can at work and going hungry on Sunday.

Now what?

Are you starting to get the picture? This, by the way, is the definition of poverty. When you hear about "Americans living in poverty," this is what they are talking about: this sort of crappy, 60-hours a week, no way out, can't make ends meet sort of existence. You are scraping by at the absolute bottom on the barrel, and if anything goes wrong you are dead. If your car blows its engine, or you get a speeding ticket and your insurance goes up, or you get sick one week, or…you are out on the street. There is absolutely no slack in your budget. Once you are out on the street, it will cost you another $4,000 or $5,000 to get back on your feet again. So you are permanently stuck.

If you have taken the time to read through all of this and really think about it, you have discovered five things:

- You must do something with your life so you can make more than minimum wage. It is *impossible* to survive on minimum wage. When you hear adults constantly talking about a "good job" so they sound like a broken record, that's why. It takes about $20,000 a year just to get by in this country (1997).
- You don't mind making minimum wage when you are a teenager living with your parents because it is gravy. Your parents are paying the rent, buying food, covering all the bills, giving you clothes and loaning you a car. You should now see that minimum wage won't cut it when you are out on your own.

- You really need your family to help you get started in "real life." How else can you handle that $5,000 start-up fee? There is no way to start a household for any less than $5,000. Your parents can help you with expenses, loan you furniture, and so on.
- If you were to actually find yourself in this position, it would be difficult to get out of it. When you are working 10 hours a day, 6 days a week, there isn't a lot of time for anything else. The only way to get a better job is to get more education. But when, exactly, are you going to get it?
- A person in this position has no freedom. You are absolutely stuck in that rut and there is no way out. You get up every day and go to work, then you come home dead tired and feel like you are trapped in a prison cell. Money is freedom.

Right now you might be thinking, "There are lots of jobs out there that pay a lot more than minimum wage. I'll get one of those jobs. It's easy." Keep this in mind: Median income for the U.S. in 1997 is $23,000. That means half of the jobs in this country pay less than that. All of the jobs paying better than that are being fought for by all the people in America who give a damn. You aren't just going to walk into an office one day and be handed an easy $30,000 a year job. There are 100 other people in line trying to get that job just like you. They would love to have that job.

From the above discussion you should be able to see a fact of life that is important:

IF YOU DON'T PAY THE RENT, YOU ARE HOMELESS

It turns out that this is the central reality from which adults derive all their decisions. Almost everything else adults do makes sense once you realize, understand and appreciate this fact of life. Right now you are oblivious to this fact of life because by living with your parents you are living in a dream world. Once you leave this dream world and start living on your own, you will be acutely aware of this particular fact of life.

Given that central reality, you can quickly derive a second fact of life:

YOU MUST HAVE A JOB TO PAY THE RENT

No matter what you do, you need a place to live and you have to eat. Therefore, you must have a job. You have two choices when you look for jobs: good ones and all the rest. The time to start preparing yourself for a good job is during your time as a teenager when you can control things like finishing high school, going to college and so on.

Given the discussion we've just finished in this chapter, here is a third fact of life:

WORKING 60 HOURS A WEEK IN A DEAD-END, MINIMUM WAGE JOB TO LIVE IN A CRAPPY APARTMENT WITH NO A/C REALLY STINKS

It may not stink the first month because you are happy to be "out on your own." However, it will begin to stink by the second month. By the third month it will REALLY STINK. There will come a day when your crappy car breaks down on a hot, hot summer afternoon. It will be about 110 degrees and 100% humidity. Since your car has no A/C, you will be hot and pissed and sweating like a pig. You will need a quarter for a phone call and you won't have one. You will walk over to a guy in a parking lot who is sitting in his $40,000 Jeep Grand Cherokee. He will roll down his power window and out will come this breeze of delicious, cool, dry air and he will ask, "How can I help you?" He will be totally confident and happy to help you. And you will say pathetically, "My car broke down, but I don't have a quarter for the phone. Do you have a quarter?" And he will say, "Here, use my cell phone." You will call a tow truck that you cannot possibly afford. As you walk away the question will flit through your head for the 600th time, "What the heck am I doing wrong?"

Which leads to a key fact of life for every teenager:

EVEN IF YOU DON'T CARE ONE BIT ABOUT ADULTS AND JOBS AND SCHOOL RIGHT NOW, YOU WILL ONCE YOU HAVE TO PAY THE RENT

You might not care about jobs and money now, but that is only because you don't have to. You are able to sponge off your parents as a teenager, so you don't have a care in the world. A few minutes after leaving your parents' house to start out on your own you will care about a job. You will care how much you make. You will care how much rent costs. You will suddenly care very deeply, because you will have no choice. That is a fact of life. If you are looking through magazines as a teenager thinking, "Wow, when I'm older I am going to drive a Corvette and live in a great big house," you need to start planning your life today. It turns out it is not as easy as you think. If it was, you would have a Corvette now.

Now let's look at your parents. What is motivating them? They are faced with these same money concerns every day. The difference is that if they mess up it's not one person who ends up on the street; it's the whole family. Even if you live in what appears to be an extremely safe, suburban neighborhood, you might be surprised at how precarious things might be under the covers. It really depends on how good your parents are at managing their money.

Let's say that your father has an extremely good engineering job. He is making $60,000 a year. His job covers his health insurance and gives him two weeks of paid vacation per year. You live in a nice, four-bedroom suburban home. You have two cars: your mother drives a nice, two-year-old mini-van and your father drives a 1978 Dodge Dart that you despise. You have a brother (also a teenager) and a sister (10 years old). Your mother stays at home.

Let's look at a likely monthly budget for the household. Let's say that the

> *If you are thinking, "Wow, when I'm older I am going to drive a Corvette and live in a great big house," you need to start planning your life today. It turns out it is not as easy as you think. If it was, you would have a Corvette now.*

house cost $140,000 when your parents purchased it 5 years ago. They paid $10,000 down and locked in a fixed rate 30-year mortgage at 8.5%. That means the monthly mortgage payment on it is about $1,000 per month. They pay about $40 per month for homeowners insurance and about $100 per month in property taxes. The house also needs to be maintained at a rate of perhaps $50 per month. This covers things like a new furnace, water damage, roof repair, repainting, recarpeting, new appliances and so on. On the car side the monthly payment on the mini-van is about $400. Car insurance is about $100 per month. Car maintenance, gas, etc. on the two cars is about $200 per month. Food is running about $300 per month. Power/water/sewer/gas is about $200 on average per month. The phone plus long distance is running $80 per month. Cable is $50.

Your parents also have other goals. If they are smart, they are saving between $6,000 and $9,000 per year for retirement. They are also putting something aside to cover future college costs. They also have some kind of life and disability insurance. Plus... Let's look at the numbers:

INCOME		
Gross annual income	$	60,000.00
Retirement witholding	$	(6,000.00)
Taxable income	$	**54,000.00**
Federal tax (28% of $40K)	$	(11,200.00)
State tax (7%)	$	(3,780.00)
Social Security (7.5%)	$	(4,050.00)
Net Annual income	$	**34,970.00**
Net Monthly income	$	**2,914.17**
MONHLY EXPENSES		
Mortgage	$	1,000.00
Homeowners ins.	$	40.00
Property taxes	$	100.00
House Maintenance	$	50.00
Car Payment	$	400.00
Car Insurance	$	100.00
Car Maintenance	$	200.00
Food	$	300.00
Utilities	$	200.00
Phone	$	80.00
Cable	$	50.00
Clothing	$	100.00
College fund	$	200.00
Total Monthly Expenses	$	**2,820.00**

You can learn a tremendous amount from this worksheet. For example, even though your father has an exceptionally good job at $60,000 per year, barely half of it ($35,000) actually makes it home. You can see that taxes take a gigantic bite out of his paycheck. That is why your parents may often rant about taxes and politicians, by the way. Anytime you have someone taking $20,000 a year out of your pocket you are going to complain.

Your parents do not have an extravagant lifestyle. They live in a respectable but certainly not elaborate home in an inexpensive part of the country (the house would cost twice as much in California, for example). They have two cars, but neither is a show-stopper. They have no luxury items like a boat or an RV or a $10,000 home theater system or a cell phone. And yet, monthly expenses almost exactly match monthly income. What this budget does not include are things like Christmas, birthdays, family vacations, dining out, movies, newspapers and magazines, ballet lessons for little Suzy, soccer equipment, school pictures, yearbooks and on and on and on. You can see exactly why your father drives a 1978 Dodge Dart. What choice does he have? Sure, he'd like a fancy car, but it's impossible. You can also see why your parents are fairly tight when you ask for anything. Where, exactly, is the money going to come from? If you want a $100 pair of sneakers, that blows the clothing budget for the month. If anything goes wrong it is a big problem. If a major expense pops up unexpectedly (for example, braces or eyeglasses for one of the kids), then your parents have to borrow the money for it, and they are going to have to cut back somewhere else to pay back the loan. The most likely thing they will cut is the retirement withholding. This explains why an extremely large percentage of adults in America (more than half) have inadequate retirement plans. The next thing they will cut is the college fund.

Why is your mother working or thinking about getting a job? To earn some extra money to cover things like Christmas and birthdays and family vacations. Why does your father sometimes complain about work

Adults and Financial Privacy

For all adults the topics of money, salary, home prices, etc. are fairly sensitive topics. That is a fact of life. No adult goes around saying, "Yeah, I pull in $60,000 a year." The fact that you have been alive 16 or 18 years and have no clue what your parents make, how much your house is worth, etc. tells you how sensitive this information is. You might be able to go to your parents and have an honest, open conversation about these topics. If so, that is great. But if not, it is not unexpected. Also, if you do have an open conversation with your parents about money, *it should be understood that the information is highly confidential.*

"Why," you might ask, "is this information so sensitive?" For most people, it occurs because they perceive salary to be a measure of their worth. Is that a good thing? Who knows? It is simply a fact and it is true, at least in the business sense. If you have two people in a business and their salaries are different, then one is more valuable to the business than the other for whatever reason. In any company salary rates are incredibly competitive. Therefore, for an adult to say to another adult, "I make $40,000 a year" gives the other adult an incredible amount of information. Understand and respect this sensitivity—you will likely feel exactly the same once you have a job.

but still go in every day? Because if he doesn't the whole family is in a very bad place. Note that there is no line item in the budget for "emergency savings." If your father loses his job, it is going to cause a tremendous amount of difficulty and there will not be a lot of good options.

Remember that at one point in their lives your parents were teenagers. They had all of the dreams you have now—nice cars, fancy trips, expensive stereos and so on. They wanted it all, just like you. All of it has been put aside so that the family budget will balance. Whenever you ask for an expensive Christmas gift and get it, that is a gift that your parents cannot give to themselves.

It is when you begin to realize the level of sacrifice your parents made to raise you and the amount of financial juggling they did to give you what you wanted that you begin to truly respect and appreciate them. That process starts perhaps at age 20 or 25, but doesn't really hit you until you are into your 30s and raising your own family. It is not

---

"The seven deadly sins. . . . Food, clothing, firing, rent, taxes, respectability and children. Nothing can lift those seven millstones from Man's neck but money; and the spirit cannot soar until the millstones are lifted."   - George Bernard Shaw

---

something you, nor your peers, ever realize or appreciate as a teenager.

The title of this chapter is "Money Really Matters." Hopefully, the examples in this chapter help you to understand why money is so important. Most teenagers live in a protected dream world that totally isolates them from the realities of financial life, and that isolation can make it extremely hard to understand why adults are so preoccupied with money, taxes, their jobs, etc. The sooner you realize how important finances and jobs are to your future well-being, the sooner you can begin planning and preparing for your own financial independence.

Please do not get the impression that money is the only thing there is to life (in particular, see Chapter 41). However, it is a fact that without money you starve. Chapter 0 talks about *designing your life*. After you design it you will want to *build* your life, and you cannot build without money. That is what makes money important to you. You get a good job (see Part 2) so that you have the freedom to do the things you enjoy.

CHAPTER 2

Teenagers Lack Experience

Y ou may have noticed that quite a bit of the information in the last chapter is new to you. For example, did you know that it will cost you about $5,000 (1997) to get your first apartment? Did you know that the power and phone companies require first-time customers to pay a security deposit? Did you know that taxes are so high? What about car insurance? Did you understand your parents' cash flow situation? Probably not. The reason you did not is simple: teenagers lack experience. Teenagers have not been out in the real world and experienced life as independent people. Teenagers dwell in a funny, intermediate state between child and adult. You might have heard the phrase, "Teenagers are naïve." It means about the same thing.

You may find it hard to believe that teenagers are naïve. In fact, you may think I am an idiot for saying it. So why do I say it, and why is it one of the key facts of life? Here is something to ponder that will help you to understand: No one can teach himself or herself to read. Think about that for a minute. If you were stranded on a desert island and if you didn't know how to read, could you teach yourself to read if a whole box of books washed up on shore? No. Once you understand what that says, apply it to your lack of experience. It is only in recognizing your naïve nature and understanding what "lack of experience" means that you can go about fixing the problem. You cannot start to become "worldly" and "informed" until you understand your naïveté. Then you can start to learn your way out of it by asking questions, reading books and carefully observing the world around you. It is the act of recognizing that you lack experience that lets you correct the problem and become an adult. The sooner you come to that realization, the more successful you can be.

Why might you find it hard to believe that you might be naïve? It is because there is a component inside your head right now that I am going to call the "Teenage Illusion Module" (TIM). I am making the TIM up for the sake of this discussion, but if you think about your brain in this

21

way it will help you to understand something about where you are right now. The Teenage Illusion Module is designed to send signals into your head telling you that you are the smartest person in the world, that you know everything and that all of the adults around you are idiots. This module forms during puberty, grows to some maximum size and then collapses in most people by the age of 23. When I was a teenager my TIM consumed approximately half of my head.

Mark Twain had an interesting saying about the Teenage Illusion Module: "When I was a boy of fourteen, my father was so ignorant I could hardly stand to have the old man around. But when I got to be twenty-one, I was astonished at how much the old man had learned in seven years." Of course Twain's father had not changed at all—it was Twain himself who changed. Twain's father became smart about the time Twain's TIM collapsed. Twain simply could not see how smart his parent was until then. That problem afflicts all teenagers. As soon as you realize, for whatever reason, that you don't have all of the answers but that many of the adults standing all around you actually do, you begin to become an adult. The sooner that transformation occurs, the better (see Chapter 3).

> *"When I was a boy of fourteen, my father was so ignorant I could hardly stand to have the old man around. But when I got to be twenty-one, I was astonished at how much the old man had learned in seven years."*
>
> *- Mark Twain*

My mother had a good friend when I was a teenager who, each time she visited, would ask me, "Are you still in the tunnel?" That question always seemed really stupid to me, and as a teenager I had no idea what she meant. The "tunnel," it turns out, is a condition caused by the TIM, and I could not see it until my TIM collapsed. Now I know exactly what she was talking about. She was talking about the tunnel vision that afflicts all teenagers because of their TIMs. As a teenager it would have been a really good idea to have asked her, "What do you mean when you say that?" rather than thinking she was an idiot.

Why does the Teenage Illusion Module form? It has to do with the evolution of our species. Think about a young bird. It lives in a nice nest. It is warm. It plays with its brothers and sisters all day without a care or concern. Its parents bring it food constantly. Why in the world would a young bird ever want to leave this pleasant place? There is no reason. In fact, it would be silly to leave a cushy situation like this. But say, about the time in life when it is physically able to leave the nest, this thing forms in a young bird's brain that generates messages like, "Your parents are idiots! You can find better food than this! You could build a much better nest than this one! And their feathers are so boring! You have much cooler feathers! It's time to get out of here!" The teenager bird hears these messages inside its head all day long, day after day. Eventually it gets so disgusted with its parents that it flies away and creates its own nest.

That is approximately what is happening inside your own head and in your own life. Evolution has wired in this Teenage Illusion Module to encourage you to leave the nest. It is a release mechanism. The problem is, we live in modern technological society and you are not a bird. In human society you cannot simply go out and pluck worms from the lawn. People succeed in this society because they are smart and because they know other smart people. That is a fact of life (see Chapter 28). Your TIM actually is doing you a tremendous disservice in this day and age because it turns out that adults hold a gigantic amount of knowledge that would be extremely useful to you. They will give you this knowledge gladly. All you have to do is ask. Your TIM, unfortunately, is telling you to ignore this wealth of information.

The size of the Teenage Illusion Module varies from teenager to teenager. I know a number of teenagers who are blessed with a properly-sized TIM. "Properly-sized" means that the TIM is large enough to encourage independence but small enough to discourage rebellion. Teenagers with a properly-sized TIM can become very successful very quickly. Things are much easier for them. It is possible to have too small a TIM. In that case the teenager never gets up enough energy and courage to leave home. Others have very large TIMs. As I said, mine was huge. Some unfortunate people have TIMs that persist through old age, never collapsing and never allowing them to see the world around them clearly.

Let's say that you are convinced that your parents, your brothers and sisters, your teachers and most of the people around you are idiots. Let's say that you believe that you are the smartest person in the universe and have all of the answers to all of the world's problems if anyone would take the time to listen. Or let's say that you are less opinionated than that and simply find it difficult to imagine that you might be naïve. That is your TIM talking. Let me try 10 questions to see if I can get you to look at yourself in a slightly different way:

- Do you have a job? *Maybe.*
- Do you have a job that would allow you to support yourself independently if your family disappeared tomorrow? Something on the order of perhaps $20,000 per year (in 1997)? *Almost certainly not.*

- If you answered the previous question with, "You don't need $20,000 a year to support yourself," then do you know what it actually costs to live a normal life in American society? *Probably not. See Chapter 1.*
- Do you have a car? *Maybe.*
- Did you pay for it? Is it registered in your name? *Probably not.*
- If your car blew its engine tomorrow and you had to spend $1,500 repairing it, could you afford to buy the new engine yourself with money you have in the bank? *Doubtful. What if the next day your car blew its transmission as well?*
- Do you own a house? *No.*
- Could you buy a house? *No, unless you happen to have $100,000 or more in your name in a bank account somewhere.*
- Could you get a loan to buy a house? *No. Absolutely not. It will probably be 5 to 10 years before you can even consider it. See Chapter 32.*
- Do you know how much medical insurance costs per year? Could you afford to pay it? Do you even see a reason to have it? *Probably not. See Chapter 1.*

Right now your answer to most of these questions is "No." When you answer "Yes" to all 10 of them you are well on your way to knowing something about how the world works. Prior to that you are naïve. Here is a funny observation: Your parents can answer "Yes" to all of these questions, yet you think they are idiots. Here is another observation: *The fact that you can answer "No" to seven or eight of these questions and still feel like you have all the answers tells you that your Teenage Illusion Module is functioning properly.* If you can hear yourself saying, "Those Questions Don't Matter!", then your TIM is exceptionally well developed.

Let's try another approach. Find someone who has an infant. Sit and watch the infant for five minutes. Notice an important fact about that infant: the infant is totally helpless. You can see that. Everyone can see that. An infant knows how to do perhaps four things: suckle, sleep, smile and cry. You and I can agree that infants are helpless. An infant is also as ignorant as a person gets. Infants have no knowledge but that which is built in.

Now let's say that every person learns things continuously, all through life, at the same rate. So if you are 6 years old you are learning a certain number of things per day, and if you are 60 you are learning at that same rate. You simply change the things you learn as you mature. Now take a look at the following graph:

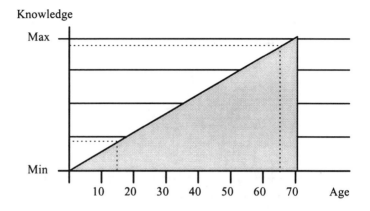

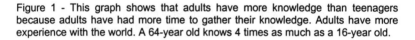

Figure 1 - This graph shows that adults have more knowledge than teenagers because adults have had more time to gather their knowledge. Adults have more experience with the world. A 64-year old knows 4 times as much as a 16-year old.

What this graph shows you is that, in the grand scheme of things, you know very little. On this graph an infant knows nothing. As a teenager you know not a whole lot more. If you are 16, you know half of what a 32-year-old person knows. You know one third of what a 48-year old knows. And so on. As you go through life your intelligence and knowledge grow continuously as you experience the world. You are on the low end of the curve at the moment.

Here is another way to think about it. When you are 16 and you talk to an 8-year old, you can see quite obviously that the 8-year old is naïve. An 8-year-old kid knows nothing about love, about life, about algebra, about money. Eight-year-old kids know about cookies and candy and toys. They know nothing. It is obvious. *When people who are 32 look at you at 16, they are thinking exactly the same thing.* A 16-year old knows nothing about careers, the job market, housing, credit ratings, child rearing, long-term relationships and so on. In the grand scheme of things, a 16-year old knows nothing. That's a fact of life.

Go back and look at your infant again. Another thing you will notice is that infants are outrageously self-centered. There is not a single cell in their brains wired for empathy, generosity or compassion. When an infant is hungry, it screams. When it is sleepy, it screams. When it is uncomfortable, it screams. If it doesn't like the person who is holding it, it screams. Very self-centered. As you go through life your self-centeredness decreases, but teenagers are still remarkably self-centered. The graph below shows a typical curve:

Self-centeredness

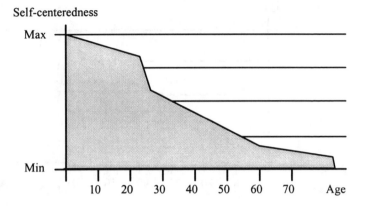

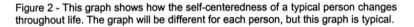

Figure 2 - This graph shows how the self-centeredness of a typical person changes throughout life. The graph will be different for each person, but this graph is typical.

The self-centeredness curve varies from person to person and also between males and females, so this curve is hypothetical. The steep drop in the middle of the graph shows the point at which a person has his or her first child. Most people become far less self-centered at that point because the act of becoming a parent changes a number of priorities in your life. In general most people become more giving, more generous, more concerned about others and more empathetic throughout their lives as they fall in love with their spouses, have and love their children, work with other people closely and so on. Look at all of the sacrifices parents make for their children and you can understand this phenomena (see Chapter 1 for details). From this graph you can see that as a teenager you are still very high on the self-centeredness curve.

Let's look at one last graph having to do with interest in sex. Many teenagers have a raging interest in sex, people of the opposite sex, dating, kissing and so on. I am sure you would agree. The spike occurs right around puberty. Prior to puberty you had absolutely no interest in sex. You can probably remember, as a child, watching any couple kissing and thinking, "YUCK! I will NEVER do that!" And yet here you are as a teenager and you probably find you can think of nothing else. The reason for that transformation is that, at puberty, your body began producing sex hormones. *Hormones* is a good word to go look up in the encyclopedia. You will be amazed—perhaps startled—at how the whole endocrine system works. These hormones cause fundamental changes in your mind and body. As you go through life the concentration and the effects of those hormones decrease. Adults understand this curve, have been through it themselves and know exactly what you have on your mind.

Interest in sex

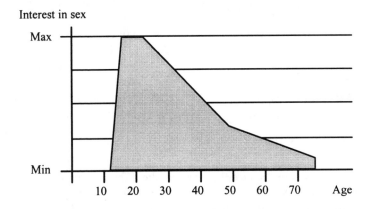

Figure 3 - This graph shows how sexual interest changes throughout life. The graph will be different for different people and also changes between men and women, but this one gives you the idea,

The point of these graphs is not to make you feel bad or to put you down. The point is to show you that people change throughout their lives. You are at one point in your life now. You are a teenager. You are just getting started. You have this unfortunate TIM in your brain. Fifteen years from now you will be at another point. You will be twice as smart, half as self-centered and half as interested in sex. A lot of other things will change as well. These changes cause adults to see the world in a much different way, and it causes them to act differently.

You may wonder why adults tend to treat you like you are naïve. You may wonder why no one listens to you. You may wonder why when you say something that you think is crystal clear to everyone, an adult will often say, "You don't know anything. You are just a kid. One day you will understand." There are two reasons for this phenomena, both derived from the previous examples:

- First, it is generally the case that teenagers do not know a lot about the real world. Teenagers lack experience. The knowledge curve shows that.
- Second, all adults have at one time been teenagers and they understand what that means. They know what you are thinking, what you are feeling, what is important to you and why it is important. They have seen their own TIMs collapse. All adults look at you and know pretty well where you stand.

So, there it is. I am telling you that you are naïve right now. You are going to do one of two things at this point. You will either cast this book aside because it is obviously written by an idiot. If you do that, please do

> *You will learn the facts of life one way or another. It's just that the earlier you learn them the faster you can take advantage of them and the more successful you will be as a result.*

me a favor: Come back and read it in about 10 years. You will be amazed.

The other alternative is to read this book and see what you can discover about your situation. Hopefully, the above examples helped you to understand a little bit about your current position. Maybe you can learn something by reading this book. Maybe, by learning about the immutable facts of life, you can work with the system instead of always butting your head up against it. You might be much happier and more successful as a result.

The goal of this book is to show you how the world works so that you can begin to take advantage of it. This book shows you the facts of life. You will learn these facts of life one way or another. It's just that the earlier you learn them, the faster you can take advantage of them and the more successful you will be as a result. If you can shut your TIM off while you are reading this book and let a few of these ideas seep in, you might be amazed by what you will learn.

CHAPTER 3

Adults Rule the World

Adults rule the world. That is a fact of life. I can clearly remember as a teenager being quite mystified about that fact. Why aren't teenagers ruling the world? Here is a simple population graph that shows you why adults rule the world. It is taken from data in the *1995 World Almanac*:

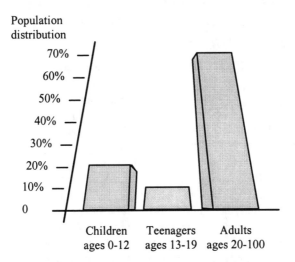

Figure 4 - The population distribution in the U.S. by age.

From this graph you can see that there are twice as many children as there are teenagers. There are seven times as many adults as there are teenagers. In other words, if a UFO flew over the earth tomorrow and beamed up all of the teenagers, the world would hardly notice. In the grand scheme of things, teenagers are insignificant.

Is that true? You might find yourself thinking, "That's not true! There are twice as many teenagers as there are adults!" The above graph is true. So why do you and most other teenagers feel that teenagers outnumber adults? It's because the world you live in creates a strange illusion for you. During most of your life you have lived in a school environment that concentrates children and teens together. Right now you spend a majority of your life in a classroom where there are 20 or 30 teenagers and 1 adult. The family structure supports the illusion as well. In your own family there might be two or three kids and one or two parents. It seems like teenagers, therefore, make up at least half the population. What you are missing is the millions of adults that do not have children. There are a lot more of them than you imagine.

By sheer force of numbers adults rule the world. But there is another thing that causes adults to be in control: they own everything. They own all of the cars. They own all of the houses and apartment complexes. They own all of the businesses and skyscrapers. They own the government. They own all of the forests and weapons. They own it all.

> *If you are going to succeed you need to learn how to fit into the adult world. You need to become an adult yourself so that you are not part of the insignificant fringe group called "teenagers."*

These are very interesting facts, and they have interesting implications. You need to learn and understand one thing from them: Adults are in charge. There is nothing you can do to change this situation.

Now, what are you going to do about it? If you are going to succeed—in fact, if you are going to accomplish anything at all, whether it be saving the environment or becoming a millionaire—you need to learn how to fit into the adult world. *You need to become an adult yourself so that you are not in the insignificant fringe group called "teenagers."* The sooner you learn to fit in to the adult environment, the better. The world simply does not make sense until you see it from an adult perspective, because adults own and operate everything.

The great thing is that you can start to become an adult today. The day you stop thinking about yourself as a teenager and start thinking and acting like an adult, you begin to become an adult. To do that, it is important to understand what it means to think and act like an adult. That is what the rest of the book is about.

CHAPTER 4

You Can Ignore
Your Peers

Building off the previous two facts of life you can generate a third: You can ignore your peers. I know this is impossible to believe. I can remember as a teenager being incredibly concerned about "being accepted" and about "being cool." You might feel the same way.

So let me tell you an important secret. All of those feelings are a part of your Teenage Illusion Module (see Chapter 2). As soon as your TIM collapses you will realize that what your peers think is largely irrelevant. They know little or nothing about the real world. Instead of pleasing your peers, you should please yourself or please people who matter. The sooner you understand this fact, the better.

Let me say it another way. Look at these two people:

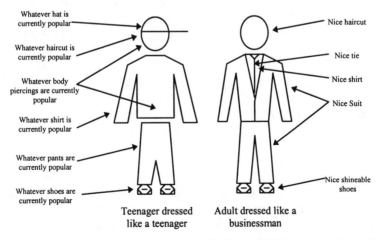

Whatever hat is currently popular

Whatever haircut is currently popular

Whatever body piercings are currently popular

Whatever shirt is currently popular

Whatever pants are currently popular

Whatever shoes are currently popular

Teenager dressed like a teenager

Nice haircut

Nice tie

Nice shirt

Nice Suit

Nice shineable shoes

Adult dressed like a businessman

Figure 5 - A comparison between the "look" of a typical teenager and a typical adult.

On the left you have a typical teenager. When you look at him you might think, "Wow. Cool. A really together guy." On the right is an adult businessman. You are thinking, "Dweeb. Business geek. Suit. Boring." You need to do a complete 180 on that. Here's why. When he is lucky the teenager on the left is able to make minimum wage sweeping floors. He owns nothing. He can make absolutely nothing happen. He knows little about the adult world. When he wants to go somewhere he has to borrow his mother's car. His major claim to fame is a high score on a video game. In the grand scheme of things the teenager is largely insignificant.

The adult on the right, on the other hand, has a good job. He owns a nice house. He gives money each year to help needy children in the community. By speaking eloquently at a business luncheon, he can generate thousands of dollars in charitable contributions for the foundation of his choice. He can get you a job if you ask him. In other words, he can make things happen. He knows how the world works.

Compare the teenager to the adult. Who is more successful? Who can accomplish more? Who can do more good for the community and the world? Who will people listen to? The more time you spend talking to your peers, the more you are like them. The more time you spend talking to adults, the more you are like an adult. Adults can accomplish a whole lot more. Adults can actually make things happen. Therefore, logic would indicate that you should be talking to adults if success is your goal.

Think about the question, "Who would you rather be like: a teenager or an adult?" You might answer it, "I'd rather be like the teenager." Why? One reason is because you *are* a teenager. Birds of a feather flock together, and all that. Another reason is because you understand teenagers and are comfortable with them. The reason you are comfortable with teenagers is because you talk to them all day. You may not do that with adults. Maybe that's because you think adults are boring and stupid. If you feel that way, perhaps you should reconsider. How can an adult who is making $50,000 or $150,000 a year be stupid? Especially when it is totally impossible for a normal teenager to do the same? You are, potentially, flocking with the wrong group. By spending time with adults and learning to understand their world, you can become a successful adult much more quickly.

The reason you might think adults are stupid is because you do not understand them. The adult world is a intricate, complex and interesting place. Because it is intricate and complex, however, it takes time and experience to understand this environment. You need to talk to adults to start learning about their environment. The sooner you start learning the intricacies, the better off you are in the long run. The sooner you become an adult, the sooner you can start reaping the rewards of being an adult.

Think about it another way. You have heard about "peer pressure." Notice that the words "peer pressure" are always used in a negative sense. Your "peers" are encouraging you to smoke. Your "peers" are encouraging you to do drugs. Your "peers" are encouraging you to have sex at age 15. Your "peers" are encouraging you to go smash your neighbor's mailbox with a baseball bat. Your "peers" are encouraging you to spray graffiti on cars. Whatever. Why in the world would you want to do any of that? What does it accomplish? Have you ever had a successful adult businessman pull up to you in his Lexus and say, "Come on, let's go bash mailboxes together! I have a bat in the back seat!" Of course not.

The Opinions of Your Peers

I was pretty nerdy when I was in high school. Therefore, my peers spent a lot of time putting me down. The mistake I made was that I actually listened to them and took their opinions to heart. Adults I knew told me I was doing great, but that didn't count for some reason. If I had to do it over again I would do just the opposite; I would spend all my time with adults and ignore my peers because my peers were wrong.

Why is it that adults don't go sneaking around smashing mailboxes? Because it is pointless. There are much better things to do once you know they are possible. You, as a teenager in America, are standing inside a $7 trillion economy (1997). That means that every year people willingly hand each other $7 trillion in return for goods and services. If you can figure out a legitimate way to get even the tiniest slice of that money to flow your way, then you will be set. You will be able to accomplish almost any goal you can imagine. "Goals?" you might be asking. This might be a good time to get some. It is probably the case that you have some already and don't realize it (see Chapter 23). Many of your peers don't have any goals, and that is why their lives are often so random and pointless. Instead of trying to figure out a better way to kill your neighbor's cat, you could instead be learning about our society and economy and figuring out a way to build a business or career that will make you a millionaire.

You can ignore your "peers" completely if you like. Simply walk away from them and never look back. You will be much better off if you spend your time with adults and become an adult yourself.

REPLACING YOUR PEERS

Now, having told you that your peers are irrelevant, you probably have at least four problems:

- You are so used to thinking about your peers as the center of the universe that it is impossible for you to think of them in any other way right now. Every single thing you do at the moment is dictated by your peers and their view of you, including your haircut, your clothes, the way you talk and so on. You are a slave to the whims of your peers. That is fine. Let the idea of ignoring them sink in for a week or two and it will feel more comfortable. Then come back and read this chapter again.
- Whether or not your peers are relevant, they are in your face all day, every day. You have to deal with them whether you like it or not.
- You don't know of any smart adults who will sit down and talk to you on a daily basis. And even if you did, most of what they would talk about would make no sense to you.
- You can see no way for you to ever become like the businessman. What in the world can you do to make $150,000 a year? Or $2,000,000 a year? What is the path? Since you can see no path, it may seem pointless to try.

You need to find ways around these problems. Here are some suggestions:

- Your peers are your friends. Everyone has friends, and that is a good thing. But choose your friends wisely. Completely ignore "negative peers." If you want to, go form a clique. The difference should be that your clique is doing the right thing, knows what it is doing and should be willing to let in other people who are wanting to learn. Form a good clique, in other words.
- Find other people your age who are reading this book. Talk to them. Compare notes and ideas.
- Get ready for a paradox: You will be looked down on by people who are below you. You are seeking an adult level of behavior, yet many of the children around you in high school will treat you like you are an idiot. Ignore them. They are worrying about video games and rock bands and cigarettes and drugs and expensive tennis shoes. All of that stuff is irrelevant. *Do you see a single successful adult around you worrying about video games and rock bands and cigarettes and drugs?* Of course not. The opinions of

---

If a five-year-old kid were to walk up to you and say, "You're really dumb," what would you do? You would ignore him. What does he know? Ignore your peers in the same way.

your peers are irrelevant. They have no idea about what you are trying to accomplish, or why. Try this: If a five-year-old kid were to walk up to you and say, "You're really dumb," what would you do? You would ignore him. What does he know? You can treat many of the people around you in high school the same way.

- Find adults who will talk to you in ways that you understand; who will take the time to put things in terms that make sense to you. Form friendships or relationships with these adults. Ask them intelligent questions. When things happen, ask them why. Form relationships like this with a number of adults.

- If you have a group of like-minded friends, form a club. Take tours of nearby factories, TV stations, businesses, colleges, hotels and so on. Find adults who are sympathetic to your cause and ask them to come speak to your club. Ask them if they will give you tours of their businesses. Ask them to tell you about their jobs. Some will say "No." That's OK; keep asking and you will find people who say "Yes." Show them this book and explain what you are trying to accomplish. There *are* adults who will understand and who will listen.

- Find situations where adults get together and join the group. Go work for a political campaign. Volunteer at a community organization. Get involved at the adult level at church. Go to meetings like the rotary club or the Jaycees and simply sit quietly in back and listen. Do not hang out with college students; many are clueless. Find groups of successful, mature adults. Start listening.

- Whenever you meet new adults, ask them to describe their jobs. Ask if they enjoy their jobs. *Ask how they got to their current job.* You will find that just about everyone went through a really crazy set of steps to get where they are. You will also find that a number of people have jobs you have never heard of before (see Chapters 5 and 6). Ask them what they would do differently if they were to do it again. You will learn a lot of conflicting lessons (see Chapter 24).

- Form friendships with teachers. Ask them questions. Ask for explanations of adult behavior. If one teacher does not seem to understand what you are saying, try another until you find one who speaks your language.

- See if you can find a successful adult who will be your *mentor*. A mentor is a person who takes the time to "show you the ropes." A mentor will share experiences from his or her business and personal life, act as a sounding board, offer suggestions and so on.

If you can find a professional adult who will take you under his or her wing, you can accelerate your development tremendously.

- Find your own way. Instead of searching for the opinions and approval of your peers, work instead to find what makes you happy. Simply be yourself and be with yourself and see what you find. You might be amazed.

Now about the last problem of the four mentioned previously; You can see no path to becoming a $100,000-a-year businessman or lawyer or engineer or truck driver (yes, truck drivers can make $100,000 per year). See Part 2 for more information.

GAINING PERSPECTIVE

Another thing you can do to gain a perspective on your peers is to eliminate a common problem of all teenagers: *tunnel vision*. As a child, and to some extent as a teenager, you have the ability to think about only what you see in your environment. Therefore, you tend to see your peers as the only people who matter. What you are missing is that there are five billion people on this planet (1997) and at school you are dealing with a microscopic percentage of the total population. To base any action off of the opinions of your tiny group of peers is meaningless.

Finding Someone Who Speaks Your Language

Here is an example of how helpful it can be to find someone who speaks your language. When I was a teenager, I was terrible at art, yet I really wanted to do "artistic" things. One thing I wanted to do was learn to draw. I took art classes, I read drawing and sketching books, but everything I drew myself looked *really* bad and very childish.

Then I found a book by Betty Edwards called *Drawing on the Right Side of the Brain*. This is the only book on drawing that ever spoke to me. Thousands and thousands of people have been able to learn to draw from this book because it breaks down the "problem" of drawing, shows why it is hard and explains how to overcome the difficulties with exercises. Prior to reading this book, despite talking to lots of people and reading many other books, drawing was a mystery to me. After reading it I understand completely.

If you talk to someone and you cannot understand them, do not give up. Simply talk to someone else. And keep trying until you find someone who *speaks your language* and is able to help you understand the answer to your question.

Let me give you an example of the first event in my life that showed me my problem with tunnel vision. During my junior year, my high school sent me to a week-long program in Washington, DC. In this program I spent an incredibly intense week learning about the system of American government with several hundred other teenagers from all over the country. The program consisted of tours, seminars, meetings with people in government, briefings, classes, lectures, banquets and discussions. We were on the run 14 to 16 hours a day. I can remember getting home from Washington after this trip, falling asleep at noon or so, and waking up the next morning almost 24 hours later. It was an amazing trip for me.

Besides learning a huge amount about the political system, I learned two other important things:

- I learned that there was this huge group of people *just like me*. The neat thing about this program, and the main difference between it and the group of people in my high school, was that *all the people who didn't give a damn had been filtered out.* All the football players, the smokers, the jerks who disrupted class, the bullies and the cool people were gone. I was in a group of people I could actually talk to and who actually talked to me. I met girls there and they would say, "hi" and actually sit with me at meals to discuss things. *It was amazing how good it felt to be accepted.*

- I discovered that my opinions were not the only ones. I can remember the very first day. It was a Sunday, and it was unstructured because everyone was arriving from all over the country. One of the things they had us do is get in a group with about 20 other people and discuss a topic like gun control. A funny thing about a high school is that the people in any given high school are pretty homogeneous. They all come from the same place and they tend to have fairly similar belief structures. For example, if your high school is in a large wheat farming community in Iowa and you look at the people at the local high school, there is going to be a lot of homogeneity there. In the discussion group there was nothing homogeneous. These were smart people from all over the country. They had well-thought-out opinions and they knew where they stood. *But they were all different.* We would discuss different topics, and people would take positions that *I had never even considered as options.* It was incredibly interesting but a little scary. Half the world felt one way and the other half felt another, and in many cases both sides were right!

When I got back to my high school I saw it in a whole new light. I could say to myself for the first time, "These people might not matter!"

Adults in Groups

Teenagers, especially in groups, can be outrageously cruel. If you don't happen to "fit in" with "the group" teenagers tend to harass you to death. It is almost as bad as chickens. I don't know if you have ever spent any time watching a flock of chickens that is able to run free in a pen, but teenagers are remarkably similar. One thing you will notice in a group of chickens is that there is a definite hierarchy. This is where the phrase "pecking order" comes from, by the way. Another thing you will notice is that if one of the chickens gets sick or is out of line, the other chickens will literally *peck her to death*. Being in a group of teenagers where you don't fit in can be a lot like that. Other people in the group will peck you.

You will find that a good group of adults has a lot more kindness, understanding, tolerance and forgiveness than a similar group of teenagers. I think the reason for this is because adults understand that they are fallible. All adults have made mistakes, they have all tried to do things and had them not work out, and they all know how that feels. Therefore, they cut each other a lot more slack. It is a much happier environment.

The same thing will happen when you get to college. Suddenly, you will be in a place where most of the people who don't give a damn are missing, and you will feel much more comfortable.

Keep these things in mind as you are thinking about your peers in school. Once you get out of high school their opinions will not matter any more, so it may be pointless to consider their opinions now. If you feel like you don't fit in at school, you might want to get involved in groups outside of school that let you be with people that are more like yourself. Or investigate the option of going to college early. Or hang out with adults and enjoy it. You may fit in much better with adults than you do with your peers because you may already *be* an adult. If that is the case, take advantage of it.

The point is, do something that helps you feel good about yourself. Join a group full of good people who are on the right track and enjoy it.

PART 2

The Facts About Jobs and Careers

You *will* have a job—that is a fact of life. By planning ahead, you can get a job that is both high-paying and enjoyable.

CHAPTER 5

You Must Have a
Job to Live Life

In Chapter 1 you saw how important money is. You need money so that you can pay rent and buy food. It is also nice to have extra money (discretionary income) that you can spend on luxuries, give to charities and so on. What you learned in Chapter 1 is that it takes a remarkable amount of money to live what is considered to be a "normal" American lifestyle. It is this simple fact that forces you to get a job.

Most people miss this fact of life until they are well into their 20s or 30s. By then it is more difficult to do anything about it. If you start thinking about it as a teenager, however, you gain a tremendous amount of control over your life. Given that you have to have a job, why not have a fun one? Why not have a job you really enjoy? Why not have a job that pays you $100,000 per year or $1,000,000 per year rather than $20,000? Why not? You WILL have a job. There is no way around it. You might as well make it a good one.

If you look at life this way, then you can start to formulate four questions at a very early age:
- What is a "good" job?
- What do I need to do to get a good job?
- What kind of jobs are out there?
- How can I get better jobs throughout my life?

If you start asking and answering these questions now, as a teenager, when you have a lot of free time and no expenses, you are doing yourself a huge favor. You can accelerate the process tremendously. By the time you are 25 you will be well on your way while the rest of your peers are still standing around trying to figure out what is going on.

41

WHAT IS A GOOD JOB?

Here are some of the things you want to be thinking about as you consider your employment options. A good job has the following characteristics:

- You enjoy it
- It pays well
- The payment model matches your personality
- It gives you the opportunity to learn and grow
- It has advancement potential

All of these elements are important. The first one, however, is the most important. You are going to be working 8 to 10 hours a day for the rest of your life. You might as well enjoy it. Chapter 6 discusses this topic in detail and shows you how to prepare yourself for a job you will enjoy. The "pays well" part is also nice but might be irrelevant if you are truly happy in your job. Given a choice between "truly happy" and "rich," most people would choose "truly happy" in an instant (see also Chapter 41). What fun is it to be rich if you are miserable?

The payment model is important because certain payment models work well for some people but not for others. There are several different payment models in use in this country. Here are a few examples:

- Volunteer work—You receive no pay for your efforts.
- Piece work—You receive a payment for completing a specific task. You might see this sort of payment model in a garment factory (where a person is paid for each piece of clothing he or she completes), but could also be considered the model for delivery companies, trucking companies, etc. that pay by the trip. Even a doctor, who charges each patient, is in a sense doing piece work.
- Commission work—Similar to piece work but applied to sales positions. You are paid a percentage of each sale you make. This model is common for Realtors, car salesmen, etc.
- Gratuity work—Some or most of your income comes from tips.
- Hourly work—You are paid for each hour you spend on the job.
- Salaried work—You are paid a fixed amount per year.
- Self-employed—You own a business (a restaurant, printing company, consulting firm, car repair shop, lawn-care service, etc.) and you take home the profits from that business (see Chapter 44).

You can have a good job under any of the different payment models listed above. For example, if you are making $50 or $75 an hour you are doing very well, and that hourly rate is common for both high-end software developers and high-end electricians, plumbers and welders. High-end sales people working on a commission basis can make a very good living under the commission model. For example, Realtors typically make 7% on the sale of a house (to be technically accurate, the listing agent takes half and the selling agent takes half and the realty office takes a cut as well, but you get the idea). Therefore, a Realtor who lists and sells just one $200,000 house every month can do extremely well. If you are an actor getting paid per show you are doing piece work, and if you are making $10,000 per weekly show you are doing very well indeed. Waiters and waitresses at a fancy restaurant can clear $40,000 per year on tips alone (1997). The point is, you can make good money under lots of different payment models. The key is to find the model that best fits your personality.

When most people think of a "good job" what they have in mind is a salaried position. A typical low-end salaried position has the following characteristics in 1997:

- Pays $30,000 per year
- Provides free or low-cost health insurance for the employee and family
- Possibly provides other types of insurance: dental, life, disability and so on
- Provides at least two weeks of paid vacation time per year
- Provides some amount of paid sick time
- Provides a 401(k) retirement plan with some level of employer matching

Careers

A good job is normally part of a good career. A *career*, according to *Webster's Ninth New Collegiate Dictionary*, is "the pursuit of consecutive, progressive achievement especially in public, professional or business life," and also, "a profession for which one trains and which is undertaken as a permanent calling." As you build up skill in a certain area it makes it easy for you to advance to new jobs in that area. The result is a long career in a certain job category.

As an example, let's say your first job is as a car salesman. You move between several different dealerships, eventually becoming a manager of sales at a large dealership. You have a career in "automotive sales" as a result. Or perhaps you move from car sales to heavy equipment sales and then electronics. You have a broad career in "sales." If you were to work in sales, then in the service department and then in purchasing, you could start your own dealership. Then you have a career as an "automobile dealer and businessperson." If you start as a car salesman to learn the ropes of sales, get a college degree in electrical engineering and then focus exclusively on computers, electronics and eventually the sale of satellite transponders to corporate clients, you have a career in "technical sales."

- Provides a good level of "upward mobility," meaning that you can see a promotion path to better positions in the future

Compared to a minimum wage hourly job, a salaried arrangement looks very nice. For example, in an hourly job you can take vacation or get sick, but your income is cut off during the time you are out. The "upward mobility" part of a salaried position is also important. Once you are in a company, you have the opportunity to rise to higher positions as you gain experience.

The fact that you are only making an hourly minimum wage right now tells you something. You are only "worth" $5 an hour. How do you earn more? What might make you more valuable? How do you find a "good job" for yourself? The following chapters will help you to understand what makes the difference between a minimum wage worker and a highly paid professional.

CHAPTER 6

Education is One
Key to a Good Job

Education is one key to a good job. In today's job market what you know determines what you earn. The more you know the more you make, especially if what you know is important to some segment of the business world. The following comes from the *1995 World Almanac*:

> Educational attainment has a direct impact on many aspects of life, but most directly on earnings. Average annual earnings for persons without a high school diploma are $14,391; with a diploma, $20,036; with a bachelor's degree, $34,096; with a doctorate, $54,982; and with a professional degree, $74,725.

What this tells you is that a college degree is important if you are looking to make more than the minimum $20,000 per year (1997) required to live a life in America. However, it is not the only way. We will talk later in this chapter about non-college jobs that pay well. Also, while a college degree is important, many teenagers miss the fact that a "college degree" is a variable thing. Certain majors in college are worthless, while some are extremely valuable. For example, if you get a degree in Computer Science right now, your earning potential is extremely high. At the same time, a degree in English literature can make it extremely hard to find a job. Not all degrees are equal.

Another thing that is easy to miss as a teenager is that "education" does not have to come from traditional sources. You can teach yourself a tremendous number of things simply by sitting down and reading books or by talking to people. The thing that makes you valuable is what you know. It doesn't matter where the information comes from.

Let's say that you were to find yourself one day with nothing to do. For example, you are sitting around on the couch watching TV and the thought crosses your mind, "This is incredibly boring; there must be

45

something better to do." Let's say you would like to improve your odds of getting a good job. You can do a gigantic variety of things, on your own, without anybody else's assistance, to drastically improve your value in the job market. In the process you can have a lot of fun. What you need to do is teach yourself a skill that is valuable. The skill might be valuable to people who hire employees, or it might be valuable to you if you were to start your own company.

The very best way to start is to look toward something that you would really enjoy doing. Let me give you an example. Let's say that you like watching TV and you like watching movies. Let's say you have been curious about how movies are made. If you like movies, learn how to make movies. *I mean that literally.* Go buy yourself a video camera and start shooting movies. Organize some friends and write a script and make a movie. It really is as simple as that.

The minute you start down this path you will be forced to ask yourself, "How do I make a movie?" It looks so easy when you watch them on TV, but it turns out it is incredibly hard to make a *good* movie. You will suddenly find that it is a lot harder than it looks to make it "feel right." It is a lot harder than it looks to create a good story. It is a lot harder than it looks to get people to do what you ask them to do in their acting. So start reading books on making good movies and see what you can discover. Learn about the equipment you need for editing and creating special effects. Then start talking to people who make movies or television shows. Get a job at a local TV station (volunteer if necessary) and start talking to people there. Or simply take a tour and meet a few people. If you *really* want to make movies, you will find this to be the most fun and interesting thing you have ever done in your life, and in time you will learn all of the skills necessary to make a good movie. Suddenly, you have something to major in at college, you have a great tool for finding summer jobs and you have started a career.

Eliminating Excuses

Many teenagers hear a message like, "Go buy a video camera" and they shut down. Or they think to themselves, "Video cameras cost $1,000. Where am I going to get that kind of money?" The answer to that sort of thought is easy: Get a job. Suddenly, a job will seem a lot more relevant because there is something that you want and need. Go to work for a couple of months and raise the money you need and buy a camera. Or borrow a camera from a relative who has an old one sitting in the closet. Or look in the classified ads and buy a used one. You DO NOT need the latest, greatest, most wonderful video camera. What you need is any camera that can take a picture. Many artists will tell you that limiting your tools can inspire great creativity. Try that approach (see Chapter 32).

The point is, find something you like and learn how to do it. Start small. Read books. Talk to people. Learn the basics and then refine your skills. Eventually, if you keep at it, you will become highly skilled at what you are doing and you will *love* doing it.

In the book *Industrial Light and Magic: The Art of Special Effects* by Thomas Smith, the author describes the techniques and people behind the special effects in movies like *Star Wars, Raiders of the Lost Ark, E.T* and *Back to the Future*. He spends a lot of time talking about the individual people who make up the ILM team and how they got started in the business. Here is a typical entry about an ILM employee named Phil Tippett:

By the time he was 13 years old, he had spent the money he'd earned mowing lawns on an 8mm Keystone camera and was making things move in front of it. He filmed walking figures made of pipe cleaners and formed stop-motion action in clay, all shot one frame at a time. By the time he was 17 years old he was being paid minimum wage to animate for TV commercials.... He began to form working relationships with some of those who in five years would become important names in special effects: Jon Berg and Dennis Muren. Dennis had been working at ILM as a special effects cameraman, and at his recommendation Phil and Jon were hired to join the *Star Wars* production team and animate the miniature chess game. When work began on *The Empire Strikes Back*, Phil began designing the tauntaun creature and animated all medium and long shots of Luke on the tauntaun.

An amazing number of people important to ILM simply started doing something on their own in films or special effects as teenagers. That's a good book to read, by the way, if you like special effects. Read the book and then watch the movies it talks about. Then try making your own movies and see what happens.

Here is another example. Let's say you like computer games. Get a computer and start writing computer games. You will find that you have to buy a compiler and learn a programming language, so do it. Don't know what compiler to use? Start talking to other programmers and see what they think. Don't know any programmers? Meet some. Don't know where to meet other programmers? Ask your math teacher. Teenagers are masters of the creative excuse; blast the excuses away by doing something to solve the problem! Just get out there and start teaching yourself the skills necessary to create a computer game. Go to a good technical bookstore and buy some books. Search the web and see what you can find there. Read and post messages on programming news groups. Then try to create a game of your own. You will find it is not as easy as it looks. So learn more. And more. And more. Soon you will know all of the skills required to create good computer games and you will be extremely valuable in the job market.

Let's say that you like music. Form a band with some friends. Don't know how to play an instrument? Learn one. Don't know which instrument you might like? Buy a cheap keyboard and see if you like that. Buy a cheap, used guitar at a pawn shop and see if you like that. Find an instrument you like and learn it. Find that you can't play an instrument? Learn about MIDI programming on computers and make music that way. Don't like computers? Would you enjoy doing marketing or production for a band? Find a band in your high school and see what assistance they need on the marketing and promotion side. Perhaps you would enjoy being a light or sound technician, and you could learn to do that. The possibilities are endless.

Do you like surfing the web? Teach yourself how to create a web site. Find a school or a company or a church that needs a web site and build them one. If you like cars learn how to repair cars, or learn how to weld and build your own car. If you like clothes learn how to sew, then learn how to design and make your own clothes. If you like money learn about the stock and bond markets and the whole money system of the United States. If you like paintings, then buy yourself a blank canvas and some paint at an art supply store and start painting. Like to read? Try writing. Like to eat? Try cooking. Like airplanes? Learn to fly. Like actors? Learn to act. Find a buddy who wants to learn how to make movies and act in his or her movies. Are you getting the idea?

USE YOUR IMAGINATION AND DO SOMETHING!

Find something you really enjoy and start doing it and learn more and more until you are an expert in that area. There is nothing to stop you. Somewhere in this country there will be a company that can use your skills, and because you are an expert that company will be happy to hire you. Do not allow yourself to make excuses. This is the age of information. If there is *anything* you would like to do, there are books, magazines, web sites, and news groups on the subject, as well as clubs where you can meet other people interested in the subject, ad infinitum. If there are not, then you should learn about the subject and write the book yourself.

If you try something and get pretty far into it and find that you do not enjoy it as much as you thought, then stop and pick something else. I can remember getting a camera for my birthday one summer. It turns out a friend of mine also had a camera and knew more about it than I did. So we spent time together every day that summer, and we each shot at least one roll of film every day or two. We'd mail the film off to an inexpensive film processing center, and we always shot KodaChrome slides or black and white film to save money. We shot *thousands* of pictures that summer, read books, talked to people, rode our bikes to historic or interesting places to get different shots and so on. And we got better and better. Finally, I submitted a photograph to a magazine and it was good enough to get accepted and published. When that magazine came out I totally lost interest in photography and moved on to something else. Why did I lose interest? Who knows?! I simply did. I learned two important lessons from that experience:

> *Find something you really enjoy and start doing it. Learn more and more until you are an expert in that area. Once you do that it will be easy to find a job you love.*

1. I now know how to take really great pictures of anything.
2. I learned that on any given roll of 36 pictures you generally only get one shot, or maybe two, that are "good." All the rest you look at and you think, "Boy, that one did NOT come out the way I expected." Ever watch a photo shoot for a model? They take hundreds of shots to get one or two good ones. In all the rest of the shots the model's eyes are half closed, or her hair looks funny, or the framing isn't right or whatever. It is normal. That is a good lesson because it applies to a whole lot of other things in life. Film directors shoot 10 times more film than they need to get a movie to look right. Designers draw hundreds of pencil sketches until they get the look they are seeking. Baseball players get up to bat and strike out two thirds of the time. In many different activities failure is a normal part of success.

The time I spent with my camera was not wasted, and my friend and I had an incredibly good time that summer learning to use our cameras and taking all those pictures.

Let's say there is nothing that you enjoy doing. Impossible, but let's just say. Then take a more pragmatic approach. Find the classified ads in the Sunday paper and look in the jobs section. See what areas have high demand, and see which jobs are paying the most. Then learn the skill with the highest demand and the highest pay. If you get into it and you find that you don't like it, then pick another area and do that until you find something you like. You might as well pick a job that pays well if you are going to pick something at random!

FINDING GOOD JOB CATEGORIES

As a child, if someone asked you, "What do you want to be when you grow up?" you probably answered, "A fireman," "A policeman," "A nurse" or "A teacher." Children only know about the few jobs they can see in their world. A child would never answer with, "An account manager for a 401(k) record keeper," "Lead buyer at a major department store," "Editor and publisher of a magazine," "Stock specialist" "Computer engineer," "Financial analyst," "Athletic therapist," "Small businessman" or even "Principal of a school." Children cannot see those things, so they never consider them. You likely carry that same narrow vision with you now as a teenager.

There are millions of high-paying jobs out in the real world that you have never heard of. In fact, you cannot even conceive of them. What is interesting is that you have certain skills—things that you are best at—that you can exploit in a good job if you know that the job is out there.

How do you find out about all of these job categories? Start asking adults around you things like:

- What do you do?
- Why do you do it?
- Do you like it?
- How did you get your job?
- What are all the jobs you have held in your career?
- What was your first job as a teenager?
- What is the salary range for your job? (DO NOT ask "How much do you make?" See the sidebar at the end of Chapter 1 for details.)
- How much training do you need?
- Where would I start if I wanted to have a job like yours?
- And so on.

You will find that many adults do not like their jobs. In general you should ignore these people and focus instead on adults who do. Seek out the adults who are really excited and passionate about their jobs and focus on them.

You can also look around you at the jobs you see on the surface and then look behind the scenes. There are good paying, interesting jobs behind the scenes of any industry. Focus on those words *good paying* and *interesting* and you will not go far wrong. Let me give you some examples:

- Behind every successful rock band there are producers, record companies, light and sound technicians, ad companies, artists, agents, songwriters, financial experts and so on.
- Behind every TV show there are producers, directors, cameramen, technicians, writers, managers, financial experts, production engineers and so on.
- Behind every pro athlete there are managers, coaches, financial experts, therapists, trainers and so on.
- Behind every house there is a foreman, a contractor, sub-contractors, heavy equipment operators, truckers, framers, roofers, plumbers, electricians, painters and so on. None of these jobs require a college degree, but they all pay well if you do them well. For example, a reliable long-haul truck driver can make incredibly good pay. So can a back hoe operator. So can a painter. If you discipline yourself to be incredibly reliable and if you treat your customers honestly, you can make great pay in any of these professions.
- Behind every computer program and web site there are programmers, database specialists, network administrators, system operators, graphic artists, technical writers, advertising executives and so on.

Even if you yourself aren't a TV star, a rock musician or a pro athlete, you can still be involved in these fields helping to make things happen.

See also the BYG Publishing web site at http://www.bygpub.com and Chapter 45.

CHAPTER 7

Good Jobs Go to
Good Employees

L
ook at how a "typical" teenager normally operates
when he or she has a "teenager-type" job. The teenager
comes into work. The employer gives him or her a
task. The teenager often does it poorly. The teenager shows no interest or
excitement in the job. He complains about having to do it. When the
employer goes to see what he is doing, the teenager is chatting with
friends on the phone, goofing off or doing something other than the
requested task. "Teenagers don't care" is the message that most adults
carry in their heads because of this sort of behavior.

Now imagine that the employer finds *you* to be completely different.
When the employer asks you to do something he gets an "OK, I'll do it
right away!" Then you do it. Perhaps you do more than required. You do
it well. You are happy about it. If it is a task that takes four hours and
your employer comes up half way through and asks, "How is it going?"
you say, "It is going well. I have just finished blah blah blah and am
starting on the blah blah blah." It does not matter what you are asked to
do; you are always ready to do it.

Now imagine what the employer thinks when he compares you to a
"typical" teenager. If you respond to your job in this way for a good
employer you will be tagged as someone who actually does things and
does them well. You will be successful very fast. It is as simple as that.

"Good jobs" go to "good employees." That is a fact of life. What are
employers looking for in "good employees"? Here are some of the
qualifications:

- Good employees take the initiative. There is a huge difference
between an employee who does things on his or her own and one
who doesn't. Imagine yourself as a boss. You have two
employees. One does nothing unless told exactly what to do, then
does it poorly. The other one does any assigned task well, but in
addition she is always happy to be helping and never sits idle. She

52

always seems to be doing something to make life easier for customers or other employees. Who would your rather work with? Who will you promote? The choice is obvious.

- Good employees take responsibility. When they are given a task they do a good job and see the task through to completion. Good employees are responsible for their own actions and the work they produce.
- Good employees understand the financial side of the business. They know what activities make the business money and focus on them. They understand their paychecks depend on the business making money.
- Good employees keep their commitments, both large and small. Simple commitments are important: returning calls, showing up on time, etc.
- Good employees know that customers (and other team members) matter. Good employees take the time to ask people how they are doing and show concern and empathy for the needs of others.
- Good employees do a job cheerfully, even if it is not their favorite. Who wants to work with a person who is complaining all the time?
- A good employee consistently does what is best for the company.
- A good employee is disciplined and stays on track.
- A good employee is a consistent performer. Tasks are done well all the time, so the employer can depend on you.
- Good employees are self-motivated. If there is a period of time where there is nothing to do, they find something useful to fill the void. Or they spend the time learning something new that will help their performance on the job.
- Good employees give credit to others on the team.
- Good employees exceed expectations. They do more than they are asked to do, and they do a better job than expected. If you never do more than you are paid to do, you will never be paid more for what you do.

Obviously no one is perfect in all of these areas. A person works to improve at them all through life. As a teenager you want to be conscious of the different areas and strive for improvement each day. That will take time because there is a lot to learn. Work to distinguish yourself as a good employee, learn new skills that make you better at your job, do more than expected, offer new ideas and do things important to the business. For example, if you work in a store, learn to treat customers in a special way. Perhaps try remembering their names and greeting them personally when they come in the store. You will be a fundamental reason for people to

Understanding a Business

Once you are working in a business, take the time to understand how all of the pieces of the business fit together. A large business with hundreds of employees is an intricate machine. Every part in the machine does something important. What role do you play in the business? Why is that role important? What does your department do? What departments does it work with, and why? What is the nature of the organizational hierarchy? Who are the key players in the business? In your division? In your department? How did they get there? If you take the time to answer all of these questions, you will learn a tremendous amount about the company you work for and about business in general.

come to the store, and your employer will notice that. You can learn to do new things so that you can perform more tasks. You can make life easier for your employer. By demonstrating these qualities your employer will assign you tasks that have more and more responsibility.

Let's say you do all of this and you find your employer is totally non-responsive to it or hyper-critical. Or you find that your job involves flipping burgers and only flipping burgers and there is no room for creativity or advancement. Then that is your cue to get a new employer. Simple as that. If an employer is consistently assigning you a toilet scrubbing job, you are probably thinking, "What's the point?" That's a good question. Get any job in a growing SMALL BUSINESS instead. Make yourself useful. Learn the trade. You will be pushed into higher levels of responsibility by default. Make yourself indispensable.

Once you are in a small business, apply the following strategy: Learn all tasks in the business so you can start a business just like it. Learn the operations, the money, the marketing, the inventory, the payroll and the processes. Learn the entire business. It is amazing how complicated a business is, and it can take several months or years or more to learn it all. The education, however, will be invaluable. Your knowledge will allow you to run any part of the business at any time. That will give you an incredibly wide range of freedom within the business.

Another strategy to apply, especially if you are in a larger company, involves *looking up*. Look up in the organization and find a position or a person you admire. Then talk to people and find out about the skills, qualifications and personality required to get that job. Talk to the person who holds the position you seek and find out how he or she got there. You will generally find it was a crazy path. Ask his or her advice on what you should do to get there. Then start accumulating what you need. It will take time. Everything does (see Chapter 34). You might as well start now.

WHAT IS IT EMPLOYERS ARE NOT LOOKING FOR

When you work in business you come across both great and poor employees. You also come across people who *could* be great employees but are missing some important point that ends up derailing their careers. One of the things a lot of teenage employees do is complain. Constantly. The problem with complaining is that no one likes to work with a complainer, and the complaining drags the whole team down. Here is an example of a letter a complainer might receive from his or her manager.

Jim,
    There was a snippet of conversation from lunch yesterday that I would like to come back to and discuss. It went something like this:
    You: I don't want to be assigned to little 3-day projects. I want to work on something long-term.
    Me: Well, you should love the XYZ project. We are in there for the long haul and have complete control.
    You: [Long pause] Well, I don't want...
    Here's something I have noticed. I am not saying this in a derogatory way but in a way that will help us understand something. Jim, you spend an awful lot of time complaining like this. It gets tiring after awhile. The people who work with you, myself included, have the impression that you complain constantly. Other people are going to be promoted right over you because they use their talents to move the company forward rather than complain.
    Let me give you an idea for another approach you could take. This approach is clearly used by Steve, Joanne, George, etc. You have a set of clear and obvious talents. You also have a certain set of things you like to do. Starting point: We ALL have to do some things we don't like so we can move forward as a team. I, for example, certainly had no desire to fly to Seattle this week. However, I want to get paid at the end of the month. There must be enough cash coming in so we can meet payroll each month. That is just a simple fact of life. So given that fact as a starting point, there are certain things that need doing in our department. Ask yourself, "What can I do, among these things, to help? What makes good use of my talents?"
    Looking at our current projects, the obvious thing is the XYZ project. I don't know if you have looked at this project but their approach is BEAUTIFUL. It is a long-term project; we will be working out at XYZ for a year, maybe two years. It definitely needs the raw talent and ability you possess, Jim. It is exactly what you seem to say you want.
    So why don't you, instead of telling us what you don't want to do, step up to the plate and say, "Hey, I think I could make a tremendous contribution on the XYZ project. I have the right skills and the ability to work creatively and effectively in that space. Would you consider letting me work on this project?" Approach it from the positive side rather than the negative side.
    What would happen? Joe Johnson would be overjoyed! I would be overjoyed! George would be overjoyed! Instead of having to drag you into something with you complaining about it, you would have actually taken the initiative to make this company a better place. Since you had made the decision to enjoy it, you would actually enjoy the work with

the XYZ company. You would be helping our company to perform in a stellar way for its largest customer.

That would be such a better way to work. You would be much happier. We would be much happier. The entire company would recognize your contribution to our success and really appreciate it because it would be so visible. You would be taking an active leadership role on the XYZ project, so you would gain a tremendous amount of respect there as well.

Think about this. It could, potentially, be a much healthier, happier and more prosperous way for you to work. This, by the way, is exactly how successful people work in this company. Simply TAKE THE INITIATIVE and HELP THE TEAM as best you can.

Your Boss

All of us have our own character flaws. Some of them we know about and are working to fix. Others we don't recognize until we are told. If you are fortunate to be working for a good manager, he or she will take the time to help you work through character flaws that are impeding your progress. Ideally your manager will do that in a constructive way, but sometimes your manager will explode instead. Try not to take it personally. Do not quit or become a recluse. Take it for what it is—constructive criticism. Use it to make yourself better. Simply accept the criticism and work to fix the problem, because it the long run it will be beneficial to you to do that.

A good manager who can deliver good constructive criticism to you, especially as a teenager, can accelerate your career tremendously. A good manager will also groom you for more important tasks in the company.

Another thing employers are not looking for is people who cannot get a job done on their own. When someone asks you to do something, what they hope you will do is complete the task without assistance. You may have heard the saying, "There is no such thing as a stupid question." That saying is untrue. A stupid question is one which you could answer yourself if you took the initiative to find the answer. When you are given a task, try to do it on your own. If you are missing a key element important to completion, then obviously you should ask for it. That is common sense. But try to discover missing elements yourself when possible. You will often surprise yourself with what you can accomplish.

Finally, employers will have absolutely nothing to do with you if you cannot work with other people. A business is made up of a team of people and this team functions as a unit. Someone who comes in acting like a prima donna or who is belligerent to or disrespectful of other team members will be asked to leave. Such a person is simply too disruptive to have around and clearly does not understand how the world works.

RÉSUMÉS, INTERVIEWS AND SO ON

To get a job you have to do two standard things: you have to create a good résumé and you have to give a good interview. There are a million books available on both topics, and your guidance counselor at school can give you an armload of information as well (see also the BYG Publishing web site at http://www.bygpub.com and Chapter 45). I want to show you something to help put résumés and interviews into perspective.

Let's say that one day the project leader of a software development company is sitting in her office and a person walks in. He is neatly dressed. He sits down and they have the following conversation:

> Him: I am wondering if there is anything I could do here to help you and your company.
> Her: Well, what do you know how to do?
> Him: My primary skills lie in the area of object oriented development using the C++ programming language. I have experience with both the Booch and Rumbagh methodologies but prefer Rational Rose as my tool for object oriented design.
> Her: Do you know MFC?
> Him: Yes, I am familiar with Visual C++ and MFC and have two years of GUI experience using MFC.
> Her: How do you like MFC?
> Him: I think it is a compromise, but overall I like it. I especially like the way Microsoft has created integrated tools that work with it. I have found I do not like the CRecordset class, however, and prefer to use a customized, three-tier architecture of my own design instead.
> Her: Really? So you have database experience as well?
> Him: Yes, I am familiar with the Sybase and Oracle database engines and have worked with both in application development environments.

What I want you to notice is the following: This is a normal person. He has no résumé. He walked into her office unannounced and sat down and simply told her what he knows. The thing is, this person is worth something like $50,000 to $80,000 a year (1997). Thousands of companies in America would hire him in an instant if he could sit down at a computer for 15 minutes and prove that he knows what he says he knows. The skill set he is displaying is extremely valuable and in high demand in 1997. Therefore, he can go anywhere he wants and get a good job very quickly.

My point is this: Your résumé and interviewing skills are secondary to your job skills. If you have a good skill set (a skill set that is in demand in the job market), if you can work comfortably with other people and if you simply show up to work on time every day and do a good job, then you are set.

How do you find out what the good skill sets are? There are at least three ways:

Networking for Jobs

I have never seen a specific statistic, but I'd say that at least half of the jobs filled in this country are filled through *networking*. Networking means, in this case, discovering jobs through a group of people who know each other. If I am a businessperson and I am trying to hire someone, the first thing I am going to do is ask my employees and friends, "Hey, do you know of anyone looking for a job who is good at..." Chances are that half of my job vacancies are filled because somebody I know knows somebody who needs a job and has the proper credentials. Why is that? First, it is easy. It is a lot easier than placing an ad in the paper and sorting though hundreds of résumés (or placing an ad in the paper and getting no responses). Second, there is a level of human trust involved. If I know you and trust you, then I know you will bring good people to my attention. That saves me a lot of time.

As a teenager you should pay attention to networking for two reasons:

1. If you are looking for a job, you can use networking in reverse. You can ask your friends, "Do you know anyone who is hiring?"

2. Since you now know that networking is a good way to find jobs, it encourages you to form relationships with adults in good jobs. That way you have more connections into the network.

- Look in the classified ad section of the Sunday paper. Find the "help wanted" section. Look for the job categories that have lots of openings and good salaries. If you are truly adventurous, send a letter to some of the ads that sound interesting to you and say, "I'm a teenager. Can you tell me what I need to learn to apply for a job like this some day?" You will be ignored by many companies, but a few will write back a nice letter and you can learn a lot. Because you are a teenager, you are allowed to write innocent, earnest letters like that. There are many people who will take the time to help you (see Chapters 4 and 16).
- Get any menial job in any growing small business and find out, through experience and by asking questions, what skills are important to that business. Learn everything you can about every part of the business.
- Start asking your parents and other adults for skill sets that would make it easy to land a good job in their companies. Ask them what types of people are making the most money. Ask them which jobs are the most enjoyable. Then shoot for those jobs.

AN EXAMPLE

I would like to give you an example of what a person can do for himself or herself as a teenager. Here is a piece of Email I received from a teenager named Paul:

> I would be interested in working for a large company writing in C or C++; however, I'm still a senior in high school. Even though I am young, I know more than most college grads. I have spent at least 8 years programming and 5 of them in C/C++. I also program in Assembly language and am familiar with Pascal. I have spent the last few months teaching myself how to work with the Windows API.
>
> I don't really expect to get the job, but some kind of response telling me what you look for in a new employee would be helpful.
>
> Thanks,
> Paul

This is the response I sent back:

> Paul,
> Your letter has been forwarded up to me by Ken. Let me take a minute here and give you some ideas for you to pursue.
> Even in the short letter you have written, you have conveyed several important facts about yourself:
> -You are smart
> -You are motivated
> -You are confident
> You will find a lot of companies are interested in people who display those qualities. One option, once you get to college, would be to find a co-op or intern position with a company (most larger ones interview on campus) and proceed from there.
> I am going to hazard two guesses though: 1) you don't want to wait that long, and 2) you might not get enough freedom in a big company—it all depends on the company.
> I would encourage you to look for a small company in your area that understands what you are trying to accomplish. That may be hard. You may have to knock on a LOT of doors before you find someone who understands what you are saying. However, I think it would be worth the effort.
> Good luck! You may not realize it now (or maybe you do...), but you will accomplish great things. The writing is already on the wall.
>
> MB

His response closed with this:

> Thanks, you don't know how long I have been wanting to hear something like this from a real business and not from my parents :)

The point is, you have to search until you find someone who understands what you are trying to accomplish. A lot of people will blow you off. Ignore them. Just keep looking until you find someone who can benefit from your talents and goals.

GETTING A PROMOTION

Once you get a job, you may not want to stay in that same job forever. You would like to advance so that you can learn new skills, make more money and take on more responsibility. Here are the most common things that people do to get a promotion:

- Learn more in your current skill area. Become more of an expert

---

Management Positions

Management positions, especially at higher levels in a large company, are some of the best paying jobs in this country. They are also some of the most demanding. If you are interested in getting one of these positions, it is important to understand what a "manager" is and what makes a good one.

Think about a minimum wage worker working in any company: a factory, fast food restaurant, grocery store or whatever. A "line" worker like this does one job without thinking. The worker is told what to do and then does it. That's it. The line worker mentality is, "I've got to flip these burgers," "I've got to solder these wires" and so on. The line worker understands nothing about the bigger picture.

A manager is treated differently. A manager is given a group of people plus a budget and told, "Please accomplish this task." A manager, therefore, needs at least four skills:

- Interpersonal skills to help in leading a group of people and making sure they are all happy, productive and interacting well with one another.

- Organizational skills to make sure that all of the people do the right things at the right time so that the project is completed on time and on budget.

- Corporate skills to make sure that the project fits in well with the rest of the company (A department is not a free-floating entity—it has to work with other departments, request corporate resources, deliver output and accept input and so on).

- Money management skills to keep track of the budget.

You do not gain all of these skills by accident. You work at all of them throughout your career, gaining experience with them as you tackle each new project or assignment. The important thing to know is that you *can* work at them. By improving these specific skills you can accelerate your rise in any company.

in the area you currently understand.

- Learn a new skill that has better earning potential than the skill you currently have. Normally, once you get a job you can learn about other skill areas that are available in the same or different industries.
- Learn what it takes to get the next job up. In every business there is normally a natural promotion path. In larger companies there are formal promotion ladders. Ask your manager for the requirements of the next job up and fulfill them.
- Learn management skills. The ability to organize projects, manage people and get the job done profitably is highly valued in all companies. Learn about management opportunities, take management courses and read books so that you can move into management roles.
- Do a good job. In all companies, the people who do a good job are the ones who get promoted. See the list of attributes at the beginning of this chapter for more information.

CHAPTER 8

Suits Send Signals

S uits are a fact of life. In fact, suits have been a fact of life for quite awhile. As a teenager, you probably have an aversion to suits—a deep dislike that runs right to your core. I know that when I was a teenager I felt that way. I felt like a total geek whenever I had to wear "nice clothes."

And yet, I wear a suit as I am writing this. I wear a suit every day. I actually choose to wear a suit and like the fact that I do. What I would like to do here is explain what caused that transformation.

Suits are an important part of the professional world. A suit is the uniform of success. *By wearing a suit you are saying, both in American culture and most other cultures on this planet, that you are succeeding.* It is as simple as that. People see the suit you are wearing, and it has an effect on them. It is that way now. It has been that way for decades. It will be that way in the future. A suit is the uniform of a successful person.

Don't believe me? Walk into any large office center, any courtroom, any large fancy hotel, any airport, any church, any meeting. Look at the people. The ones who are successful and thinking and rising are wearing suits. All of the hourly people, the gofers, the teenagers, are not. The sooner you understand this simple fact of life, the sooner you can take advantage of it in your own way.

Many people ask, "But why? Why have people chosen this ridiculous outfit as the outward symbol of success, goals and intention? It is expensive, cumbersome and absolutely worthless in any sort of inclement weather. Why? What possible purpose does a tie serve, for example? Why ties?" The answer is simply BECAUSE. It is completely random. It makes no sense. But that is how it is. You can accept it and take advantage of the effect suits have, or you can reject it. By accepting it you tend to accelerate your development.

62

Let me give you an example that will help you understand the effect. Let's say you are an agent at an airline ticket counter, a police officer, a clerk at a hotel, a service station attendant or whatever. Two people are standing in front of you. One is a smartly dressed person in a suit. The other is a slouching teenager in torn and dirty clothes. Something needs to happen. Who is going to get priority? The one dressed in the suit. Almost always. You might say, "But if the clerk is another teenager the slouching teenager will get the nod." That *may* be true in some situations. Since there are seven times more adults than there are teenagers (see Chapter 3), it is irrelevant. The odds heavily favor the suit wearer.

A suit is the uniform of a successful person. Don't believe me? Walk into any office, any courtroom, any fancy hotel, any airport, any meeting. Look at the people. The ones who are successful and thinking and rising are wearing suits. All of the hourly people, the gofers, the teenagers, are not. It is as simple as that.

Look at your own reaction to suits. When you see people wearing suits you think of them as "adult" and "meaning business" and "mature" and "in control." By wearing a suit you give off those same signals to everyone else. "Why?" *Who cares?* It is a fact of life. That is how our culture is wired, so begin to take advantage of it. Why does an object in mid-air fall to the ground? Because it does. You plan your life around that fact. Suits are the same way.

Let's say you listen to this discussion and you decide to investigate its validity. You could do that. It would be a very interesting experiment for you to perform. It would be easier to try if you are in college, but you could theoretically try it in high school. First of all, get a suit. You are going to find this is not easy if you don't already own one. A nice suit, shirt, tie and shoes will run you $300 to $1,000 (1997), depending on what level of quality you are looking for. Go to a nice department store that is having a sale; you can't go far wrong. Buy a good, conservative suit. That means a darker color like charcoal or dark blue. Get a nice shirt, a nice tie and nice, shineable shoes. Now wear this outfit all the time, every day, everywhere you go, for a month. I am not kidding. It will take you a week at least to feel comfortable in it. It will take another week for you to forget you have it on. Your friends will harass you mercilessly for a period of time as well. Ignore them. Tell them you are trying an experiment. During the third and fourth week, after you and everyone around you have settled down, watch the difference a suit makes in how people treat you and how you feel. It will be subtle, but you will notice it. You will find that people you know, especially adults, treat you differently. You will find that strangers treat you differently as well. They treat you with a different level of respect. You will find that a suit also changes what you say and how you act. It is very surprising.

The other thing you will notice is that a huge number of other people are wearing suits. All of them are adults. All of them are successful—business people, entertainers, high-end sales people and so on. Every important person on TV is wearing a suit. Every person in charge of things is wearing a suit. You ignored all of these people before because you were in the "flunky teenager" category. Suddenly, they become visible because you are a member of their club. There are certain environments where suit-wearers tend to congregate, and now you will fit right in. You will find that the people wearing the suits are the ones who are successful.

A lot of teenagers look at the "adult world" and decide they can be more adult-like and "grown up" by wearing lots of makeup or smoking or drinking coffee. They are TOTALLY missing it. You fit into the adult world by wearing a suit and acting like an adult.

OTHER RULES OF THE ROAD

While you are wearing your suit, it is good to know the other "rules of the road" in the adult world. People expect a certain level of behavior from suit-wearers, and you may be unfamiliar with them. Here are a number of the most basic:

- When two adults meet, they shake hands—This is a very odd

Defining a Suit

The definition of a suit for a man is extremely clear. A suit is a jacket and a pair of pants cut from the same cloth, along with a dress shirt and a nice tie. For a woman a suit is a jacket and a skirt or pants in matching material, along with a nice business-like blouse.

One step below a suit is "sports jacket" or "blazer" worn with a pair of nice slacks (or for women a skirt). Men wear a nice shirt and tie, while women wear a nice blouse. The jacket and the pants/skirt are made of different materials/colors and do not match.

One step below that is "business casual." It consists of a nice dress shirt and nice slacks, but no tie for men. For women pants and skirts are interchangeable, with skirts considered slightly more dressy. No jeans, no T-shirts, and usually no "polo shirts" either, but that depends on the environment.

custom, especially when you are first learning it. However, it is universal in American culture and many others. Two adults on first meeting will offer their right hands and shake. You might say, "Hi, my name is John Smith. I am glad to meet you," as you are shaking. The first 100 times you do this it will feel awkward. Practice, practice, practice until it is totally natural. Practice with your parents if you have no one else.

- Offer your hand—Even if the other adult does not, always offer your hand to shake. If the other person fails to respond, it means he or she is uncouth. Say something to make them comfortable in their uncouthness, such as, "I'm glad to see you! Let me shake your hand." The other adult might be clueless or distracted rather than uncouth. By offering your hand you send the signal that you are in control.

- Always lead with your own name—A person who states his or her name clearly right up front is saying to the world, "I am John Smith, and I am proud, confident and honest." If you weren't confident you would be afraid to state your name. If you were dishonest you would try to hide your name. Always state your name up front.

- Shake hands firmly—When you shake hands, do so firmly and look the person in the eye as you are shaking. This is another sign of honesty and confidence.

- Smile—Who wants to talk to unhappy people?

- Remember the person's name—People like it when you remember their names. Practice this skill. A time-honored technique used to remember a person's name is to repeat it. For example, "Hello, My name is John Smith." "I am glad to meet you John; my name is Mary Johnson." "I am glad to meet you, Mary..." If you forget someone's name it is OK to ask them to repeat it. Say, "I'm sorry, I have forgotten your name." It happens to everyone.

- Get a haircut—There is nothing more ridiculous to an adult than a person in a suit who has a non-suit haircut. Get a professional, business-like haircut to go with your suit. You may feel silly when you first look at it. Here is a fact: You and maybe a few of your friends are the only people who feel that way. The whole rest of the world expects a haircut that matches the suit. In this same category goes, "Shine your shoes." If you are going to do this, do it right.

- If you want to speak with an adult, offer to make an appointment. Say something like, "Is this a convenient time, or could we schedule a time that would be better for you?" Adults are busy people. Their time is valuable. Show up on time for your appointment. It is important to keep all of your commitments, both large and small. Adults notice people who do not keep small commitments because it often means the larger ones won't be kept as well.

- Speak clearly—Speak as an adult would speak rather than using teenage slang. You can learn the "institutional language" that adults use by spending time in institutional environments. As with any foreign language, the more time you spend immersed in the culture the better you get at the language.
- Watch your language—Cussing is out. So is yelling.
- Be polite (see Chapter 22).

What you will notice is that if you dress like an adult and act like an adult, people will assume you are an adult and treat you like one. This treatment can have huge advantages,

The Psychological Effect of Suits

I spend a lot of time with clients. I may go to a client's company and work there for a week or a month at a time. I always wear a suit. In many smaller companies I will be the only one in the office wearing a suit. You can best see the psychological effect of a suit in these situations. If a stranger walks in and sees me, the stranger will automatically make the assumption that I am "in charge" simply because of the way I am dressed. I am the one in the suit, so obviously I know what is going on! If you watch, you will notice that you make that same assumption in many situations. By wearing a suit you can take advantage of this effect.

especially for a teenager. In a business environment wearing a suit sends a signal to those around you about your attitude and intent.

PART 3

The Facts About Love and Marriage

You might have noticed that, as a teenager, your brain and body seem to be obsessed with members of the opposite sex. This section explains "the facts of life" and what they mean to you, both now and in the future

CHAPTER 9

Love is THE Fact of Life

Love is a fact of life. For all human beings, and especially for teenagers, it could be said that love is THE fact of life. It is one thing that is central to all human existence. You might have come to this realization already. Simply by looking into your own mind and noticing how much of your time it spends thinking about people of the opposite sex, fantasizing about people of the opposite sex, dreaming about people of the opposite sex, wondering about people of the opposite sex, feeling depressed about people of the opposite sex and so on, you get a good idea of how important this topic is in the human realm.

Because it is so important and so central to human existence, love is something that can be extremely confusing and frustrating. I know that as a teenager love was extremely confusing and frustrating to me. I had a huge number of questions about the whole space, including (If you are a girl, please replace "girl" with "boy" in the following questions):

- Why do girls hate me?
- Why do I feel so awkward around girls?
- Why is it that I think about girls all the time, despite the fact that I would rather not?
- Why does it hurt so much?
- Why does it seem like a lot of people don't have these problems? Why does it seem like they are able to walk up to girls, talk to them and the next minute they are going out together and having a really great time? Why are a lot of those people athletes?
- Why are pretty girls like they are?
- Why do a lot of girls seem attracted to guys who are obviously idiots and who treat them badly? I would treat a girl great, but that seems to make no difference. Why?
- What is jealousy, and why do I get so angry about it?
- Will I ever find someone who I can marry?

- When?
- Why can't it be now?
- How will I know when I have found the girl I should marry?
- Now that I think about it, what is marriage again? Why do we have marriage? Why don't we all just go around having sex with whoever we feel like all the time?
- For that matter, what is love? I mean, what the heck is going on here to begin with?
- Why does it seem like adults don't have these problems?
- Why do my parents say they are "in love," but it looks so different from what I mean when I say I am "in love"? In other words, why does their love seem so boring, why do they have fights and why do they never hold hands?
- And so on.

You might have asked one or two of these questions yourself. Obviously, this is a pretty big and complicated space.

One way to begin to get a handle on love and to begin to understand it better is to try to tackle it one piece at a time. We will start with the fundamental facts of life concerning love. Once you understand these facts you have a foundation. Then you can move on to other areas.

THE FACTS OF LIFE CONCERNING LOVE

The first and most fundamental fact of life about love is: love is something that is fundamentally wired into the human brain. There is nothing that you can do about it. You cannot turn it on and off. It is there, it is active and that's the end of it. In fact, it is nearly impossible to separate love from human existence. Especially as a teenager, they are one and the same.

The second fact of life is that there are different kinds of love, and we need to agree on what we are talking about when we say the word "love." Here are some of the different kinds of love that you might be familiar with:

- Parental love—Parents love their children, and this sort of love, devotion and caring is different from all other types of love. When done well, parental love could be called perfect.
- Christian love—Jesus said, "Love your neighbor as yourself," and many people are able to do that. They love and care about those around them because they are fellow human beings.
- Friendship love—A deep friendship between two people often involves a level of trust, devotion, commitment and caring that is love. So two women or two men or a man and a woman who have known each other for 20 years and have been through a lot

together can say they love one another. There is not a bit of romantic or sexual attraction involved.

- Material love—You might hear someone say, "I love that car!" or "I love that movie!" It is love applied to an object. In this case the word "love" can mean a range of things from "I really like it" to "I must have it" all the way up to, in extreme cases, "I will (literally) kill myself if I don't get it." Another word for this is infatuation.
- Lustful love—To some extent lustful love is a form of material love, but it is applied to another person and tied almost completely to a sexual infatuation. So a girl might say, "I love Tom Cruise!" Or a guy might say, strictly on the basis of a girl's looks, "I love that girl!" This is lust.
- Romantic love—When most teenagers think of "love", this is what they are talking about. It is the combination of friendship, sexual attraction and the search for someone to marry. It is the search for the one person with whom you can raise your family and spend the rest of your life.

This chapter is about "Love," and you understood it to mean "romantic love." That was a correct assumption, and in the rest of this chapter the word "love" implies the romantic meaning. However, it is good to recognize that there are all these other forms as well. Sometimes people get confused between them, and that can cause problems.

Love is tied to sexual attraction, especially at the teenage level. That is the third fact of life about love. The link between love and sexual attraction is strong and important. Many people will tell you that love and sexual attraction can be separated. And that is true. But when you separate them you have friendship love, not romantic love. Or you get lust—the sexual attraction without the friendship.

Which leads you to a fourth fact of life; sexual attraction is a fact of life. There are four important facts about sex that are easy to miss:

1. Both men and women have entire sections of their anatomy devoted to sex and reproduction. This should come as no surprise to you. You have feet. Feet are a part of your anatomy devoted to walking. You have ears. Ears are a part of your anatomy devoted to hearing. You have a part of your anatomy devoted to sex and reproduction as well. Just to get it out in the open here so there is no confusion: In males it is the penis and testicles, and in females it is the vagina and female reproductive system, including the uterus, fallopian tubes, etc. In men the sexual organs produce sperm and provide a delivery mechanism, and in women the sexual organs accept sperm, produce eggs and provide an environment in which a baby can develop. When

sperm and egg meet in a woman, a child is formed. Simple as that. Miraculous and totally mystifying, but simple.

2. The sex organs produce sex hormones, which flow through the blood stream and affect certain parts of the brain as well as the sex organs themselves. In women the hormonal part is quite complicated because the female reproductive system is quite complicated and amazing. You can learn a lot by looking all of this up in a good book or encyclopedia.

3. The brain has physical structures and systems specifically devoted to sex. Certain components in this system respond to the sex hormones flowing in the blood stream. Other parts respond to visual or tactile stimulation.

4. There is a biological desire to reproduce that, if you feel like thinking about it this way, can be considered to be the core of human existence. You could say, "Humans exist in order to give birth to other humans," and that is true in a biological sense. You can get a better handle on this by thinking along these lines. Why do bacteria exist and do the things they do? To create other bacteria. No one would argue with you on that. Why do fruit flies exist and do the things they do? To produce other fruit flies. Plants? Fish? Mice? Dogs? Chimps? Same thing. And thus humans. Humans exist to produce other humans. Of course humans are wildly complicated and interesting, especially when compared to a simple bacteria. We do lots of other things besides reproducing. But we are still living things and living things live, fundamentally, to reproduce.

When you take all four of these things together—the sex organs, the hormonal system, the brain structures and the biological imperative to reproduce—you can see why sex is so important to people. You can also see another thing: *Sex is not like anything else.* Let me say that again because it is an important fact of life:

SEX IS NOT LIKE ANYTHING ELSE

When you find yourself asking things like, "Why do I think about Christina all the time?" this is the reason why. Sex simply is not like anything else. It is absolutely fundamental to human existence.

A lot of people simply do not understand that sex is different from everything else. They will say things like, "Eating is completely natural and you do it every day without thinking about it. Sex is the same way! It's just like every thing else! Do it and have fun and don't worry about it!" That is an approach to life, but it is not true. Sex is not like everything else. Eating, for example, cannot create a new human life. Sex can. When someone tries to equate sex and eating, it is impossible to take them seriously.

Having said all of that, there is a fifth fact of life that people often completely ignore. It is funny that people ignore it, because it is so simple and obvious. It is this: The purpose of sex is to create a baby. That is another thing that needs emphasis:

THE PURPOSE OF SEX IS TO CREATE A BABY

You cannot separate sex from babies. The reason our bodies are equipped with sexual apparatus is to have babies and reproduce. If you try to separate sex from babies you are ignoring the obvious, because they cannot be separated. A lot of the "problems in today's society" are caused by the fact that people forget this linkage.

It is the baby part of sex that leads to love and marriage. Babies link sex, love and marriage together.

The sixth fact of life is fairly simple: Love is a mechanism in our brains that encourages coupling. We "fall in love" to form a strong couple. "Falling in love" is another thing that is wired into our brains. It is a mechanism that ensures the survival of the species. You can now see that we have made a full circle, back to the first fact of love at the beginning of this section.

One of the more frustrating things about love is that it is a fairly messy emotion that has a number of rather strong psychological side effects. In order to form a strong coupling, the love mechanism seems to disconnect a variety of normal mental functions. "Falling in love" often means a loss of perspective and a focusing of attention that can drive those around you crazy. Everyone has heard the expression "Love is blind." It is also true that love is irrational at times. You cannot afford to be irrational, and yet a part of your brain is hooked up to make you that way. You need to take that into account in your own life.

The seventh fact of life is marriage. Our society (you can think of the word "society" to mean "the group of people we live in") has taken our natural coupling tendency and formalized it into a thing called *marriage*. A man and woman marry with the intention of staying together for life. Within that bond they have children and raise them.

Finally, here is the eighth fact of life. Sex feels good. You may be aware of this fact already. Part of the wiring between the sex organs and the sexual parts of the brain is a direct connection to the brain's "pleasure center" (time to pull out the psychology book). This connection is no doubt designed to further encourage the reproductive urge by providing direct positive stimulation for reproductive behavior. Many people (both teenagers and adults) seem to miss three important facts about the pleasure of sex:

- Much of the pleasure of sex is psychological.
- It is possible for sex to feel bad.
- The fact that sex is pleasurable doesn't mean that it is always appropriate.

All three of these facts are important. Inside a loving relationship between a husband and wife who care deeply about one another, for example, the pleasure of sex is highly magnified. By the same token, having sex with a prostitute is degrading and can actually feel bad. Ask anyone who has tried it. "Cheap sex" and "one-night stands" and "sex on the first date" all tend to fall into that same category. It often feels bad. It is inappropriate. It is also dangerous because of the disease problem [AIDS, herpes, syphilis, gonorrhea, clamydia and so on (all good things to look up in an encyclopedia)]. Teenagers today know all about these diseases.

> *Eating cannot create a new human life. Sex can. When someone tries to equate sex and eating, it is therefore impossible to take them seriously.*

The fact that something is pleasurable does not necessarily make it good. Many people live many years before they realize this simple fact.

So, here you were looking for an answer to questions like, "What is love?" and you get a six-page answer. That is why love is complicated, by the way. Love is important as far as our bodies, our brains, our biology and our evolution is concerned. There is a lot more to it than meets the eye. Look at all of the different topics discussed in this chapter:

- Reproduction
- The definition of love
- Sexual attraction
- Sex organs
- Hormones
- Babies
- Brain structures, like the pleasure center
- Marriage
- Sexually transmitted diseases

These are all facts of life. The thing you will notice is that they are all intertwined, and that makes everything complicated. Love and marriage and sex and babies all go together. As a teenager it is at first difficult to see all the interconnections.

Teenagers get into problems in the love/marriage/sex/babies arena because they do not understand the interconnections. Or they happen because teenagers (and adults, for that matter) purposefully ignore them. For example, why does society frown, in general, on premarital sex? Because the purpose of sex is to have a baby, and a baby needs a stable family to raise it. Teenagers, because they have never had a baby, miss the connection between sex and babies. Your parents are saying, "Wait! Wait! Wait!" because they understand the baby part (they had you, for example). They understand the need for a strong, life-long couple to take care of the baby and to provide it with a stable family. Marriage is the mechanism to provide that coupling and stability. Your parents also understand that babies represent a huge financial commitment. The hospital bill alone for a normal childbirth is $5,000 to

Sex without love is meaningless.

$10,000. Do you have that money (along with the money to cover all the other expenses associated with a new child) in the bank? If not, then you are not ready to have a baby.

Can you separate sex and babies? Can you separate sex and love? Can you separate sex and marriage? These are good questions. The answer is "Yes." But consider the following:

- When you separate sex from love, babies and marriage, you get prostitution. Sex without love is meaningless.
- When you separate sex and babies from love and marriage, you get unwed, teenage mothers. This creates problems for the mother, the child and the people who end up supporting the mother because she cannot support herself.
- When you separate sex and love from babies and marriage, you get premarital sex, recreational sex and people living together. None of this seems bad on the surface, and many teenagers you ask will say, "Go for it!" Find a person, fall in love and have sex. Adults would say there are reasons to wait, and we will talk about them in Chapters 12 and 13.

It is only when you put love, marriage, sex and babies together that you have something complete and whole and beautiful. It is pretty deep, I know. Think about it for awhile and then come back and read through this section again.

CHAPTER 10

Relationships are Random

I n the previous chapter you learned that love, sex, marriage and babies are all intertwined. You also learned that love and sex are both firmly wired into your brain and your anatomy. This explains why love, sex and marriage are such "big deals."

That is all well and good. It explains why we have love and sexual attraction. However, none of it explains why Christina won't go out with you this weekend, or why Darren doesn't know you exist. That kind of stuff all falls into the category of "relationships," and, unfortunately, this part is messy. Here are some of the relationship questions mentioned at the beginning of the previous chapter [If you are a girl, please replace "girls" with "boys" in the following questions]:

- Why do girls hate me?
- Why do I feel so awkward around girls?
- Why does it seem like a lot of people don't have these problems? Why does it seem like they are able to walk up to girls, talk to them and the next minute they are going out together and having a really great time? Why are a lot of those people athletes?
- Why are pretty girls like they are?
- Why do a lot of girls seem attracted to guys who are obviously idiots and who treat them bad? I would treat a girl great, but that seems to make no difference. Why?

So we need to talk about relationships and the facts of life around them. Unfortunately, I have some bad news: The relationship part of being a teenager is totally random. As random as lottery numbers and rolling dice. *It turns out there are no rules.* That is a fact of life. The quicker you learn it and accept it, the better.

How can relationships be totally random? Let me give you an example that will help to explain the way the world works. For this example I am going to use the menu at a fast food restaurant.

Think about the menu at any fast food restaurant. Think about the main entree section. Let's focus on four of the main items: cheeseburger, Super Burger, Fish Sandwich and Chicken Nuggets. Now imagine that it is lunch time, you have just walked in the restaurant to order lunch and you are trying to decide what you are going to have. You look at the menu, and the following monologue floats through your head:

> Hmmm. Let's see. Lunch. Wow. I'm really hungry. What do I want? Let's see. No cheeseburgers. Too boring. A Super Burger is just a big cheeseburger. No Super Burgers. No Fish Sandwiches, either. Who eats those, anyway? I just had Chicken Nuggets yesterday, so that's out. Well, maybe a Super Burger does sound good. I'm really hungry. I think I'll have a Super Burger today.

And so you choose a Super Burger. Simple, right? You make decisions like this every day and you never give them a second thought.

Now I want you to imagine that the restaurant works differently. Instead of you looking at a menu and making a choice, each sandwich comes up to you and talks to you personally. You walk in the restaurant, sit down at a table and a cheeseburger walks up and says, "Hi, would you like to have lunch with me today?" You say, "No." A Super Burger comes up and says, "Hi, would you like to have lunch with me today?"

Now I know this scene creates a funny mental image. But I want you to think about this from the point of view of the sandwiches. What if they all take your rejection personally?

You say, "No." A Fish Sandwich comes up and says, "Hi, would you like to have lunch with me today?" You say, "No way. I hate Fish Sandwiches!" A Chicken Nugget comes up and says, "Hi, would you like to have lunch with me today?" You say, "No." Then you think about it and call the Super Burger over to the table again and say, "Yes, let's have lunch."

Now I know this scene creates a funny mental image. But I want you to think about this from the point of view of the sandwiches. *Let's say they all take your rejection personally.* So when you say "No" to the Chicken Nugget, the Chicken Nugget sulks back to the kitchen thinking, "Boy, I really blew that one. I am such an idiot. That guy hates me. Hates my guts. Why did I even go up to his table? I could tell he was going to say no. When will I ever learn? I shouldn't go up to tables any more.

Why does everyone hate me? And why this guy? I really liked him. I hate this whole thing. It stinks. Maybe I should just kill myself. Or maybe I'll go live in a vegetarian monastery. At least then I won't have to think about it any more. I hate this."

From the Chick Nugget's point of view, the whole transaction was a total rejection. You, on the other hand, are looking at the "relationship" between yourself and the Chicken Nugget differently. Do you hate the Chicken Nugget? No. Do you have any feelings at all against the Chicken Nugget? No. Are you rejecting the Chicken Nugget? No. Obviously not; you had Chicken Nuggets just yesterday. But you did have them yesterday, so you don't want them today. Therefore, you said, "No."

The point is this: When you said "No" to the Chicken Nugget it meant nothing. It meant that you did not want to have Chicken Nuggets for lunch today. It did not mean a single thing to the Chicken Nugget but that. For the Chicken Nugget to take it personally and read anything into it is pointless, because it was not meant personally and in fact has no meaning at all. *The fact that you said "No" to the Chicken Nugget was totally random!*

Now let's say you are a guy. You call up a girl and ask her out and she says, "No." What should you read into that? Nothing. It is as meaningless to you as it is to the Chicken Nugget. She simply did not want to have lunch with you for whatever reason, those reasons are totally random and there is nothing you can do about it. Take it at face value and walk away. To take it personally and beat yourself over the head with it is pointless.

"OK," you say, "but why is it that the last three girls I have asked out said 'No'"? That occurs because relationships are a "numbers game." That is an expression used in sales. Let's say you decide to go to a car dealership and get a job as a car salesperson. It is your first day. A couple comes on to the lot and you talk to them; they decide not to buy a car and drive away. You say, "Oh well." Another couple comes on to the lot. You talk to them, they decide not to buy a car and drive away. You say, "Hmmm." A guy comes on to the lot, you talk to him, he decides not to buy a car and drives away. You say, "I'm not doing very well." Another couple comes on to the lot. You talk to them, they decide not to buy a car and drive away. You say, "I really stink at this."

At lunch you go talk to the manager and you say, "I stink at this. I quit." He would say to you, "You aren't doing anything wrong. It's a numbers game. Just stick with it for a month and you will see what I mean." So you stick with it for a month and you do see what he means. What he means is that you have to talk to 10 or 15 people before someone buys a car. In the month you talked to 150 people and they bought ten cars. What that means is that you got rejected fourteen times for every acceptance. And that is how it is. It is only after you have tried 150 times and been rejected 140 of those times that you begin to see the pattern. The first day was rough because you couldn't see the pattern due to lack of experience.

Should a car salesman be mad about the rejections? No. Should he take them personally? No. Do they mean anything? No. Not everyone who comes on to his lot is going to want to buy what he sells. That's a fact of life. On the other hand, are there techniques he might be able to use to improve the ratio? Yes. He learns those techniques by asking other successful sales people, reading books on sales, experimenting with new techniques to see how they work and so on.

Asking people out is a numbers game as well. That is a fact of life. You will be rejected many times for each acceptance. When you are 30 and you have asked many people out you understand the pattern and are more comfortable with it. You know that when a person says, "No" it is meaningless. But when you first start asking people out it can be really depressing because you don't understand.

The funny thing about asking people out is that it is a pretty bad numbers game. Let me show you why. Go to a mall or shopping center and sit on a bench where a lot of people will walk by. Take a pad of paper and a pencil. If you are a guy, I want you to look at every female that walks by. If you are a girl, look at every guy. Here is what I want you to do. On the pad of paper I want you to make two columns. In the left column you are going to put a mark as each person walks by. This will let you count all of the people you are looking at.

So if you are a guy, I want you to put a mark in the left column for every female that walks past. Now, as each female walks by I want you to look at her and decide if you would like to go out with her. If so, put a second mark in the right column. You are doing this based strictly on appearance alone, which I realize is superficial, but I want you to do it anyway. So the first female to go by will be 60 and you will make a mark in the left column. You will say to yourself, "Too old," so you will make no mark in the right column. The next female to go by is 5, so you make a mark in the left column and not in the right. Now the third female to go by is about your age, but you do not find her attractive. Again mark the left column but not the right. Eventually, a female will walk by that you might consider asking out. Put a mark in both the left and right columns.

What you are going to find is that there are a lot more marks on the left side than there are on the right. That is one thing that makes dating a numbers game. But there is something else that makes it a numbers game, and that is the fact that *it goes both ways*. Let's say you find that your ratio on your sheet of paper is 20 to 1. (Or it might be as high as 200 to

1—it depends on the person and the environment.) For every 20 females that walk by, one is "acceptable" to you.

Let's say that is a consistent ratio for all people: 20 to 1. Let's say you call a girl up. What you must keep in mind is that she has a 20:1 ratio as well, and *you may not be on her list.* There is only a 5% chance that you are on her list, in fact. Why might you not be on her list? Who knows? Why did you find only one out of every 20 girls attractive? Some were too fat, some were too thin, some had stupid hair, some wore ugly shoes... You are as fickle as anyone else. Why do some people like Chicken Nuggets and some like Fish Sandwiches? *BECAUSE.* There is no reason! It is totally random! It is the same way for guys and girls.

What you can begin to see from this discussion, if you do the math, is that the probability of you liking someone and them actually liking you back enough to go out with you is pretty minuscule. If the average for each person is 20 to 1, then that means there is a 1 in 400 chance of any given female actually saying, "Yes" when any given male asks her out. Pretty bad odds!

So what is "love at first sight"? It is that rare, one-in-a-million shot that you look at someone and think, "Wow, if only this person would go out with me, I would be in heaven," and the other person looks at you and thinks exactly the same thing. In that case it is a perfect match. It doesn't happen very often because the odds are really low, but it does happen occasionally.

Given that asking people out and dating is a numbers game and is also totally random, there are a few conclusions you can draw. You can also answer a lot of questions. Let's go through some of them.

Why do some guys get all the girls? Let's say a guy is really handsome. When he calls up a girl and asks her out, his probability of success is higher. It is not 100%, but it is higher. That is a fact of life. Fortunately, only a tiny percentage of the population is startlingly attractive. The rest of us have other gifts. Live with it.

Is there anything you can do to improve the odds of success? Yes. Some car salespeople are better than others. Part of it is natural talent. But all the rest is learned through experience. Experience means practice—the more people you ask out, the easier it gets. If you have people skills and lots of people like you, the odds rise quite a bit (see Chapter 15). If you are confident in yourself, the odds also rise (see Chapter 14).

You can also learn to recognize signals. People give off signals when they like each other (and when they don't). Teenagers are notoriously bad at recognizing the signals because they are new to the game. Adults can see from a mile away when two teenagers like each other because they understand the signals. Start watching the people around you at school carefully and you will begin to see these signals everywhere.

"Why do I feel so awkward?" That is a combination of lack of confidence and lack of practice. Let's say you are 14 years old, you are a guy, you have found a girl that actually likes you, you have gone out on several dates and it is time for your first kiss. And this is the first kiss of your life. Or you are at a dance and a slow song comes on and this is the first slow dance of your life. Then it is possible that this moment will feel awkward. How do you know you are doing it right? How do you know people won't laugh at you? I would point out that the first time you do *anything* it generally feels awkward. What happens as you get older is that you learn to accept "first-time awkwardness" as a natural part of being human. Everyone feels that way. When you are an adult, everyone knows that everyone feels that way. But as a teenager, everyone is pretending—for some reason—that they know it all.

The awkwardness also comes from seeing people of the opposite sex

Small Talk

Have you ever noticed that when adults meet they will often start by talking about something innocuous like the weather? Why do they do that? You can answer that question with another question: Have you ever noticed how uncomfortable it is to sit down next to someone (especially someone you would like to get to know better) and have absolutely nothing to say?

To say that someone is "good at small talk" is to say that the person is able to sit down with a friend or a stranger and have a worthwhile and interesting conversation with the person starting from scratch. For some people, this is easy because it comes naturally (just as, for some people, drawing comes naturally). For most people, however, small talk is uncomfortable. This is especially true if you are shy.

Small talk is a natural human skill. Like walking, running or writing, we are all able to do it at some level. However, the way to get much better is to *practice*.

If you start practicing small talk, you will notice that the hardest part of having a conversation is *starting the conversation*. During the startup phase you have to find something that the two of you are interested in talking about. Then you can build to a full conversation. The reason why people start talking about the weather or current events is because they are innocuous and common to everyone. That makes it a good place to start. As you practice small talk you will find your own starting points that work for you. You will also learn how to keep a conversation rolling by asking questions and showing interest. After several months small talk will seem much more natural and easier, and you will actually enjoy it because you will be able to meet new and interesting people.

as somehow "different." Let me give you an example. Let's say you are a guy and you are in the library and you are minding your own business. A girl that you would like to know better sits down near you. What are you going to do at that point? You can say, "Hi. How's it going?" and see what happens. You would do the same thing if she were a guy. There is a very strong probability that nothing will happen. On the other hand, you might end up having a nice conversation. However, there is no reason to quiver in your seat and worry about it. Just talk to her and see what happens; if nothing happens, don't worry about it. She is just a girl.

Or is she? Is she *just* a girl? You may see her as the most beautiful goddess in the world, and therefore the *only* girl in the world. Talking to her in that case becomes something different. What is happening when you talk to a girl you really like is that the same terror signal discussed in the Fear section of Chapter 14 kicks in. Any mistake and you will lose her. Since she is the only girl in the world, it's a big risk. So you freeze up.

What can you do to get beyond this problem? One thing you can do is remember that there are a lot of fish in the sea. At this moment in your life this girl seems important. But if you were to go down to the mall and watch people walk by, you would find that there is at least one girl a day who catches your eye. You would find that there is about one girl a week who makes your heart beat faster. And there is one girl a month who makes you ache. You are overlooking these others when you focus on one person.

The other thing you can do is practice. I can remember a funny thing I did when I was in college because I felt so awkward around women. This is a true story. I decided I would work on my conversation skills, so I went to a nearby park. A lot of older people frequented this park, sitting on benches and enjoying the view. All of them seemed to like to talk. So I could sit on a bench with a 70-year-old woman and have a conversation with her. Because she was 70 there was no pressure. The first few times I did this, I was surprised to find that it was awkward. Really awkward. *I had nothing to talk about!* I had no idea how to start or have a conversation with a stranger (see the small talk sidebar). But after awhile, I overcame this problem and got to where it was extremely easy to have a very pleasant conversation with anyone 70 years old. Then I started moving down the age scale. Pretty soon I could start and maintain a natural conversation with just about any stranger. *This did not happen overnight.* It took several months of practice. I learned all sorts of things from this experience.

One day I went to the park and there was a very attractive woman sitting on a bench in the sun. I sat down next to her and guess what? We had a very nice conversation for 20 minutes. And it was completely natural. Did we then fall in love, get married and live happily ever after? No. It's kind of silly to expect that. What we did do was have a relaxed, pressure-free conversation. That was a major milestone for me. My practice sessions in the park made it much easier to talk to women, and to people in general. One day I went to a party with some friends. I saw a very attractive woman there. Her beauty made me ache. I was able to walk up to her and have a completely natural conversation with her and feel totally comfortable. The next time I saw her she remembered me and we talked again. And the next time we talked together we decided to take a walk. Coincidentally, we walked in that same park. And one thing led to another, and we fell in love and got married.

That sort of natural progression is how the world works. Compare it to how you might deal with members of the opposite sex. You find someone you are attracted to. You start dreaming about him or her. You do this for several weeks until you are ready to burst. You work up all your courage, make an extremely nervous and nerve-wracking phone call, ask him or her out on a date and... you get rejected. Your despair is infinite. The next time you see that person your humiliation is so great you run in the opposite direction. Is this a healthy pattern? No.

It turns out most adults do things completely differently. Instead of dreaming about someone and getting all worked up about it, most adults simply walk up to each other and have a natural conversation. The conversation is totally pressure-free and largely meaningless. Some signals may or may not be given off. One or the other may already be in a relationship, for example. A fact like that comes out naturally. The two adults talk several times like this, casually, meaninglessly. If there is some positive interest and there are no overt negative signals, the guy might say, "Hey, I am going to go get some coffee; can I get you a cup?" And the woman might say, "No, thanks." In that case the woman was able to say no in a way that is totally harmless. Or the woman might say, "That sounds great; mind if I tag along? I could use the break." And from that one encounter comes another and another, and the relationship forms in an extremely natural and smooth way. If it doesn't work out it doesn't work out, and there is never any nervousness or rejection. Try it as an approach some time. You will be amazed at how much nicer it can be. Or continue with the cold calling; just be willing to accept a high rejection ratio and don't be upset by it. It is a fact of life.

BREAKING UP

One of the fundamental problems with relationships and "falling in love" is that you open yourself to the hazards of breaking up and getting dumped. You may have heard the saying, "It is better to have loved and lost than to have never loved before." That sounds great until you are the one being dumped—then it's a whole different story.

The thing that hurts so much about being dumped is that you feel like you have been betrayed. You may also feel like you will die. To lose someone you truly love is, at times, nearly unbearable. Here is a letter from a typical person in the throes of those feelings:

> Everything was perfect. We met in high school. I was her first boyfriend and she was my first girlfriend.
> For five years I have given her my love, my soul, my trust and my commitment. Until two weeks ago, I thought that this woman was going to be my soul mate.
> Now she wants to date other people. She's curious about what's out there. She felt that her life had been missing something.
> Knowing her for so long and loving her so much, I felt that she had just stabbed me right in the heart. It was so unexpected. I didn't know what to do except try to convince her that I still love her and hope that she will change her mind.
> It didn't do any good. I just found out that she is seeing someone. I was terrified. I felt betrayed. I felt emptied.
> [Source: Miss Manners, February 16, 1997]

There are situations where you can look at your boyfriend or girlfriend, you can "feel" that "something" is seriously amiss and you can say to him or her, "Is something wrong? If something is wrong please tell me and I will fix it." And the person will look you right in the eye and say, "Nothing is wrong. I'm fine." And then a week later he or she dumps you and you find out there has been "someone else" for a month. Most people experience something like this at least once in their lives, and it is bewildering.

Why does that kind of stuff happen? It happens because relationships are random. There is no explaining why someone falls in love with you in the first place, and there is no explaining why someone falls out of love with you, either. It just happens. When it happens, the only thing you can do is accept it, be thankful for the good times and walk away. That can be incredibly hard to do, especially the first few times you get dumped; but it is the only thing you can do (see also Chapter 24).

CHAPTER 11
Men and Women are Different

Men and women are completely different. As a teenager it is very easy to miss this simple truth. As soon as you accept it relationships don't make any more sense, but the fact that they make no sense begins to make sense.

One way to understand the fundamental differences between men and women is to look at their anatomies. Men are equipped to impregnate women. There is no cost to a man in impregnating someone. Women, on the other hand, are equipped to be impregnated and produce babies. As soon as a woman gets pregnant she has just signed on for a 20 year tour of duty taking care of the resulting child. Her goal, going back millions of years, is to help that baby survive. For a woman pregnancy carries an extremely high cost. Furthermore, the woman's mind and body also know, instinctively at some level, that a baby needs two people to survive. Women are therefore designed to wait for a strong commitment prior to getting pregnant. In our culture that commitment is called "marriage," and women are smart to wait for it. Many men seem to have little or no such programming.

This basic anatomical difference, by itself, leads to rather strong differences in priorities between men and women. In addition, men and women clearly have different programming in other parts of their brains. For example, men are much more aggressive, in general, than women, while women tend to be much more nurturing. Men are more individualistic, while women are more social. Men tend to rely more on rational thought, while women rely more on feelings. These observations are generalizations, of course, but they are fairly obvious. You can see these tendencies in children at play. Girls play with dolls and work with each other socially, while boys wage mock wars with one another. Neither mode is "better" than the other. They are simply different, and they have their own places. For example, you cannot deal socially with a wild tiger who is attacking your village, so an aggressive approach works

85

better. On the other hand, an aggressive approach does not work at all with children.

You may have seen the tongue-in-cheek posters or T-shirts that purport to show the differences between men's and women's brains. All that the posters are trying to say is, "In general, men and women have different things on their minds." For example, if you look at who's browsing in the tool section at the hardware store, you will find that most of the people are men. Men tend to be more interested in tools than women are. Men also tend to be more interested in cars, sports, computers and so on. On the other hand, if you look in the cosmetics section at a department store you will find that most of the customers are women. Women tend to be more interested in beauty, fashion, and shopping than men are. Neither sex is "better" than the other, but there certainly are significant differences in preferences.

Another way to understand the differences between men and women is to look at the sexual anatomy and endocrine (hormonal) systems of males and females. Obviously, there are physical differences. In addition, the hormonal cycles of men and women are different because a woman's body is designed to produce babies, while a man's is not. Here is a simplified description of a woman's hormonal cycle:

> Assume that the start of the menstrual period marks the start of the cycle. The pituitary gland, a small endocrine organ in the brain, begins secreting a hormone called the follicle-stimulating-hormone, FSH. FSH is responsible for stimulating the development of an ovarian follicle and the egg it contains. A follicle has the ability to secrete the hormone estrogen, so once it develops the estrogen levels in the blood rise. Estrogen has a number of effects. For example, the glands lining the cervix secrete mucus and the uterine lining builds up.
>
> About a day prior to ovulation the estrogen level in the blood peaks. The peak triggers a change in the pituitary gland, causing it to secrete another hormone called luteinizing hormone, LH. Ovulation occurs because the level of LH causes the follicle to release the egg. The egg may be fertilized by sperm over the next 24 hours. If not, menstruation starts approximately two weeks later and the cycle repeats.

This certainly is not a simple mechanism. Men have a similar system, but in men the hormones act on different organs to produce testosterone instead of estrogen. Testosterone and estrogen have completely different effects on the brain and body. Given the differences in the hormones flowing in their blood streams, the expectation that males and females

Good Books	A good book to read for more information is *Men Are From Mars, Women Are from Venus* by John Gray. See the references section for more information.

will respond similarly to *any* stimuli would be naïve. It is important to recognize that neither sex is "better." They are simply wildly different.

Knowing and accepting that there are all of these differences can make you much more alert and understanding in any relationship that you undertake.

CHAPTER 12

Marriage is Forever

arriage is a fact of life. In our society it is the structure
people use to create a stable family unit. A man and
woman marry with the intention of staying together
for life. Within that bond they usually have children and raise them. This
arrangement is good for the children. It guarantees that the two parents
are totally committed to the children and to each other.

I can remember thinking as a teenager that marriage would be natural
and easy. You fall in love and then you get married and you live happily
ever after. Right? It turns out that that view of the world is a little naïve
because it leaves out the most important part. To my teenage mind
marriage was about love. To an adult, marriage is about *commitment*. It is
about *staying in love* and staying together for a lifetime despite the fact
that both partners are individuals who change over time. Marriage itself is
easy. Two people can *get* married any time they want. The challenge of
marriage is making it work for a lifetime.

The question you might have as a teenager is, "What could possibly
be hard about being married? What could possibly be 'challenging' about
it? Once I find a person who I am madly in love with and who is madly in
love with me, marriage will be easy. Our love will keep us together no
matter what happens." What I would like to do in this chapter is suggest
to you several reasons why marriage can be challenging, and show you
why marriage is a big step that should not be taken lightly.

UNDERSTANDING THE CHALLENGE OF MARRIAGE

The first few months of most marriages is easy. This phase is called
the "honeymoon phase" and may last up to a year. The honeymoon phase
exists because the couple is enjoying the significant advantages of being
married: living together, being together constantly, looking toward the
future as a team, planning a family, sexual intimacy, trust, closeness and

so on. The honeymoon phase is also aided by the effects of romantic love, which tend to mask problems and differences. The honeymoon period starts to end as the couple comes to the realization that marriage *lasts a lifetime*. Let's look at some of the things that make a life-long marriage interesting:

- Marriage is a lifetime commitment. This commitment can have a tremendous number of advantages: stability, financial strength and unity, infinite trust, etc. However, it can have a paralyzing disadvantage if one or both parties decides to abuse the commitment. Imagine a person who is told, "We are giving you your job for life—you can never be fired." Most people will continue to do a good job, but a few people would take that message as a cue to become extremely lazy. Marriage can cause the same effect. Both partners have to work hard to avoid complacency.

- Marriage means that everything is shared. Sharing means that every major decision involves a team decision. If both parties do not agree, then conflict arises. Most people enjoy having a certain amount of freedom in their lives. Marriage instead forces a great deal of compromise. If two people have different spending habits (i.e., one likes saving money and the other likes spending it), it can cause immense strain.

- Marriage involves being with the same person for long periods of time. While the couple is still "in love," this is easy. Once romantic love's effects wear off and the relationship is driven more by friendship than sexual attraction, however, little habits can become irritating. Imagine living in an RV with your best friend for 10 years. After awhile even your best friend can become annoying. Countering this natural effect requires skill and creativity.

Marriage is something like a big amplifier. When things are going well, the team effect of marriage makes them go very well. When a marriage works it is a source of infinite peace and joy. However, when things are not working marriage tends to amplify things in a negative direction. It can make bad things worse because it can create a trap.

Have you ever noticed that many married couples spend a lot of time fighting? Have you ever wondered why that happens? It happens because at any given moment the two people in the marriage may want to do two different things that are mutually exclusive. For example:

- You want to go to your best friend's wedding while your spouse wants to go to "the big game" on the same day.

- You want to go to church but your spouse wants to stay home on Sunday morning.

- You want the house to be neat but your spouse does not care.
- You want to buy a new car but your spouse wants to save the money and continue fixing the old one.
- You want to live close to your family but so does your spouse, and the families live 1,000 miles apart.
- You want to buy a new riding lawn mower but your spouse wants a new sofa.
- You want to paint the house blue but your spouse prefers yellow.
- You want to spend extra time at work but your spouse wants you to be home for dinner.

Imagine facing one or two situations like this every day, day in and day out, for 50 years. *That* is what makes marriage challenging. *That* is why you want to pick a good marriage partner. If you can find someone who will work with you daily and love you enough to solve all of the "little problems" that arise naturally in a marriage, then you will have a successful marriage that brings you joy throughout your life.

FINDING A GOOD PARTNER

Because marriage is so strongly tied to family, because it is so permanent, because it is such a big step and because the cost of entry and exit is so high, adults put a lot of emphasis on it. So does the community. When you and your spouse get married, you are both proclaiming to the community your lifetime commitment together. You also are declaring, to some extent, your adulthood, your independence and the start of your household. The community understands how big this step is and responds with wedding gifts intended to make it easier to start the new household. You can imagine a young couple getting married in a small town 100 years ago. The couple starts its household and its family, and the community of adults chips in with wedding gifts to make the startup easier. Recall from Chapter 1 how expensive it is to get started. Wedding presents help you get over the hump.

You can now see that marriage is a big deal. It is not a party one weekend—it is a lifetime commitment to your spouse. Your parents want you to choose the "right" person:

- A person who will help you to make the marriage work
- A person who is stable and kind
- A person who is slow to anger
- A person who is a good worker and who has a good job
- A person who will be a good mother or father

These qualities are universal. Here are some of the attributes of a good marriage partner:

- Trust—When both partners trust each other implicitly, they are able to go through life with a tremendous amount of confidence and freedom.
- Loyalty and commitment—Trust is built on a foundation of loyalty and commitment between the two partners. Many people get married with the concept that, "If I don't like it, I'll sleep around or get divorced." This is a recipe for disaster in any marriage. Marriage is about total commitment to your partner.
- Helpfulness—Partners in a good marriage help each other constantly and accelerate their lives that way. Married life can be much easier than single life if both partners work together.
- Friendship—Partners in a good marriage are good friends and gather strength and joy from that friendship.
- Kindness—Partners in a good marriage are kind to one another out of love and friendship.
- Patience and understanding—Partners in a good marriage understand and forgive each other for the mistakes that come from being human.
- Acceptance and support—Partners in a good marriage accept one another and support each other constantly.

If a couple can maintain these qualities within the marriage, then success is much easier. Maintaining those qualities, it turns out, takes quite a bit of discipline. If one or more of these fundamental qualities is missing, then you can say with some certainly that the marriage will fail.

There are quite a few things that can cause a marriage to fail:

- Disagreements over money—If one person is frugal and the other is free-spending, the conflict that arises can be extremely difficult to manage.
- Laziness—If one partner is not willing to put in the effort required to make a marriage work or keep the household functioning (financially or operationally), then the conflict that arises can cause a lot of stress.
- Stubbornness—If one or both spouses refuse to compromise, then the marriage likely will not survive. Marriage depends on compromise.
- Infidelity—The fundamental contract in marriage is "lifetime commitment to a single partner." If one partner breaks this contract, the marriage is over.
- Disagreements over children—If one spouse wants children and the other does not, you simply should not be married. It is impossible to reconcile this difference because one partner is guaranteed to be dissatisfied.

- Physical or mental abuse—The partner being abused should leave to maintain his or her own health and safety.
- Addiction—Alcohol or drug addiction will destroy any marriage.

As a teenager thinking about marriage you probably do not have all of this complexity in mind. How could you? However, it is important that you come to this level of understanding and take marriage seriously. When you get married you are committing to your chosen spouse *for the rest of your life*. You are making that commitment, generally, in order to start a family. Keep that in mind and you can understand why your parents see dating and marriage as such a big deal.

The Advantages and Disadvantages of Marriage

Having discussed all of this, you can see that there are advantages and disadvantages to being married. The advantages include:

- Unconditional love, stability and consistency—You don't have to worry about dating, breaking up, etc. There is one person you love and will love you for the rest of your life.

- Lower cost of living—A married couple tends to have more free time and/or more money because the cost and work of a household are shared by two.

- Confidence—It is very reassuring to know that there is a person who loves you and only you no matter what and who lives to be with you. That sort of commitment can give you a tremendous comfort and confidence.

- The potential for children—Inside a stable marriage it is possible and extremely easy to have and raise children.

There are also disadvantages:

- You are locked in with a single person—If you like to be with a different person every week, marriage is not for you.

- You give up a great deal of freedom—Every decision will now be a compromise between two people.

- You are going to have to work to maintain and build your human qualities—Trust, loyalty, commitment, kindness, patience, etc. are not easy. You have to work at these skills every day in a marriage to become better at them. If you are not willing to put in the effort, you will fail in the marriage.

If you find that you cannot deal with one or more or the disadvantages, then that tells you that you should not get married.

CHAPTER 13

Teenage Sex is an Option

S hould you pursue or have sex as a teenager? This is an option, and you get to make the decision. Like any other decision, however, there are things you should keep in mind. Here are three of the more important:

- Fact #1: If two people have unprotected sex long enough, they will get pregnant.
- Fact #2: This comes from the October 1996 issue of *Scientific American* magazine: "Six out of 10 women having abortions used protection." What that says is two people who have *protected* sex have a pretty good chance of pregnancy as well.
- Fact #3: If two people have sex and one of them is carrying a sexually transmitted disease, then the other person has some probability of getting the disease, even when the couple uses protection.

Think of these three facts as "disadvantages." They tend to be good reasons not to have sex as a teenager. None have them have ever stopped anyone from having sex, however. You can look at the rate of infection for STDs, the number of abortions performed every year and the number of unwed teenage mothers to see that.

To any adult the three disadvantages make it "obvious" that teenagers should not have sex. What adults generally forget is that for many teens the brain and body are sending signals that indicate otherwise. The question for you as a teenager is, "Should logic win this one?" Your body has a desire to reproduce. To your body sex is important. Can you discipline yourself enough to live with the urges and wait until you get married? That is the question.

Here are two things to keep in mind as you are making that decision:

1. By having sex you are making a hidden commitment to the child that results. The purpose of sex is to create a baby. Therefore, by having sex you are saying, "I am willing to care for the baby."

93

2. Babies carry with them a lot of baggage. They need constant attention, they cost a lot and they require two people. Therefore, once you and your friend create a baby you will need to get married, and then the two of you will need to care for the child for the next 20 years. That means you will give up a tremendous amount of personal and financial freedom. Spend some time with someone who has a baby and see how much work is involved before you underestimate the amount of care a baby requires.

If you decide to have pre-marital sex, do it with the understanding that once a child is conceived you are responsible for the care and well-being of your mate and the child for the next 20 years. The hospital bill alone for a normal childbirth is $5,000 to $10,000. Do you have that money? If not, then why would you have sex? The correct path is to find someone you are madly in love with and want to spend the rest of your life with, then decide that the two of you want to have a child, then get married, then save up enough money to provide for the baby and then conceive a baby. Have a baby within a strong marriage that is ready to support the child: It is best for the baby and best for the parents.

As an unmarried teenager there is one other fact that you should keep in mind. You generally don't hear much about this fact, but it is important. You are doing your thing right now. You are meeting people, going out, having fun. That is all fine. You have this vague notion in your head that one day you will get married. That is also fine. But eventually you will find someone who you want to marry, and it will become much less vague. You are going to be deeply in love with this person. You are going to be with this person for the rest of your life. That is a fact.

On the night of your wedding you are going to be with that person in bed. There are two options on that first night you are together. Either it will be the first time for you, and therefore it is going to be special. Or it will not. If both of you are able to come to bed and learn about sex with each other and share that throughout your lives, it is a good thing. It is an incredible gift to give to someone. Maybe your partner cannot give it to you. That is OK. You can still give it to him or her.

In general, teenage sex is like drugs (see Chapter 37). It seems like it should feel good when you do it, but longer term it often feels bad. It is a "cheap thrill" that has little or no value. It also tries to separate sex from babies, which is impossible (see Chapter 9). Keep in mind that the purpose of sex is to create a baby, and that a baby is an incredibly long-term commitment. You should not be attempting to create a baby unless you are willing to make that commitment. If you want to make that commitment, you should be getting married first for the sake of the baby. That is a fact of life.

PART 4

The Facts About Attitudes and Values

You are in total control of your attitude and your values. You can choose to be happy or sad, optimistic or pessimistic, shy or boisterous, honest or dishonest or anything in between. The only person who has any control over your attitude and values is you. This section will show you some of the possibilities.

CHAPTER 14
You Can Be Confident

Y ou may recall from the preface that when I was a teenager I felt like an idiot much of the time. That is true, but it is funny because I had the highest SAT score in my class. You may recall from the chapter on sports (Chapter 36) that I felt like a geeky weenie and a loser much of the time in anything that had to do with athletics. That is funny because later in life I was able to ride my bike over a hundred miles in a single day. You may recall from the chapter on love (Chapter 9) that I felt like everyone hated me. That is funny when I consider how many people love me now. So the question you have to ask yourself is, "What was wrong with this guy when he was a teenager?" It is the same thing that is "wrong" for a huge number of teenagers—it is a lack of confidence. Psychologists might throw in things like a lack of "self-esteem" as well.

Whatever you want to call it, it is a fundamental disbelief in your own worth, value and abilities.

It turns out that lack of confidence is a terrible thing. It robs you of a tremendous number of opportunities in your life. It wastes time. It causes emotions that hurt and tear you down. In extreme cases it causes people to commit suicide.

If you are in the huge army of unconfident teenagers now, I know exactly what you would think if I were to say to you, "You are a good person—be confident!" You would think, "Yeah, that's fine for you to say, but it doesn't apply to ME. I AM a loser. I AM an idiot. I AM a weenie. I am miserable and I hate it." Or maybe you are less extreme than that and are merely mildly disgusted with yourself at times. What I would like to do in this chapter is try to show you a different way to look at the world. It may not work for you today, but I would like for you to think about it. Then come back and read this chapter again next week. And again the week after that. And keep thinking about it. About 10 weeks from now (or if you are stubborn, 10 years from now) you will begin to

97

see the light and things will change. My goal is to help you start the process. It is usually the case that the change to confidence causes a change towards success.

THE BASICS

Let me start with a simple statement of fact: You are a human being. As a human being you are no different from anyone else. You have strengths and you have weaknesses. You have talents and you have faults. You have advantages and you have disadvantages. In that you are equal to everyone around you. You are just as valuable and you are just as worthwhile and you are just as important as everyone else. That is a fact of life. The only thing that stops you from thinking you are an equal to everyone else is a failure to believe these simple facts. You lack confidence in yourself and your value as a human being.

I know you are looking around you and seeing people and thinking, "But he has all this natural athletic talent, and she has all this natural intelligence, and he has..." And that is all true. What you may also be thinking is, "And I have none of that, and I'm not really good at *anything*." That is not true. You too have a set of natural talents that are just as good and just as important and just as eager to be developed. There is no difference between you and everyone else except for the fact that they have *found* and *accepted* and started *exploiting* their talents, and you have not. Primarily the part you are missing is *acceptance*.

Here are three quotes to help you get some perspective. The first is from the book *Industrial Light and Magic: The Art of Special Effects* by Thomas Smith:

> In 1974, George Lucas was in trouble. Universal Studios, which had made a small fortune from his movie *American Graffiti*, had turned down his next proposal, *Star Wars*. United Artists, too, had said no. There were a few flickers of interest at 20th Century-Fox, but George couldn't quite build that flicker into flaming enthusiasm. The studio executives just didn't understand his vision for the film.

This is George Lucas, the man who has created many of the best-selling movies of all time. Here he is with this great idea in his head called *Star Wars*, and he is already successful from *American Graffiti*, yet he is being rejected multiple times.

The second quote comes from the book *The Sam Walton Story* by Austin Teutsch:

> In the five years Sam Walton spent in Newport, he made the store one of the best. People from all over north-central

Arkansas came to buy products that were once only found in Little Rock to the south or Memphis, Tennessee to the east. Bobby socks, white leather shoes and hair tonic for that just-right ducktail of the 1950s made Sam's store the most desirable place to go. The previous owner also began keeping his eye on the store's progress and liked what Sam had done to it, especially in the areas of size, appearance and greatly increased profits. He would eventually deal Sam Walton his first lesson in business. The previous owner had two aces up his sleeve. One, he was well-liked in the community and was a hometown boy. His own son was coming back from the war, having been missing in action for years... The boy returned with nothing to do but work for his father. But the father used a clause in the business contract to oust Sam Walton from the ten-year option in order to give the Ben Franklin store to his son.

This is Sam Walton, the creator of Wal-Mart, the richest man in the United States at the time of his death. The quote is talking about his very first store. He had poured all of his savings and five years of effort into

Good Books

A good book to read for more information is *The Sam Walton Story* by Austin Teutsch. See the references section for more information.

that store and built it up to a true success, only to have it taken away by a bad clause in a lease.

The third quote comes from the autobiographical book *Be My Guest* by Conrad Hilton:

I, personally, was living out of my suitcase, rushing from one hotel to another, from one town to another, borrowing my fare where I could, always trying to raise a dollar here, a dollar there and not having much luck... At that very moment the Moodys in Galveston were preparing to foreclose. They considered my position hopeless. I was clearly in default on payments on my $300,000 loan. The Hilton hotels were their collateral. Within a few weeks they took over my hotels. They now owned the roof over my wife's head, over my mother's head, controlled the fate of my loyal partners. I had nothing left.

This is Conrad Hilton, founder of Hilton Hotels, a hotel chain that now has over 40,000 employees and serves 40,000,000 guests annually.

There are millions of stories like these from millions of successful people. What is my point? My point is that you feel unconfident, stupid and unsuccessful right now because you are looking at your "failures" and focusing on them. What you are missing is that *Things go wrong, even for successful, confident people.* It happens to everyone. It happens equally to successful and unsuccessful people. It happens to young people and old. It happens constantly. No matter where you are. No matter what you are doing. No matter how hard you try. Things go wrong. The difference between confident people and unconfident people is how they react to problems. Confident people dig through problems, rebuild and move on. Unconfident people wallow in them, are miserable and die. It is as simple as that. That is why you need confidence. Right now you are choosing to be unconfident because you are looking at your failures rather than looking at your potential for success in the future.

The difference between successful people and unsuccessful people is that the successful people keep trying and keep trying and keep trying until they succeed. Then we look at them and say, "Oh, that was easy for you!" But it was not. People do occasionally win the lottery. That is luck. The

> *Things go wrong, even for successful and confident people. That is a fact of life.*

rest of the people on this planet work to achieve their goals and dreams. And they work hard. Confidence in your own abilities and self-worth is what gives you the strength to keep slogging through the hard times until you see a light that says you are on to something. What's funny is that if you look at it the right way and recognize it for what it is, the slogging can be interesting. The slogging is what makes the goal worth achieving. You can focus on the journey rather than the destination.

Confidence vs. Arrogance

There is a big difference between confidence and arrogance. Confidence is an understanding that you are OK and valuable. Arrogance is shouting it from the rooftops like you are the most important person in the world, and feeling that you are better than other people. You do not have to be arrogant to be confident. They are completely different things. Most truly successful people have confidence but none of the arrogance.

SELF-HATRED

One thing that is the opposite of confidence in yourself is hatred of yourself, or *self-hatred*. This is a very strange emotion, it is outrageously common in teenagers and it can be extremely hard to get out of the rut it creates. However, you cannot hate yourself and be confident. The two things are mutually exclusive.

The alternative to self-hatred is self-acceptance. Self-acceptance is, quite simply, accepting yourself as a good and worthwhile person and *loving yourself* the way you are. You are just like any other person on this planet: just as good, just as worthy of love and success, just as talented, just as important. When you can accept that for yourself and start liking and loving yourself, you can become confident.

There are a number of things you can do to get out of the self-hatred rut and build your confidence. They take time, but they are worthwhile. Here are several:

- Make a big list of your strengths. List all of the things that you are good at. If you can think of absolutely nothing you are good at, then start extremely small. Think, "I am good at setting the table." How can you not be good at that? And if somehow you feel you are not, figure out a way to get good at it and accept that you are good. Get a book on napkin folding or center-piece arranging and set the nicest table you can imagine. Think, "I am good at putting on my socks." How can you not be good at that? Think, "I really brushed my teeth well this morning." Of course you are good at a huge number of things, big and small. Make a huge, long list of all the things you are good at. Read it and update it every day.

- Accept compliments. I mentioned in the preface that this was really hard for me. When someone gives you a compliment, *any compliment*, large or small, for whatever reason, say, "Thank you." That is how you accept a compliment. If you are feeling good that day, say, "Thank you, I really feel good about the way that turned out." Accept the compliment. Then reflect on why you received the compliment. DO NOT say, "Well, he sure was an idiot to compliment me on that." Think, "Wow, this is great!" Reflect on the compliment and replay it and accept it and understand why you got it. No one gives you a compliment without a reason.

- Confidence can be boosted by a win or a success, so try to increase the odds of success. That is one reason why athletes are confident. They win games, and they accept those wins.

- Each day when you come home, make a list of at least five things you did well during the day. Some days that will be hard. Dig deep on those days; "Today I helped Mrs. Jones with her groceries." "I got to all of my classes on time." "I did a good job studying for the test." Whatever. Keep these lists in a notebook, and occasionally go back and read your lists of things you did well each day. Look for patterns and add them to your list of strengths.

- Every person has a super hero power. You may find that hard to believe, but it is true. Think of yourself as a super hero. What are you best at? What is your super hero power? Ask your parents or other adults what they think.

- Lead with your name. EVERY time you meet someone lead with, "Hi, my name is John Smith." That will feel EXTREMELY uncomfortable the first 100 times you try it. *DO IT ANYWAY.* On the phone. At the store. Everywhere. Say, "Hi, my name is John Smith," until it is comfortable and natural and easy. You are John Smith. You are proud of that fact. You are confident and honest. That is what you are saying. Even if it makes you feel completely stupid, DO IT. Smile when you say it.
- Some people have a real problem with mistakes replaying in their heads. You are walking along, living your life and this BIG STUPID MISTAKE that you made two years ago replays in your head and makes you feel like an idiot for five minutes. Why does that happen? It happens because you see something or hear something or think something that somehow triggers the memory. It happens to everyone. It happens a lot when you are a teenager. Let it pass. It is just random debris in your head and it is meaningless. Instead of letting it make you feel bad, just say, "Oh, here is one of these silly memories replaying itself; let's just let that tape finish up and then we will load a better one." Remember that mistakes replay for everyone. You are not alone. Then write it down. Keep a journal and write, "My mind replayed that memory of me spilling orange juice on Mary Sue at Kenny's party and her screaming at me in front of everyone." Look at it. Yes. So. It happened. That's life. Get over it. It is meaningless. Next time you will be more careful with your juice.

EVERYONE makes mistakes. Mistakes hurt because they are embarrassing. The difference between confident people and unconfident people is that the confident people say, "Wow, that was dumb. Let's figure out a way to not do THAT again." Confident people also are able to laugh at themselves and their occasional stupidity. Unconfident people think, "God that was such a stupid idiotic thing to do and I am worthless and stupid and ignorant and no good and why am I like this and God I hate being me and when will I ever learn and ..." See the difference?

The thing is: IT IS YOUR HEAD! Let me repeat that:

IT IS YOUR HEAD!

You can control what your head says to you. Confident people have it say one thing. Unconfident people have it say something else. Get yours saying good things instead of bad and you are on your way. When your head says stupid things (like replaying stupid mistakes), let it get past that and then plug in a good thing. A strength. A win. Replay something good. Do not forget that IT IS YOUR HEAD and you control what it says every day.

FEAR

Fear is a fact of life. Like anger and love, it is an emotion wired into your brain that you cannot get rid of, but that you can do a lot to control. Fear is the opposite of confidence. Instead of being confident that you can do something well, you are afraid you will mess it up or that something bad will happen. Here's an example. Let's say I ask you to walk down a normal sidewalk that is a block long, and I offer to pay you $100 if you do it without falling off the sidewalk. The sidewalk is four feet wide. This is the standard width of any sidewalk in any suburban subdivision or park. You would say to me, "No Problem!" You can obviously walk on the sidewalk without difficulty. You do it every day. You would probably run to the other end and then collect your money.

Now let's say I take that same sidewalk and I put it between the twin towers of the World Trade Center in New York City and I ask you to walk across between the towers. You are now 1,400 feet in the air. The wind is blowing. The simple, obvious act of "walking on the sidewalk" becomes suddenly terrifying. What's the difference? There is no difference, conceptually. But if you trip on a suburban sidewalk you skin your knee. Trip when you are 1,400 feet in the air and you plunge to your death. Your brain factors the risk in and produces a large "terror" signal.

That same terror signal kicks in in a lot of different situations. Anytime a mistake will blow something important you have the potential for fear or anxiety. This is why we admire great athletes. Think about a golfer. He is on the 18th hole of the Masters tournament in Augusta, Georgia. Fifteen million people are watching. If he makes this putt he wins. If he misses it he loses. The thing we respect at that moment is not his ability at golf. We honor him for controlling his fear and making the putt. Sports teach you to control your fear under pressure when the stakes are high (see Chapter 38). It is not easy.

One thing you can do to control fear is practice. If you were to practice walking on sidewalks at various heights and work your way up to the World Trade Center, rather than trying the World Trade Center first, it would be a lot easier. You could start at 10 feet, then 20, then 100, and so on until you were ready for 1,400 feet. By practicing you build your skills and confidence. You learn about different situations that can arise and you learn how to control them. Eventually, you get to where you have seen all the possible failure points and have faced fear hundreds of times and you can handle it.

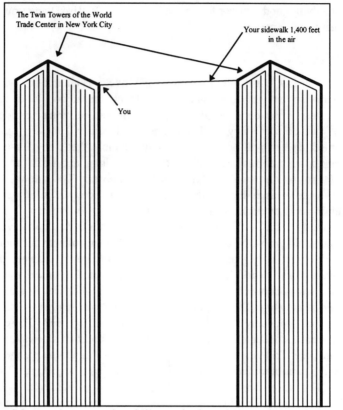

Confidence gives you the ability to look at fear, understand it as a human emotion and use it.

THE MIND OF A CONFIDENT PERSON

What I would like to do here is give you some insight into the differences between the minds of confident and unconfident people. By seeing how they differ and seeing how much more comfortable a confident mind can be, you may be encouraged to switch over to confidence. The big thing to keep in mind is that there is nothing to keep you from being confident. It is all in your head. If you decide tomorrow to be confident, you can start the process of becoming confident.

Let's start with the first big difference between a confident person and an unconfident person. In their minds there are two completely different things happening. Here is what an unconfident person's head is saying:

My God, I am the dumbest, stupidest person ever to be born. I cannot believe how stupid I am. I can't believe that idiotic mistake I made today. That was so stupid! I wish I was dead. I will never be able to do anything right...

Compare that to what is flowing through the head of a confident person:

Wow, today is going really well. I really like the way I was able to talk to Jerome today. I think I really made an impression on him. It is really amazing the way I am learning to handle those kinds of situations. In another year I will be a master of diplomacy! I think my goal for the next time I talk to him should be...

There is a very simple difference. The unconfident, self-hating person is focusing on the problems, the mistakes and the stupidity and ignoring what went right. The unconfident person replays mistakes from the past constantly and beats himself with them. The confident person is focusing on the good things and the things that went well and is looking toward the future and how things will get better. There is no magic. It is a simple choice: focus on the bad from the past or focus on the good in the future. If you are unconfident you have made the negative choice. Start the process of switching to the positive side and you will see a big difference. A confident person is simply saying, "I am good. I am normal. I am OK." All the time.

A confident person gets those messages from a simple source. Look at any celebrity or famous person:

- Any US senator or representative
- Any TV or movie star
- Any sports star
- Any Olympic athlete
- Any successful businessperson

A confident person looks at people like these and thinks, "They all started out as infants, just like me. They all learned things as they went along, just like me. They all made mistakes, just like me. They all had to start at the bottom, just like me. Look at where they are now. I will be there, just like them, one day. What can I do today to help myself get there?"

An unconfident person looks at those same people and says, "They are SO lucky! I could never be like them. They have all this natural talent and I am SO stupid! I hate being me."

The confident person is the one who has it right. All of these people were born as infants, just like you. There was nothing special about them when they were born. They had talents, but they also had problems and difficulties. They all went through the process of being children and then teenagers. What made them successful? They simply found something they were good at and worked and worked and worked until they got where they are today. EVERYONE has talents. Your goal is to find yours and start developing them.

I can tell you a funny story about my sister. My sister did not have a really fantastic life until she was about 25. When she was 25 she went to work in a print shop as a gofer. While she was there she discovered a computer called a Macintosh. She LOVED this thing. She could use it easily and create great things and she felt good when she did. She developed her talent as a graphical artist and now has a great job in advertising. Finding her talent gave her the chance to develop into a successful person. What you are looking for is something in your life that makes you feel that same way. If you have not found it yet, then keep searching and enjoy the ride (see Chapter 6 for details).

What do unconfident people do when they make mistakes or get rejected? They wallow in it for days. A confident person accepts it and looks forward to trying something else tomorrow. Why wallow in it? What does it accomplish?

A confident person accepts failure and understands that it a necessary part of success. You cannot be successful unless you fail and learn from your failures. All successful people failed on their way up. The difference is they learned from their failures and applied the lessons in positive ways.

A confident person learns from criticism rather than dwelling on it and applies it to becoming better. If the criticism is invalid then the confident person simply ignores it and moves on. A confident person does not get defensive. There is no need to. Let me give you an example. Say someone walks up to you and yells at you, "YOU HAVE BIG GREEN HORNS GROWING OUT OF YOUR HEAD!!!!" Your response would be, "No I don't. Don't waste my time." There is no reason to be defensive or insulted because the statement is obviously untrue. It's the same thing with invalid criticism. It is invalid, so you can ignore it.

A confident person is willing to try many times and many ways to accomplish a goal. An unconfident person tries once, and if that doesn't work he quits.

Finally, an unconfident person is constantly tearing himself down, directly and indirectly. "I am so stupid," is a common refrain. A confident person instead builds himself up with positive messages. Confident people do make mistakes, but they are perceived as chances to learn rather than chances for self-destruction.

Do you see how the minds of confident and unconfident people differ? To be confident you need to start from a basic foundation that says, "I am a normal human being. I have strengths, but I also make mistakes. I am no different from anyone else." Then, from that base, focus on the good things that happen to you rather than the bad. Since you have a choice, and since good and bad happen in about equal proportion, focusing on the good is much easier.

Confidence around Members of the Opposite Sex

A confident person deals with members of the opposite sex much differently than an unconfident person. Imagine that you are confident and you are sitting next to an attractive member of the opposite sex in the cafeteria. First, you would be completely comfortable. You know you are important and valuable, you know that there are many fish in the sea and you know the person sitting next to you has a life, too. You would say, "How's it going?" Simple as that. The person would respond in some way. You might have a conversation from there or you might not, and it wouldn't really matter. If you seemed to be hitting it off, you might say, "I'm glad we met. Can I call you?" The person would say yes or no. There is no anguish, fear, pain or loathing in this picture. Confidence—an underlying faith in your own value—gives you the ability to experience life in that way.

Here is one more thing to think about. Imagine that you were to go back to the third grade and retake all of your third grade tests. They would be easy, right? Or imagine that you are frequently accosted by a bully, but one summer you go through Army boot camp (including weapons training, martial arts, night combat and so on). When you got back to school in the fall, how would you feel if you had the opportunity to deal with the bully again? You would feel a lot more confident. That is what makes adults seem more confident. They have been through all sorts of situations, so they know how to handle things. It is also what helps athletes to be confident. They see the same situations over and over again in their sports and learn how to handle them. In your own life you can actually do things to help yourself become more confident. You can practice. You can try things over and over until you succeed. You can imagine yourself a year from now and then deal with the situations you see today from that perspective. Try some of the techniques mentioned in this chapter and see how they change your outlook over time.

CHAPTER 15

You Decide to Be Happy

Happy people are a lot more fun than unhappy people. That is a fact of life. Most normal people, given a choice, would rather be with a happy, smiling, fun person than with any other type of person available. Say, for example, I were to give you a choice of being trapped for two days in a cave with:

1. A complaining person
2. A miserable person
3. A bitchy person
4. A happy and optimistic person

Most normal people would take the happy person any day.

Since it is a fact of life that the person you spend the most time with is yourself, and since it is also a fact of life that other people would rather be with a happy person, there are a lot of good reasons for you to try to be happy.

I would like you to imagine the following scene. You are walking down the sidewalk toward a bus stop. You notice that coming down the sidewalk in the opposite direction is another person. You notice that this person is about your age, of the opposite sex and very attractive. You notice that this person is stopping at the same bus stop. You have several possible approaches as you come to the bus stop yourself:

- You can walk by with the thought, "I'll go around the block and catch the next bus."
- You can stop and stare at the ground, saying nothing.
- You can get to the bus stop and complain about how cold and miserable the weather has been.
- You can get to the bus stop and say something like, "Good morning! How are you doing today?"

If you are the other person you have a lot of possible options yourself, but which of these four people is the most approachable and interesting to you? Which of the four would you rather talk to if you are

108

in the mood to talk? Which of the four seems like you could have fun with? Which of the four invites you to start a conversation? The happy person has the best probability of interaction. The highest probability of potential success lies with the happy person.

Each morning when you wake up you have a choice. You can decide that you are going to focus on the negative things during the day and be miserable, or you can focus on the things that are going well and be happy. You can, in other words, *count your blessings* and have a good day, or you can complain.

Happiness involves a fundamental difference between optimists and pessimists. You might have heard the story about two people who see a partially-filled glass of water on a table. The optimist sees the glass as half-full. The pessimist sees it as half-empty. The optimist focuses on the positive and looks toward a future in which things will get "fuller" and better. A pessimist, by focusing on the negative, looks for things to get "emptier" and worse in the future. Therefore, optimists are happy and pessimists are miserable. It is as simple as that.

An appropriate saying to remember when thinking about optimism and pessimism is, "You get what you expect." Over the long run that saying is exactly right, and therefore optimists win. If you expect things to get better they tend to get better. Why, when looking at a glass where two interpretations are equally valid, would you want to choose the negative interpretation rather than the positive interpretation? By choosing the path of an optimist you look at the world positively and things get better.

A teenage friend of mine described an unhappy person she knew at her high school in the following ways:

- She is insecure.
- She is unconfident.
- She has no self-esteem.
- She can't be alone.
- Everything that happens is the end of the world—very melodramatic. If one little thing goes wrong the world is ending. She panics a lot.
- She blames herself for everything.
- She is depressed a lot.
- She complains about everything constantly.
- She puts herself down a lot.
- When she does something wrong she blames someone else.
- If people don't come up and talk with her she gets upset
- She feels no one likes her.
- She talks about running away but never does because her parents would get mad at her.

- She can't wear an outfit without changing it three times and calling two people, then puts herself down once she has it on to get sympathy.
- *She is never happy.*

The problem for this unhappy person is that people stopped wanting to be near her. And why should they want to be near her? What does her complaining and misery accomplish?

Can an unhappy person fix this sort of problem herself? Yes. She

---

Finding Yourself

What is it that will make you happy for life? What will cause you to wake up each morning and look forward to the day? What will allow you to enjoy being with yourself? What will make you believe that you are unique and important so that you are confident? This sort of happiness involves "finding yourself."

When somebody says, "I found myself" what they mean is, "I have discovered what it is that makes me unique." It means learning, through trial and error or accidental discovery, what it is that really makes you happy—what it is that you truly excel at. *Everyone* has something they are best at; something that leads them to true contentment. Some people find this thing very early in life, but for others it takes longer.

The other part of "finding yourself" is "accepting yourself." This part involves accepting that you are a good and valuable person and that you are just as good and valuable as everyone else.

You do not "find yourself" one afternoon. It is a process. Although there is often a day or a month or a year when you "get it" and discover a great deal, you can learn something new and interesting about yourself each day if you are listening.

Here is a funny way to think about finding yourself. Imagine that "you" are a city that you have never been to before. There are all sorts of interesting places in this city—beautiful parks, fun places to shop, interesting places to visit. But since it is a new city for you, you don't know where any of these things are. You explore the city each day and you learn new things—parts of town you really enjoy, places with beautiful scenery and also places in need of repair and renewal. Over time you become comfortable with the city and you learn your way around. When people visit, you act as tour guide and you are proud of the city.

It is the same way with your body and mind. You have just started "exploring it," but each day you will learn more about yourself and what you are able to do. You get comfortable with yourself, learn your way around and accept that you are a beautiful place to live. That is what it means to "find yourself." You are finding what makes you good and unique.

would have to come to a point where she says, "Wow, I am unhappy. I don't want to be unhappy anymore. How can I fix this problem?" The solution is straightforward. She must look at the good things happening in her life and focus on them. By doing this she could start down the road to happiness. From a basis of positive thought she could then stop putting yourself down (see Chapter 16) and see what she had to offer. It is extremely important for her to:

1. Focus on the positive.
2. Stop complaining.
3. Stop putting herself down.

To be happy, start with this simple exercise: Smile! No matter how miserable you feel, smile anyway. Think about the positive things in your life and smile about them. Then make a conscious effort to listen to the words that come out of your mouth. Edit them when they are unhappy. When you hear complaints coming out of your mouth, stop speaking. When you hear misery coming out of your mouth, stop speaking. When you hear self-criticism coming out of your mouth, stop speaking. If you do this effectively, there may be a several-day-long period of silence. That is OK. Simply be quiet. Now, with nothing coming out of your mouth, consciously start to look at what is playing in your head (see Chapter 16).

> *"I have learned to be content whatever the circumstances"*
>
> -The Bible: Philippians 4:11

> *"True contentment is a thing as active as agriculture. It is the power of getting out of any situation all that there is in it."*
>
> - G. K. Chesterton

What is your head playing that makes you say these things? Slowly start to replace what is playing in your head and what is coming out of your mouth with good things instead of bad. Whenever you notice that you are thinking about complaints, misery and self-criticism, replace those thoughts with positive ones instead.

Here is an experiment I would like for you to try for just one full day. Pick a day on which you will be happy. On this day you will consciously choose to banish all complaining, all misery, all unhappiness and all guilt. You are just going to be happy, even if you have to fake it. When you wake up in the morning remind yourself that you are having a good day. Pick out your best looking clothes and wear them. To start the day make a long list of all of the good things in your life. If you have trouble then dig deep, like, "I have running water, while many people on the planet do not." Then go out into the world with a great big smile on your face, even if you have to fake that smile. Whenever you see someone, smile broadly and say, "Hi! How are you doing today?! I am glad to see you!" Smile and greet strangers with "Good morning!" When you go to the store smile and say, "Hi! How is your day going?! I am having a great day today!" If one of your miserable friends says to you, "What are you so happy about? Shut up." Say, "This is just turning out to be a great day for me!" and walk on by. If strangers say, "Shut up with your happiness!" ignore them and move on. What you will notice during your day of happiness is that a lot of people you interact with will be a lot friendlier. They will talk to you. They will ask you why your day is going so well. They will smile too. They will want to be with you. They will want to catch some of that happiness.

Now imagine being like that every day. Happiness generates a field that causes other people to be happy, which creates other happiness fields... Just one happy person can infect hundreds of others with happiness. People want to be around a happy person.

Happiness is a conscious choice. You can decide to be happy and you can be happy. It is no harder than being miserable—it simply requires you to change where you focus your attention. Focus your attention on good things rather than bad and you can be happy. I can remember the day I figured this out. It was like a huge weight being lifted off of me. I didn't have to be miserable! It was a magnificent revelation. Of course, things did not change overnight. But that is the day the change began.

FINDING HAPPINESS IN UNHAPPY SITUATIONS

Let's say that you find yourself in a situation right now that is making you unhappy. Maybe you don't like the school you are going to, or you have a class you are doing poorly in, or your boy/girlfriend has dumped you. You are miserable. How can you get past this unhappy event and be happy?

The first thing you need to do is gain control of the situation. You do that by the simple act of *recognizing that you are unhappy and deciding you want to change the situation.* Say to yourself, "I am unhappy." Now ask yourself the question, "Why am I unhappy?" Answer it at several levels. For example, if you are unhappy because your parents have sent you to a summer camp you do not like, think about what is making you unhappy. What is it *about* summer camp you do not like? Be specific.

Now ask yourself two more questions:
- What can I change?
- What are the good things about camp that I am ignoring?

There might be specific things that you do not like about camp that you can change. If so, come up to a higher level (Chapter 22) and talk with someone about your options (Chapter 24). In addition, start being thankful for and enjoying the good things. Make a list of them.

What you are left with are the things you cannot change. Figure out what you can do to cope with them. Try to gain perspective on the situation. Talk to people and see how they have coped in similar situations. Look for a book about the problem you are facing. Read it.

By understanding the situation, changing the things you can, counting your blessings and coping with the things you cannot fix, you will find that you are happier, in control and much more mature.

DEPRESSION

If you find that no matter what you do you *cannot* be happy, then it is possible that you are suffering from depression. Depression is a psychological state characterized by feelings of extreme sadness and dejection, an inability to concentrate, insomnia and hopelessness. The most serious effect of depression is suicidal tendencies (see Chapter 40).

Consider the following statements and see if you agree or disagree:

- I sometimes or often consider ending my life.
- I have trouble sleeping or sleep too much.
- I am often tired.
- My weight has gone up or down recently.
- When I think about the future I feel hopeless about it.
- I cannot concentrate on things I am trying to do or get focused on anything.
- I don't enjoy anything. I am never happy. I don't laugh or smile anymore.
- I am worthless. Nobody needs me or wants to talk to me.
- I feel sad and dejected.
- I feel like crying.

If you look at this list and find that a majority of the statements hold true, it is possible that you are suffering from depression and should talk to a doctor or counselor about it. There is a difference between "not feeling very happy today" and "being profoundly sad for several weeks or months," especially if it is leading you to think about suicide. Between ten and twenty million people suffer from depression, and tens of thousands of people commit suicide every year as a result. By talking to a doctor or a counselor you can learn about the disease and the treatment options.

CHAPTER 16

Being a Teenager
Has Pros and Cons

One thing you will begin to notice as you go through life is that everything has advantages and disadvantages. For example, owning a car has the advantage that you can go wherever you want, whenever you want. It has the disadvantage that a car costs lots of money and causes quite a bit of pollution. Having a pet has the advantage of companionship but the disadvantages of pet care (feeding and walking) and vet bills. Living in California has the advantage of nice weather, but the disadvantage of a high cost of living.

In the same way, there are advantages and disadvantages to being a teenager. The problem many teenagers have is that they don't recognize the disadvantages so they can avoid them, nor the advantages so they can exploit them.

Let's start with the disadvantages and get them out of the way. You may have noticed some or all of the following disadvantages to being a teenager:

- Teenagers tend to be more naïve than adults. That means that you don't have as much experience with the real world, so you make mistakes and people tend to take advantage of you. People who know more than you can exploit your naïveté (see also Chapters 2 and 42). The key defense you have against this problem is to ask adults lots of questions so that you avoid making mistakes.
- Teenagers have less money than adults. It is hard to do things in this society without money, so that limits your freedom to some extent. Your key defense against teenage poverty is to get a job. The money you make gives you freedom.
- Teenagers under 18 generally live with their parents. That means you have to follow your parents' rules, so you cannot fly to Paris on a moment's notice. On the other hand, it generally means that they cover your expenses. They also give you love, protection and guidance.

114

- The wiring of your teenage brain tends to skew your priorities in odd ways. It also can make you moody and skittish at times. I heard an adult recently describe his 14-year-old daughter in the following way: "She's 14, which means I never know exactly *who* she will be on any given day." His point was, one day she is happy and chatty and full of life, while the next day she might be bitter and nasty and the next day she might be silent and sullen. Your emphasis on members of the opposite sex and what your friends think is also caused by the wiring of the teenage brain. Sometimes it takes an incredible amount of effort for you to bring these tendencies under control. See Chapter 2 for details. Your key defense against problems of this sort is recognizing that you have these tendencies and working on things like anger and patience.

- Everything is a "first": first date, first kiss, first car, first job, first prom, first apartment, first... Because everything is a first you have no experience, so you tend to make mistakes. These mistakes sap your confidence and make you unsure of yourself. Again, your key defense is talking to adults or other teenagers who have experienced the things you are about to experience so you can learn from them. You should also recognize that the first time you try anything it is likely that things will not go as expected. Plan for this and things go more smoothly.

- You don't have enough knowledge to understand a lot of what is happening around you. It might seem, for example, that most adult conversations are occurring in a foreign language. The newspaper may seem irrelevant. And so on. Your key defense is to begin talking to adults and learning about their world. See Chapters 3 and 4.

- You may be nearsighted. You may tend not to look past today, so you may miss the future ramifications of many of the things you do. This means you tend to make decisions that have bad long-term consequences. Your key defense is to think long-term, and to learn from others about potential future consequences of your actions.

It is good to be aware of these disadvantages because you can take action to lessen their effects. Your primary tool to control naïveté, for example, is to ask for advice from more experienced adults. Your primary tool to control nearsightedness is to ask adults for another perspective. You leverage the knowledge of adults to help prevent mistakes.

Now let's look at the advantages, which are many:

- You have a lot of free time. As a teenager you have few direct responsibilities or entanglements, so time is plentiful. This means you can do things that require lots of time. You can learn to play a musical instrument, learn a foreign language, learn any new skill, become extremely proficient at a sport and so on. You might be asking, "Why should I learn a foreign language?" Because when you are older and have the money you might want to travel to a foreign country. Think about your goals for the future (see Chapter 23) and prepare for them now while you have the time.

- It is easy to exceed expectations. Most adults expect teenagers to be slack. If you are not you can surprise people and gain benefits.
- Many adults will allow you to make mistakes and ask questions that they would not allow in another adult. You can walk up to any professional adult and ask innocently, "Can you tell me about your job and how you got here?" Instead of being annoyed, most adults will think, "Ah, now here is a teenager trying to better him/herself. Let me do what I can to help."
- You are not encumbered by many of the financial obligations adults have (see Chapter 1), so you have a tremendous amount of freedom. At age 18 or 19 you can, if you choose to, pack all of your belongings into the back of your car and move wherever you want. Adults have less freedom because they have a lot of obligations (mortgages, jobs, etc.) and it would take an 18-wheeler to hold all their stuff. You can get a entry-level job in any occupation on the planet because you don't need that much money to support yourself. Then you can learn that occupation from the ground up.
- You have a lot of energy. Teenagers by default have a tremendous amount of energy. You can run faster, play longer, stay up all night, etc. Adults tend to have less energy and enthusiasm, so you can run circles around them.
- Everything looks "easy." One of the *good* things about being naïve is that lots of things look easy. Things that adults will not try because they are "impossible" (starting a new business from scratch, for example) often look easy to a teenager. This sort of risk-taking and exuberance can really pay off sometimes.
- Your mind is a blank slate. You can fill it with whatever you want as quickly as you are able. There are no limits to what you can accomplish provided that you can motivate yourself to get started. You can choose any career you like (see Chapters 0 and 6). Your options are wide open.

The important thing to do, as a teenager, is to recognize the intrinsic advantages available to you and exploit them for all they are worth. Try making up a list of other advantages and see if there are ways for you to capitalize on them.

CHAPTER 17

Appearance Counts

Appearance counts in the way you present yourself and your ideas. For many people this is a disconcerting and seemingly unfair fact of life, but it is a fact of life none the less. You can have the best idea in the world, but if the way you choose to present it looks bad it is very likely to be rejected. To better understand this phenomena, consider the following questions:

- Why is it that if someone at school wears "geeky" clothes everyone makes fun of him and avoids him?
- Why is it that if a blind date were to pull up to your house in an old, dirty, beat up car you would likely pretend you are not at home?
- Why is it that if you walk into a restaurant and the first thing you see is a bunch of dirty tables and a rat scurrying across the floor you are likely to walk out?
- Why is it that if you walk up to a bank or business in a big, impressive building you feel more comfortable than if it is in a small, unkempt shack?
- Why is it that police officers wear uniforms and drive big cars with official-looking logos painted all over them?
- Why is it that many napkins and other paper products that want to tout the fact that they are "recycled" are died brown and have little fake flecks in them, even through it is just as easy to manufacture recycled products so they are as white as any other piece of paper?
- Why is it that when you hand in a paper at school that you have hand-written, while the person next to you hands in their paper laser-printed, well formatted and bound in an attractive cover, you feel somehow inadequate?

- Why is it that so many advertisements include pictures of attractive models?
- Why is it that something like $50 billion is spent per year on package design? Not on the packages themselves, or on what goes inside the packages, but just on the design of the packages.

It's because appearance matters. You know it. Everyone knows it. Every human being on this planet responds to the outside appearance of things at some level. It is said that you can't judge a book by its cover, but it is a fact of life that the cover is the first thing we see. And because of that the cover is important.

It is the same way with "your package." People judge you by how you look and what you say. They start forming their judgments from their very first contact with you. When you walk up to a person for the first time, their initial impression is formed by how you look:

- Your clothes
- Your haircut
- Your posture
- Your facial expression
- Your handshake
- The way you introduce yourself

Because of this phenomena, you get to precisely pick the image you portray to others. Simply by picking your clothes, your haircut, your posture and so on you can determine how people will initially see you. For example:

- If you wear an old, stretched T-shirt, dirty jeans, long stringy hair and a five-day-old beard, people will initially think of you as unkempt and unreliable.
- If you wear torn and dirty jeans, a shirt with the sleeves ripped off, a nose ring, closely-shaved hair and snake tattoos on your arms, people will initially think of you as violent and dangerous.

Would you expect them to think otherwise? People see these things, they recognize them as a part of a pattern and they react to them. For example, they see the nose ring and the snake tattoos and think, "Other people I have seen in my life who wore a nose ring and snake tattoos tended to be violent, unstable people," and they react to you in an appropriate way. On the other hand:

- If you are a man and you wear a nice suit, a business-like haircut and shined shoes, people will think of you as a reliable, professional person.
- If you are a woman and you wear a pretty dress, elegant jewelry and an attractive hairstyle, people will think of you as a sophisticated and worldly person.

It is obvious that people should feel this way. It is very likely that you feel exactly this way yourself when you look at others. Why should they feel differently when they look at you? A key conclusion for you to draw from this discussion is that if you dress and act like a teenager, you will be treated like a teenager. However, if you dress and act like an adult, you will be treated like an adult. You don't have to be a rocket scientist to figure that out.

The same phenomena holds true for anything you produce. Whenever you do anything that you are going to present to other people, make sure the appearance is the best you can achieve given the resources available to you. Alternatively, work to make the packaging extremely and obviously unique and creative. The "creative" approach has the unfortunate possibility of back-firing, but that is always the risk you take with creativity.

For example, if you are writing a paper on Egypt for a school project, you should first make sure that the paper is well written, accurate and meeting the requirements for a good grade. That is the "content" part of the paper, and obviously you want the content to be good. Then you should work on the packaging. You can provide "the best packaging available to you" by making sure that the paper is neatly type, properly formatted and bound in a nice cover. Alternatively, you could provide "creative" packaging by buying or making your own papyrus and hand-writing it with a calligraphy pen. Be sure to note in this example that

Beauty

A lot of teenagers take a statement like, "Appearance Matters" and immediately translate it into "Beauty Matters." You feel that way because beauty does matter to some extent in the weird world of High School. However, it is important to understand that "physical beauty" and "success" are totally unrelated in the real world. Think about these outrageously successful people:

- Most famous sports figures
- Many actors and commedians
- Nearly any President and First Lady
- Nearly any politician
- The vast majority of successful business people

Most people are not "physically beautiful" in the "fashion model" sense. And yet they are all highly successful. The point: If you don't look like a fashion model it really doesn't matter. What matters is how you present yourself (your clothes, your bearing, your expression, your language), what you know, and what you accomplish with your individual talents and skills.

there are two parts to this project, and to every project you undertake in life: the *content* and the *appearance (or packaging)*. You must provide both to be successful.

Because appearance is so important to human beings, you need to keep it in mind at all times. It applies to both how you present yourself as a person and how you present your work to others.

CHAPTER 18
Virtue Triumphs Over Evil

Y ou might recall from super hero comic books the proclamation, "Virtue triumphs over evil!" The good guy typically says this, or something like it, right after he puts the bad guy behind bars. And it is true. In the long run, the forces of good always triumph over the forces of evil.

---

vir·tue (vûr′chŏo̅) noun
a. Moral excellence and righteousness; goodness. b. An example or kind of moral excellence: the virtue of patience.
Chastity, especially in a girl or woman.
A particularly efficacious, good, or beneficial quality; advantage: a plan with the virtue of being practical.
Effective force or power: believed in the virtue of prayer.
[Source: The American Heritage Dictionary]

Virtue triumphs over evil both for individuals and society as a whole. In general, people who live good and just lives do better than people who do not. Good people have more friends, are more successful, are happier and live longer than people who are not. If you look at the people around you in society, on TV, at your school and so on, you will find that in general people who follow the path of good succeed, while those who follow the path of evil fail. Sure, there are exceptions, but those exceptions are almost always in the short term. In the long term those who follow the path of evil pay for it, while those who do good are rewarded.

Let's look at two questions to better understand this phenomena:

- Is it true that good triumphs over evil? Do people who follow the path of goodness generally succeed? And do those who follow the bad path fail? In general this is the case. Think about Adolf Hitler. He was evil incarnate. The entire world fought a war to stop him and he lost. Think about criminals. Eventually they are arrested and put in jail. Think about drug dealers. They die from taking the drugs they sell. Or they are killed by other drug dealers. Or the police capture them. Think about dishonest people. Eventually, they are caught in their dishonesty and pay the price. People who do the right thing are rewarded. Those who do not pay for it. Either they pay for it directly (by going to jail, for example), or they pay for it when their conscience starts bothering them.

- Why is it that good triumphs over evil? Why is it that this is such a consistent fact of life? Why is it that you can reliably predict the future of a person's life based on his goodness or evilness? First, most people are fundamentally good and they do not tolerate bad. Society as a whole has an interest in promoting goodness, so it does. When someone lies to you, for example, you find you cannot trust that person. Therefore, you stop doing business with that person. So do other people. The lying person goes out of business or loses his job. The second reason is that bad acts often have bad consequences associated with them. That is simply how the world works. You might do something bad once and get away with it. Maybe twice. Maybe many times. But in general the natural consequences of bad acts catch up with you and you reap what you sow.

The fact that virtue triumphs over evil is an excellent reason to work toward goodness in your own life. By following a "good" path you bring to yourself the rewards of goodness. Another reason is your conscience, and the fact that you have to live with yourself.

con·science (kòn'shens) noun
a. The awareness of a moral or ethical aspect to one's conduct together with the urge to prefer right over wrong: Let your conscience be your guide. b. A source of moral or ethical judgment or pronouncement: a document that serves as the nation's conscience. c. Conformity to one's own sense of right conduct: a person of unflagging conscience.
The part of the superego in psychoanalysis that judges the ethical nature of one's actions and thoughts and then transmits such determinations to the ego for consideration.
[Source: The American Heritage Dictionary]

Although the idea of a conscience may sound old-fashioned to you, and perhaps even silly, it is important. Your conscience is what distinguishes you from an animal. When an animal acts, it acts instinctively. It does things in response to signals directly wired into its brain. So when a male dog finds a female dog in heat, he mounts her.

When a rattlesnake is surprised by something it bites the intruder to kill it. When a larger animal comes upon a smaller or weaker animal that has food, the larger steals from the smaller. These are all instinctive reactions to situations. As humans we are different because we have a brain that lets us think, reason, consider and override instinct. The thing that makes us unique as humans is our conscience—our ability to differentiate between good and bad. We are most human when we are most conscious of our actions. We are at our best when we consider what we are doing and choose the right thing.

WHAT IS RIGHT AND WRONG?

In the little decisions you make during each day of your life your conscience guides you in the search for what is right. It also guides you in the larger things you do. Think about the following situations and how you might react to them:

- I'm at a store and I *really* like this hair clip (wallet, pen, whatever) but I don't have any money. No one is looking. Should I just stick it in my pocket and walk out the door?
- The star quarterback started talking to me at lunch. He has an unbelievable body and everyone loves him, including me. We started dating. We have been out three times and now he wants to have sex. Should I sleep with the star quarterback tonight?
- I broke the window. Should I tell someone?
- Should I ask my best friend's girlfriend out? I know she likes me and I like her.
- Should I sneak out of the house tonight to go out with my friends?
- I have a test today. My friend Jim took the test earlier today, and we know the teacher will use the same questions when I take the test. Jim is a genius and he owes me a favor, so he wrote down all the correct answers on a sheet of paper. It would be easy to memorize them because the test is multiple choice, and no one would ever find out. Should I use the answers Jim gave me on this test?
- My father is a house painter. I go with him to people's houses and paint with him sometimes. We are at this rich person's house today, and there is a really nice watch on the dresser. Dad is getting ready to take it, I can tell. I know he has taken things from other houses and he always gets away with it. Should I go along with dad and let him take it? I know that he would love to have that watch.
- I found my Sister's diary today because she accidentally left it on her bed. Should I read it?

- I found a wallet at the mall. Inside there is $225. Should I return it? Should I take the cash as my reward and return the wallet? Should I keep the cash and throw the wallet away?
- My friends are going to bash mailboxes in the neighborhood tonight. Should I go?
- Should I skip class today?
- I'm pregnant. I can't possibly tell my parents. When I told the father he stopped talking to me. Should I have an abortion?
- Everyone teases Mary because she is poor and wears stupid clothes. I don't like the way they treat her, but my friends say I'm in love with her if I keep quiet. I'm not in love with her, I just think we shouldn't tease her. Should I tease her like everyone else to get them off my back?
- I accidentally dinged the car next to me with my door because the wind blew it open suddenly. Does it matter?
- I would like to buy a pair of new shoes. Should I take the money I need from Mom's purse even though I haven't asked her about it?
- My friends are going to put a tack on the teacher's chair. Should I play along?
- A bunch of my friends are going to a party where there will be lots of cocaine. The guy who is having the party is a friend of a friend. My friends tell me that cocaine feels *incredibly* good. Better than sex. Should I go with them and try it?

In each of these situations you have a choice. You can do the right thing or the wrong thing. Many teenagers have trouble making the correct choices. Here are three reasons why a lot of teenagers would have trouble figuring out the "right" thing to do in the above situations:

1. Many teenagers would never stop to think about it. They would just *do* something (usually the thing that "feels good" or is "easiest" at the time), and that something is often the wrong something because what "feels good" in the moment is often wrong long-term.

2. If they did stop to think about it, many teenagers would have no way to decide on the "right" thing. Many teenagers have no *moral framework* that allows them to make the correct decision. Lacking a moral framework, their conscience does not work correctly, or it does not work fast enough. So maybe two days later they start to feel guilty about what they've done, but by then it is too late.

3. Many teenagers have a conscience, and it works correctly and plenty fast, but other pressures override it. For example, if "everyone" is doing something and they are in a group, they will let the group's behavior take precedence even when they know

the group is doing the wrong thing. They do this because they want to "fit in" and be accepted.

How do you build a moral framework and a conscience that will help you to see the difference between right and wrong? How do you make the right decisions on a daily basis? In theory your parents and teachers have helped you to build a good moral framework throughout your life. There are a couple of things that can cloud the issue, however.

For example, maybe your parents don't have a great moral framework themselves. That could slow you down, but probably won't. Much more likely is the fact that you are receiving thousands of conflicting messages each day from television (see Chapter 37) and your friends. Let's take an extreme example. You probably *know* it is wrong to murder someone. There isn't a lot of thinking power necessary to understand that murder is wrong. Yet by watching television as much as you do you have seen thousands of people murdered. Murder can solve all sorts of problems, according to television; everything from an uncooperative parent to a pesky teacher to a rival for your boyfriend or girlfriend can be solved by murder, at least on TV. Even with all of those messages on TV saying, "Murder can solve a lot of problems" you probably still understand that murder is wrong. However, notice how many drug dealers and criminals use murder every day without a bit of hesitation. Somewhere they have gotten the message that it is OK. And think about smaller things, where it is not so clear-cut. Because you get so many conflicting messages from television, it can be very hard to accurately tell if something is right or wrong at any given moment unless you have a strong moral framework to guide you.

BUILDING A MORAL FRAMEWORK

In order to *know* what is right and wrong you need a moral framework. You need a clear and simple set of criteria that you can use in any situation to tell you if something is right or wrong. You then need to learn to use your framework to make decisions. Here is a set of five simple questions that you can use to start building a moral framework and a conscience. In the situations you face you can ask these five questions to decide what is right or wrong:

1. Will what I am about to do hurt someone else? If it will, it is wrong.
2. Will I break a promise or a commitment I have made to someone else by doing what I am about to do? If it will, it is wrong.
3. Does what I am about to do have known destructive or negative consequences? If so, it is wrong.

4. Is what I am about to do illegal? If so, it is wrong.
5. Would I be ashamed or embarrassed to tell *anyone* about what I am about to do? If I were to get caught doing this, would I know I was doing wrong? If so, then it is wrong.

Now let's look at each of these rules in detail and discover why they are useful rules to include in your moral framework.

The first rule is fairly straightforward: Don't hurt other people, either physically or mentally. For example:

- You do not want to be murdered.
- You do not want to be beaten.
- You do not want other people to steal your stuff.
- You do not want to be betrayed.

You are a human being. You do not like to be hurt. Because you do not like these things to happen to you, you have to assume that everyone else feels the same way. Therefore, if you want the world to work in such a way that you aren't murdered, beaten, robbed or betrayed, you have to do your part by not doing these things to other people. This is where the golden rule comes from: *"Do unto others as you would have others do unto you."* Another way to say it is, "Don't do to other people what you would dislike having done to yourself." In both the positive and negative senses it means the same thing. By following this simple rule you can decide what to do in all sorts

> *Do unto others as you would have others do unto you.*

of situations. Should you steal or shoplift? No. Should you tease other people? No. Should you read your sister's diary? No. And so on. Simply ask yourself, "Would *I* like it if someone did this to *me*?" If not, then don't do it.

The second rule has to do with your personal accountability. If you make a promise or commitment to someone, then you need to keep it. It is as simple as that. This topic is discussed in much more detail later in this chapter.

There is another thing having to do with personal commitments that is easy to miss: *hidden commitments.* For example, when you buy a pet dog you are taking on the hidden commitment of feeding, sheltering and caring for that dog for the rest of its life. The dog, after all, depends on its owner for these things. The act of buying the dog and becoming its owner is what signed you up for these duties. Once you buy the dog you are responsible for fulfilling all of the duties of dog ownership, whether you understood them when you bought the dog or not.

The third rule in your moral framework asks, "Does what I am about to do have known destructive or negative consequences?" Drugs fall into this category. They have clear, known, well-understood and common negative consequences. Therefore it is easy to see that drugs are wrong. The same applies to smoking because of its know health effects. Promiscuous sex has the destructive consequence of sexually transmitted diseases, including AIDS. These diseases have known negative consequences, so promiscuous sex is wrong. Also keep in mind that the purpose of sex is to create a baby, and a baby carries a huge implied commitment to clothe, shelter, feed, love, educate and nurture the child throughout its life.

The fourth rule asks, "Is what I am about to do illegal?" If it is, then it is wrong by society's standards. If you think the law is wrong, then you should work legally through proper channels to change it. As long as the law exists it is wrong to disobey it because any illegal activity has known negative consequences (arrest, fines, jail, public humiliation, etc.) You have the right to change the law (see Chapter 35), so work on that instead of defying the law. If you are right a majority of people will feel the same way and changing the law will be easy.

The fifth rule asks, "Would I be ashamed to tell *anyone* about what I am about to do?" Let's say you are about to cheat on your girlfriend or your spouse. You would be ashamed to face your girlfriend or your spouse if you got caught, so it is wrong. Let's say you are about to cheat on a test. If the teacher caught you there would be bad consequences (failing the test, expulsion) and you would be ashamed to face the teacher, your classmates and your parents. Therefore, cheating is wrong. Let's say you are about to bash mailboxes. If you got caught by the owner of the mailbox or your parents, you would be ashamed. Therefore, it is wrong. And so on.

If you apply the five simple rules to any question of right and wrong, the answers you generate will tell you the right thing to do. Will they tell you the easy thing to do? No. They will tell you the right thing.

In her book *How Could You Do That?!*, Dr. Laura Schlessinger (who also has a popular radio call-in show) relates the following story (© 1996 by Dr. Laura C. Schlessinger. Reprinted by permission of HarperCollins Publishers, Inc.):

Mike, twenty-seven, called with this dilemma. Mike and I began our conversation with his denial that this issue tweaked any feelings in him at all; he said he had been brought up not to express feelings. I worried aloud about the danger of not internally acknowledging feelings such as guilt, shame, regret and pride, without which our decisions are made more from expediency than honor. It was then that he consciously acknowledged that a coming decision might, just might, end up hurting his feelings.

To avoid getting mucked up in the "details" I suggested we talk about Mike's dilemma without ever revealing the specifics.

"This is something I would kinda want to do, but..."
"Mike, do you think this is the right thing to do?"
"Yes."
"Then, when you have kids you are going to recommend this for them to do?"
"No."
"Then how can it be the right thing to do if your wouldn't tell your kids to do it?"
"Hmmm."
"So, you know it's not the right thing to do, but its adventurous or something like that and you'd like the experience?"
"Exactly."
"Mike, do you believe that after you do this thing you would admire yourself?"
"No, I don't think I would admire myself."
"Then, why would you choose to do something you wouldn't admire yourself for? What would be the point? What could be so good that it would be worth that price?"
"Yeah. And I do stand to lose some things, too."
"So, it might be fun and adventurous, but there is some potential loss attached to it. You could be hurt, you would be ashamed to tell your children, and it would diminish you in your own eyes..."
"Correct."
"So, what's your decision...are you going to do it or not?"
"I'm not going to do it."
"Thank you for your call."
"Thank you."

Does it matter what the specific dilemma was? I don't think so. And not using the details as mitigations and rationalizations helps keep you focused on what you will have to live with over the long haul: the long-range consequences and your conscience. That is the primary tug-of-war: the immediate desired gains or avoidance of undesired losses *vs.* the longer-term sometimes barely foreseeable issues of responsibility and honor. That's precisely why character requires so much courage.

I work to focus my on-air dialogs on the essentials of right and wrong and pride and guilt and shame, because it brings the future to the now—where it can more adequately compete with the expediency and excitement of temptations. In this way conscience is now introduced into the decision-making process.

Are there ever exceptions? Can you ever break any of the five rules? Yes, there are exceptions. Let's say you get married. In your marriage vows you promise, "Until death do us part." However, after a year of marriage your spouse begins taking heroin and starts beating you. In a case like that you have an obligation to break the commitment because your basic rights as a human being are being violated. You have the right to press charges against your spouse and get a divorce because you should expect that you will not be beaten by others. You also should expect that your spouse will not break the law. When these rights are violated, you have the right to take action. Another example: What if you have been dating someone for six months, but you realize that you do not want to marry this person and it is time to move on. Breaking up is going to hurt your partner. Should you stay in the relationship? No. The reason

> **Good Books** A good book to read for more information is *How could you do that?!* by Dr. Laura Schlessinger. See the references section for more information.

you date is to find a marriage partner. Once you realize that marriage is not in the cards it is time to break the relationship. There is no way to avoid it. In theory your friend should be able to understand that. If not, there is nothing you can do about it.

A problem arises when people use excuses and exceptions to attempt to validate legitimately bad behavior:

- "It's OK to cheat on this test because it is nothing but memorization and memorization is stupid."
- "It is OK to steal this item because the store has all sorts of money and I don't."
- "It is OK to lie to my friend because if I don't it will hurt her feelings."
- "My girlfriend won't mind if I go out with her best friend because we aren't really getting along right now anyway."

In all of these cases the word "because" is supposed to erase the fundamental wrongness of the act, but it does not.

One of the biggest problems many teenagers face is *self-centeredness*. As described in Chapter 2, infants are naturally and completely self-centered. Many teenagers are still remarkably self-centered and shortsighted. In many situations you face, a good additional question to ask yourself is, *"Am I being selfish or self-centered or shortsighted here?"* If the answer is yes, then it is likely that you will want to reconsider your approach. It can be hard for a teenager to get past all of the excuses and explanations and mitigating factors to understand the basic selfishness of an act. In that case it is good to ask an adult you trust to help.

ANOTHER WAY TO TELL RIGHT FROM WRONG

Another way to tell right from wrong is to try to choose a word or set of words to describe the thing you are about to do. If you find that the words you choose have a bad connotation, then you know the action is wrong. If you would not want yourself described using those negative words, then you know that the action is wrong. On the other hand, if you would be proud of your action and proud of the words used to describe it, then you know that the action is probably right. Here are lists of right and wrong words to help you describe yourself and the actions that you are considering:

Good Words (virtues)	Bad Words (Vices)
Caring	Callous
Clean	Dirty, filthy, defiled
Compassionate	Pitiless, merciless, harsh
Confident	Uncertain, weak
Considerate	Inconsiderate, neglectful, rude
Controlled	Savage, stupid, wild
Courageous, brave	Fearful, cowardly
Courteous	Impolite, rude
Creative	Unoriginal, boring
Detached (absence of prejudice or bias)	Biased, prejudiced, racist
Determined	Indecisive, waffling
Disciplined	Wild, disorderly, mismanaged
Enthusiastic	Boring, tired, old
Excellent	Inferior
Faithful	False, disloyal, treacherous
Flexible	Stiff, rigid (not always bad things...)
Forgiving	Vengeful, spiteful
Friendly	Antagonistic, hostile
Generous	Greedy, miserly, selfish, stingy
Gentle	Cruel, harsh
Helpful	Ineffectual, useless
Heroic	Cowardly, fearful
Honest	Cheating, dishonest, lying
Honorable	Disgraceful, degrading, despicable
Humble	Arrogant, conceited, egotistical, haughty
Idealistic	Apathetic, stoic
Integrity	Dishonest, corrupt
Intelligent	Ignorant, stupid
Joyful	Gloomy, depressed, dejected
Just	Unjust, partial, unfair

Kind	Brutal, cruel, mean
Loving	Abhorrent, hateful
Loyal	Treacherous, unfaithful
Mature	Childish, immature, inexperienced
Merciful	Cruel, merciless, ruthless
Moderate	Gluttonous, greedy, piggish
Modest	Excessive, extravagant
Obedient	Disobedient, defiant
Orderly	Confused, disorderly
Patient	Hasty, hotheaded, impatient
Peaceful	Conflict, disruptive
Purposeful	Irresolute, vacillating, wavering
Reliable	Unreliable, disloyal
Respectful	Disrespectful, insolent, impudent
Responsible	Irresponsible
Reverent	Disrespectful
Self-disciplined	Undisciplined, wild, disorderly
Steadfast	Disloyal, unfaithful, treacherous
Tactful	Rude
Thankful	Dissatisfied, ungrateful
Trusting	Doubtful, jealous
Trustworthy	Deceitful, disloyal, treacherous
Truthful	False, lying, dishonest, deceitful

One thing you will notice is that as people become mature, they normally take on virtues and shed vices. Adults are respected because of the virtues they incorporate into their personalities. Teenagers tend to be much more haphazard in their behavior and hence they are not respected.

PEOPLE MAKE MISTAKES

All of this is fine. It sounds great on paper. In fact, it sounds easy on paper. Anybody can be moral and good when the situations are not those that you face personally. When something is happening to you, especially with one or several people standing around you demanding that you do something that you know is wrong, it is much more difficult. In real life, in real situations—especially when you are young—it is easy to make mistakes. What do you do after you do something that you know is wrong? What if you did not realize something was wrong when you did it, but now you do?

People make mistakes. That is a fact of life. There are two things you should keep in mind about mistakes:

1.   You can admit the mistake and then work to correct it.

2. A mistake does not absolve you of guilt or responsibility. You are still responsible for the consequences of the mistake.

You can admit your mistake and say, "I'm sorry," if you have hurt someone. You can return something and take the consequences if you have stolen something. You can turn yourself in if you are guilty of a crime. Will it be easy? No. Are you likely to lose something in the process? Yes. In many cases the consequences are irrevocable. If you sleep around and a year later find you have AIDS, that's a problem that you cannot fix. That brings us to a fact of life that is important:

If you think about your actions ahead of time and do the right thing to begin with, you will not have to pay the consequences later

It is as simple as that. The advantage of having a conscience and listening to it is that it keeps you out of trouble. If you get lucky and avoid the consequences of a wrongful act, then you should be thankful that you were able to learn a lesson before it was too late. Then work on making sure the mistake does not happen again.

> *"Our lives teach us who we are."*
> - Salman Rushdie

As you become an adult your moral framework and your conscience strengthen. Matters of right and wrong become obvious. That is one of the important things that distinguishes an adult from a teenager, and one of the things that lets adults be sure of themselves.

HONESTY IS THE BEST POLICY

Your moral framework is most often tested in the area of *honesty*. Honesty is therefore the cornerstone your *reputation*. Upon this cornerstone you base your *character*.

Each day you come into contact with people and they interact with you:

*   People ask you questions.
*   People ask you to do things.
*   You say things.
*   You offer to do things.
*   You act in certain ways in certain situations.

> hon·es·ty (ŏn′ĭ-stē) *noun*
> The quality or condition of being honest; integrity.
> Truthfulness; sincerity
> *Synonyms: honesty, honor, integrity, probity, rectitude.* These nouns
>   denote the quality of being upright in principle and action. *Honesty*
>   implies truthfulness, fairness in dealing with others, and refusal to
>   engage in fraud, deceit, or dissembling.
> [Source: *The American Heritage Dictionary*]

It is from these very simple interactions with people that people form their impressions of you. It is from the combination of many interactions like these with a variety of people that you form your public reputation.

In everyday life you have the option to be completely honest:

- You can tell the truth.
- You can keep your promises and commitments.

In doing these two simple things, you will find that:

- People will learn that they can trust you.
- People will learn that they can rely on you.
- People will learn that you are responsible.
- People will learn to have confidence in you.
- People will learn that you are dependable.

> char·ac·ter (kăr′ek-ter) *noun*
> The combination of qualities or features that distinguishes one person,
>   group, or thing from another.
> A distinguishing feature or attribute, as of an individual, a group, or a
>   category.
> Moral or ethical strength.
> A description of a person's attributes, traits, or abilities.
> A formal written statement as to competency and dependability, given
>   by an employer to a former employee; a recommendation.
> Public estimation of someone; reputation: *personal attacks that
>   damaged her character.*
> [Source: *The American Heritage Dictionary*]

In other words you will earn a good reputation, and that reputation will bring you strong friends, important business associations and a great deal of inner peace. People—all people—would rather deal with an honest person than a dishonest one. That is a fact of life.

Once you get away from the truth, people's trust in you falters. For example, if you tell someone a lie (even a small "white lie" that avoids confrontation or an awkward situation) and you are caught in it, then the next time that person needs to rely on you he or she will have a problem. A collection of lies, large or small, leads to a situation where no one can trust you. Then you are stuck.

The act of being honest all the time is difficult. For example, it requires you to confront people on occasion. It requires you to find diplomatic ways to tell people things they do not want to hear. It forces you to admit to things you would rather hide. In every case it is better to take the discomfort up front rather than delay it and compound it with a lie. That can be a hard thing to face at the point of confrontation or admission, but it is a fact of life.

rep·u·ta·tion (rĕp'ye-tā'shen) *noun*
The general estimation in which a person is held by the public.
The state or situation of being held in high esteem.
[Source: *The American Heritage Dictionary*]

CHAPTER 19

You Can Say No

When someone asks you a yes or no question, you have the right to say "No." That is a fact of life. Saying "No" may not always be easy or pleasant, but it is always an option. There are two things that can make it a lot easier to say no:

- If you know what you want and someone offers you something that you do not want, it can be extremely easy to say "No." If, for example, you are on a diet, you are in a restaurant and the waitress offers you desert, you can easily say "No" because what you want is to be thin.
- If you have set pre-defined boundaries on your behavior and you have made a commitment to yourself to never cross those boundaries, it can be easy to say "No."

In the previous chapter you learned about right and wrong. One problem you might notice about "doing the right thing" is that it can be *extremely* hard to say "No" to certain activities. This is especially hard when you are in a group and everyone else is doing something that you believe to be wrong (or simply not right for you). One of the best ways to do the right thing is to set rigid boundaries that you will not cross so that you can be resolute when temptations arise.

Here are some boundaries that you might want to consider setting as a teenager. By respecting these boundaries and never crossing them for any reason you can save yourself a tremendous amount of difficulty.

- I will not smoke.
- I will not take drugs.
- I will not have sex until I am married.
- I will not destroy other people's property.
- I will not hurt other people.
- I will not lie.
- I will not break promises I make.

Memorize these boundaries. Repeat them every day. Write them on an index card and tape them to your bathroom mirror if you need to so that you see them every morning. When someone asks you to break one of these boundaries, simply say, "No, thank you." It is as simple as that. Initially your friends might think you are weird. Either they will get used to it or you will get different friends. In either case the transition will be natural.

Similarly, you can make a list of things that you want out of life, and you can then easily say "No" to things that do not conform with what you want. For example:

- I am going to college.
- I am honest.
- I have a good relationship with my parents.
- I will marry someone I truly love.

See also Chapter 23, on goals. Think about your life and come up with a list of your own desires.

Boundaries Make Decisions Easy

My father had a lot of problems with alcohol during his life. It did him absolutely no good. I learned my lesson from watching his experiences and set a simple boundary: I will drink no alcohol. This decision has made life extremely straightforward for me. Whenever anyone offers me an alcoholic beverage I simply say, "No, thank you." I don't have to think about it and there is no way anyone can sway me—the answer is always "No."

You already have lots of boundaries like this. If I offer you a big handful of rat poison and say, "Would you like some?" your answer would be "No." The new boundaries you set for yourself are simply extensions of the pre-wired boundaries you already have in place.

CHAPTER 20

Every Action Has a Reaction

Every action has an equal and opposite reaction. That is a fact of life both in the physical world and in the world of human society. Another way to look at it is to use the words "cause" and "effect." Every effect has a cause. One other way to think about it is to say that everything you do has short- and long-term consequences. When you do something you should expect the natural consequences, whether they are good or bad.

There is nothing you can do to stop the consequences of an action. Good actions generally have good consequences. Bad actions generally have bad consequences. You might miss the consequences on occasion. For example, you might do something that you know is wrong and "not get caught," but if you repeat the action several times the consequences will catch up to you. That is a fact of life. This is the primary reason why good triumphs over evil.

Because actions generally have predictable consequences, you know the following:

- If you smoke you are likely to get lung cancer.
- If you take drugs you are likely to get addicted.
- If you have unprotected sex someone is likely to get pregnant.
- If you drive 110 miles an hour down a dark, twisty road you are likely to get in an accident.
- If you shoplift you are likely to get arrested.
- And so on.

In each of the above examples, you can be sure that the effect will generally follow the cause each time. You might get lucky, but the odds are against you.

On the other hand:

- If you deal with all people honestly, it is likely that people will trust and respect you.
- If you do your homework you are likely to get good grades.

- If you work hard and get a college degree, you are likely to get a much better paying job.
- If you save your money consistently over a long period of time, you are likely to accumulate tremendous wealth.
- If you read a good book every week, you are likely to obtain wisdom.
- And so on.

There are no surprises here, just simple cause and effect relationships. Teenagers have a tendency to ignore the effects. Adults tend to take the effects into account. That is what makes them more mature.

Think about the following four teenagers:

- A teenage girl is sitting in her room. She is thinking, "What am I going to do tonight?" What she comes up with is a plan to wear a lot of makeup and a short, tight skirt and flirt with college guys down at the pier to see what happens.
- A teenage guy is sitting in his room. He is thinking, "What am I going to do tonight?" He decides to get together with some friends, get a six-pack from somewhere and drive around spray painting cars in a nearby neighborhood.
- Another teenage girl is sitting in her room. She is thinking, "What am I going to do tonight?" The phone rings. She decides to get totally wasted with some friends down at a bar that will let teenage girls in the back door.
- Another teenage guy is sitting in his room thinking, "What am I going to do tonight?" He decides to go to a party with some friends because there will be a good supply of pot and beer there.

What is wrong with these pictures? What are these people doing, and why? What purposes do their actions serve? And what are the likely consequences of these actions? Any successful adult, or any successful teenager for that matter, looks at people like this with stunned amazement because what they are doing seems so utterly pointless. In all cases it also seems dangerous, and the cause/effect chains are well known. These actions make no sense.

There are clearly two problems that these four teenagers face:

1. Because they lack experience, these four teenagers cannot see the potential consequences of their actions. Any adult, for example, can see that the first teenager, with her makeup and tight skirt, is asking for any number of potentially dangerous consequences including pregnancy and STDs. The adult understands these consequences because the adult has seen (on the news, through stories accumulated from friends and acquaintances, from personal experiences, etc.) what the effect

of certain stereotypical actions are. The teenager probably has no clue about any of this because she simply has not lived life long enough to create a firm experience base. She cannot see the obvious consequences of her actions.

2. These teenagers obviously have no goals. If any of these teenagers had any sort of long-range plan for their lives they would be heading down a completely different road. They would be implementing their plans instead of wasting time. Lacking plans these four teenagers live life totally randomly, doing whatever comes to mind at any given moment (see Chapter 23).

Something else that is missing here, at a more subtle level, is a sense of *value*. Not values, but *value*. What is fun, for example, about spray painting other peoples' cars? No one who owns a car can understand that. Even these teenagers, 10 years from now, will be cursing the people who spray paint *their* cars. They will have a totally different perspective on the whole thing because 10 years from now they will have paid $30,000 for a really nice car.

Here's an example. Take a 25-year-old person. Since he was 15 he has dreamed of owning a beautiful Corvette. At age 25 he has actually saved up enough money to buy a gorgeous red one. One day he parks it in front of a friend's house. That night two 15-year-old teenagers come by and smash one of the rear view mirrors with a brick. That sort of thing makes any adult *ache*. AT THAT MOMENT the 25-year old understands exactly how it feels to have something you have worked for destroyed, and so the 25-year old immediately understands the *value* of things. A 15-year old who has never worked hard to achieve anything has no sense of value. In the same way, the girls above are not valuing their bodies and pride, and the boy smoking pot is not valuing his brain and body.

Teenagers don't have all of the cause/effect chains wired into their heads yet, so they cannot see the possible repercussions of their actions. Adults can see the repercussions vividly and account for them in their thinking automatically. There is a classic pattern with anger—after you have been angry about 1,600 times and you see that it never comes to good, you begin to see a trend and control your anger (see Chapter 26).

Everything you see in your world is an effect that has a cause. Teenagers often cannot see or even imagine the cause. If you live in a nice house now, that is an effect. The cause is likely the fact that your parents worked hard and saved money and sacrificed until they were able to afford the house. It might have taken 15 years to get to that point. You see it and take it for granted, but they see it completely differently.

Let's say you drop out of high school at age 16 because you are strung out on drugs. There are natural consequences to that action. In general, you will end up living a life of poverty. Your actions directly cause the effect of poverty. Let me show you a reverse example as well. Say you took every cent in the world away from a rich businessman, gave him plastic surgery so no one could recognize him, stripped him of all identification, erased his name and address from his brain, dressed him in rags and dumped him on the street in Peoria, IL. How long would he be homeless? Not very long. He has worked hard to cram a tremendous amount of knowledge about people, finances and business into his brain. That knowledge is valuable to many people, or it would allow him to succeed in starting a new business himself.

Many people have not taken the time to discipline themselves and learn a skill. They have no earning power in the marketplace; therefore, they are poor. That is cause and effect at work. It is brutal, but consistent. You cannot get something for nothing.

What if you are considering an action and you legitimately do not know what the potential consequences are? Then you should ask your parents or another adult you can trust. They have seen a lot more of the real world and can likely tell you what the common consequences for a particular action would be. What if you would be ashamed to talk to your parents about it? Then that probably tells you everything you need to know. But if that is the case, ask an impartial, mature adult (friend, teacher, counselor, etc.) and see what they say. Then *listen*.

Understanding Consequences

I can remember a lot of funny scenes from my childhood. My friends and I did all sorts of things that normal kids do. For example, we would play hide and seek and tag. We dug holes in the back yard looking for fossils. We had dirt clod fights. All normal and harmless stuff. However, I can remember three scenes that are a little different.

- I can remember that my dad had a flashlight that used a great big 6-volt battery. My friends and I needed a flash light. The battery was dead, so we cut off one end of an extension cord and wrapped the wires around the terminals of the battery. Then we plugged it into the wall. It "made sense" to us. Batteries contain electricity and wall sockets contain electricity, right?

- I can remember my neighbors had a big, empty freezer in their garage. They kept it plugged in for some reason, and one day we started putting grasshoppers in it. We would put a grasshopper in, and then we would bring it out several minutes later and see if it survived. Sure enough they did, and it was fun to watch them thaw out. There was a point where we considered putting one of *us* in the freezer, but something distracted us that day and we never tried it.

- I can remember my friends and I decided to build a soap box derby car. We had a couple of old "Big Wheel" tricycles with broken front wheels but perfectly good back wheels and axles. The only problem was getting the axles out of the plastic body. One of us got the bright idea of burning the plastic bodies away from the axle. Even *I* was surprised by how big the fire got, and I wasn't disappointed when my dad came to help put it out.

The problem in all three of these scenes is that there was a lot of danger in what we were doing. We didn't know of the danger because of lack of experience. Having never seen a Big Wheel burn, how could we know how big the fire would get? Having never seen a battery explode, how could we know there was that possibility? You go outside in the winter all the time, so what would be the harm in putting a kid in a freezer for awhile? What we didn't know about was oxygen and suffocation.

Part of being a kid or a teenager is making mistakes (lots of them) in order to learn things. The thing you have to be careful about is the consequences you don't understand because of lack of experience. Asking someone with more experience is a good way to uncover the potential consequences ahead of time.

CHAPTER 21
Certain Mistakes Will Ruin Your Life

There are certain mistakes that you can make as a teenager that are harmless. For example, you can get a speeding ticket and it will have no long-lasting effects except for the $1,000 you will end up throwing out the window on insurance. Or you can fail a class through laziness and likely recover the next quarter. Your teenage years are a time to make lots of mistakes so that you can learn from each one.

However, there are other mistakes you can make that have much longer-lasting effects. The effects can be so long-lasting that they negatively affect the rest of your life in one way or another. Your life ends up being much harder than it would have been if you had prevented the mistake from occurring in the first place. The following mistakes are the most common *serious mistakes* or *unrecoverable mistakes* that a teenager can make. Make these and you normally dig a hole so deep you never fully recover:

- Drugs—Once you start taking drugs you start a long, downhill slide that has a good chance of ending in addiction. See Chapter 37 for details.
- Getting pregnant—If you get pregnant as a teenager, you have several choices but none of them are good. You can have an abortion and feel guilty the rest of your life. You can put the child up for adoption and wonder for the rest of your life. You can keep the baby and close the door on thousands of opportunities. Every one of them is a compromise that will have long-term negative consequences. A child will restrict your freedom for the rest of your life in ways that you cannot imagine, whether you are the mother or the father. See Chapter 9 for details.
- Dropping out of high school—Once you drop out of high school you basically shut the door on any sort of real job. You can get a GED later, but it will take a lot of time. It would be much easier to

142

simply stick with high school and get a diploma while you have the time and opportunity as a teen.

- Starting a criminal record—A criminal record follows you throughout your life. Imagine any employer faced with hiring you once you have a criminal record. When it comes time to choose someone for the job the decision will always be, "Let's see, this person has a criminal record so we can forget about him." Why should an employer take the chance? It makes it *extremely* hard to get a job, and that slows you down the rest of your life.

Getting Attention

How do you feel about the following statement?

"I tried to commit suicide, but I didn't really mean it. I was just trying to get some attention."

This statement comes from a teenager trying to rationalize a suicide attempt that failed.

Suicide is a rather odd way to get attention, although it surely works. People *will* notice you when they find your apparently-dead body lying on the floor! But what do they do with you the next day? You have gotten their attention, but now they cannot trust you anymore because they think you are mentally unbalanced.

This same line of reasoning is what leads many to juvenile delinquency. They aren't getting enough attention, so they decide to "act out" by doing something bad enough to get arrested. It does cause people to focus attention on you, but it is the wrong kind of attention. Now what? How do you ever get back on track?

The problem with doing something spectacularly bad to get attention is that it is a self-destructive behavior. For example, cutting off your arm is a way to get attention. But then you have only one arm for the rest of your life! Why would you do that? It makes no sense. The "act" has nothing to do with the goal you are trying to achieve. Attempted suicide and juvenile delinquency and teenage pregnancy are all ways to get attention, but they fall into the same category. They will affect you negatively for the rest of your life, so they are pointless.

If you feel like you aren't getting enough attention, start by recognizing that fact and stating it in English. "I am not getting enough attention, and it makes me feel bad." Then set a goal (see Chapter 23) like, "I want to solve this problem." Then talk to your parents or an adult friend and search for options to reach that goal (see Chapter 24). But don't let, "Maybe I should try to commit suicide" bumble into your brain and then lead you in the wrong direction. It doesn't solve the problem and has a lot of negative long-term consequences that you will pay for the rest of your life.

- Running away—As discussed in Chapter 1, running away guarantees homelessness. If you are in an impossible situation at home, look for some sort of alternative besides running away. For example, if you have an aunt or uncle, grandparents or a sympathetic family of a friend, try that. Or call a teen crisis line, such as (800) 999-9999, and see if they can help you.

You have the rest of your life ahead of you. Don't make a stupid mistake as a teenager that ruins it for you.

PART 5

The Facts About Success

There are a number of things you can do to help yourself become successful. This section explores some of the most important facts of life.

CHAPTER 22

You Can Create a
High-Level Vision

Y ou can create a high-level vision of any space that you
occupy. This vision allows you to evaluate yourself as
well as those around you. It allows you to analyze and,
in many cases, truly understand the problems you face. It allows you to
become much more strategic in your thinking. Many people never get to
the point where they even realize this fact of life. That deficit limits them
throughout their lives. Once you realize that it is possible, you can
practice this skill and use it to accomplish things both great and mundane.

Surprisingly, I realized this fact for the first time during a racquetball
game. Let me tell you how it happened so you can understand what I am
talking about. I am certainly not a stellar racquetball player. However, I
do enjoy playing the game. I had played for about a year, and one day I
was playing with a good friend of mine. There came a particular shot in
this game: In that shot I was suddenly able to watch the ball and *think
about it*. I can distinctly remember the moment because it was as though
a new part of my brain popped into existence and started processing
events. It was almost like a new me could stand, at a higher level, and
think about the game. What this new part of my brain said was, "OK.
This is *good*. Look at how the ball is tracking. Now look at where you
are, and notice where Mike is standing. If you move to *here,* you will
able to reach the ball *there*. That will allow you to *place* the ball when
you hit it right into the *far back corner*. He will never be able to reach it."
During this time the action of the game seemed to slow down, and I could
actually see and move and think at the same time. I was in fact able to hit
the ball into the back corner, well out of reach of my friend.

From that moment on my game improved dramatically.

What was amazing about this event was the fact that I had never
before in my life actually been able to think about the game. Prior to this
moment my brain simply tracked the ball and forced my body to hit the
ball. I simply *reacted*. My conscious mind had never been able to

147

participate. There was simply too much to do for my conscious mind to move to a higher level to analyze things. It is just like when you are learning anything new—it demands all of your concentration. Once you get good at something though, you are able to do it subconsciously without thinking. This is what allows you to walk, chew gum and talk to a friend while avoiding traffic as you walk down a busy sidewalk. You are doing the walking and chewing and avoiding subconsciously, and your mind is able to consciously process the conversation.

What this newfound ability in racquetball allowed me to do is to think *strategically*. Instead of flailing away at the ball in a reactive mode, I could watch the ball and my opponent, think about them and plan my actions. When you watch a skilled tennis star or basketball player do what they do, you are seeing a person who is able to think perhaps at several different levels about what his own body is doing, what his opponents' bodies are doing, what the ball is doing and what is necessary to win the point or make the basket. These higher-level thinking processes may be conscious or unconscious, and they make the brilliance of star athletes possible. At the same time, people who seem totally clueless about what they are doing and how the world works have never reached the point where they can effectively think about the world and themselves at this higher level. *Everything they do is a reaction to immediate input rather than a step in a longer-range plan.*

Once I realized that this was possible in racquetball, it became possible to use this skill in a number of other places. For example, when having a conversation with someone a part of you can move to a higher level and watch the conversation, thinking about the goals and objectives of both people who are talking. This skill is incredibly important in critical meetings and conversations, and it gives you a definite advantage over people who cannot work that way.

Is it always possible to work from a high-level view? No. And that is an important fact. It is easy to drop out of a high-level position and back to "reactive mode." Some of the things that can trigger this downward transition include fatigue, anger and newness. At the same time, however, there are things you can do to force yourself up to a higher position. One of the best things you can do is ask yourself a simple question: "What am I trying to accomplish here? What is my goal?"

Let's say that you are talking to a friend and your friend is angry. You have two choices. You can react angrily. That is certainly the easiest thing to do but almost always the least productive. The other thing you can do is say to yourself, "This person is a good friend of mine, and I trust her. But something is obviously angering her. What is my goal? My goal is to do what I can to solve the problem and allow our friendship to grow." Now ask her: "What, exactly, is the problem here? I see that you are angry. What is causing the anger?" Something is causing your friend to be angry. It could be a legitimate problem, it could be a misunderstanding, it could be a lack of communication or it could be a variety of other things. By understanding the true cause of the anger and working to eliminate it, you can prevent a major fight. Sometimes the simple act of listening rather than reacting fiercely is enough to defuse the situation so that you can both work toward a solution.

If you are trying to work with someone to accomplish one of your own goals (see Chapter 23), then by moving to a higher level you can often understand how to create a win/win situation. Ask yourself questions like: "What does this person need? What does this person want? What is important to this person? What would make this person happy?" In answering these questions and aligning them with your own desires, you can often reach a solution that makes both sides happy. You can work at a higher level during the conversation. You can think about the situation privately and try to come up with creative options (see Chapter 24). Draw or write options on a piece of paper and analyze them. For example, say you get a job at a fast food restaurant. While you are on the job you notice the manager has a lot of problems staffing weekend nights. You might come up to a higher level and ask yourself, "How can I help solve this problem?" You might volunteer to work three out of four weekends per month in return for extra pay, then negotiate a wage increase that works for both of you. Or you might suggest to the manager a broader program where all people working the weekend shift get extra pay. Look for creative solutions to the problem from a higher level.

Let's say that you have a problem that is causing you a tremendous amount of dismay at the moment. One way to get a handle on it is to move to a higher level and analyze all of your options, listing the advantages and disadvantages of each. See Chapter 24 for a discussion.

The ability to move to a higher level is something that requires discipline and practice. You have to have the discipline to remind yourself to move upwards, and you have to practice so that it becomes easier each time you do. Try analyzing problems ahead of time or while you are within them from a higher level and you will find that things are much clearer and easier to understand.

APPROACHING CONCEPTS FROM A HIGH LEVEL

Many times when you think about a concept, problem or situation, its solution is much clearer if you raise the *level* of your thinking. Often this approach means thinking generally rather than specifically, or thinking in an extremely large way rather than in a narrow way.

Here is an example. Let's say that you decide that, as a way to make money, you are going to walk along the boardwalk at the beach and collect aluminum cans out of trash receptacles. You do it for awhile and you learn about this aspect of life. You learn which trash receptacles generate more cans, where you can take the cans to be paid, how much you get paid for the cans, and so on. Let's say that you are able to do this and make $10,000 a year if you do it full time.

Now that is fine. However, you might be able to come up to a higher level, see the space in a larger sense and learn something from that raised position. Here's a progression you might go though in your thinking:

- Way to think about your life #1: I pick cans out of trash receptacles at the beach.
- Way to think about your life #2: I sort trash into two categories: aluminum cans and everything else. The aluminum has value, so I sell it to a recycling center.
- Way to think about your life #3: I provide a sorting and transportation system for post-consumer aluminum waste.
- Way to think about your life #4: I currently implement one piece of the American recycling infrastructure, a system that allows the country to reuse post-consumer products and packaging for the betterment of both the environment and the world's scarce resource base. I currently specialize in aluminum, providing both a sorting and transportation capability.

There is a huge difference between version #1 and version #4. Notice how we have been able to move from an extremely low vision to an extremely high vision of the activity. The funny thing is that as we move up the hierarchy there are more and more opportunities to do other things. For example:

- If you see yourself as a person who sorts trash (version #2), it might be possible to sort the trash into a number of different categories and do all kinds of other things. You could potentially recycle paper, glass and plastic in addition to aluminum. You could do research on the distribution of materials in the trash you sort and publish research papers on it. You might purchase (or encourage the city to purchase) special multi-hole trash cans that let the consumer do the sorting for you (you've seen these, where there are separate holes for bottles, cans and everything else). Perhaps you could then subcontract with the city to maintain and service these receptacles and make money both through the contract and the value of the recyclable materials. If this lowered the cost of clearing trash from the beach, the city might go for it.
- If you see yourself as providing both a sorting and a transportation activity with a specialty in aluminum, this might get you into other

forms of transportation. For example, you frequently make runs between the beach and the recycling center. Perhaps you could purchase a special aluminum can hauling truck that lets you stop not only at the beach but a number of other facilities along your route. For example, you might stop at bars and convenience stores along the way picking up all their empties and paying them a portion of the recycling revenue. Then you expand the route to include larger portions of the city until you cover the entire city. Then you move on to provide the same service to cities nationwide. You eventually become the country's largest provider of aluminum recycling services.

- If you see yourself as one part of the nation's recycling infrastructure, then you might end up eventually creating a company that brokers services between producers of a variety of waste and the different recyclers in a region. You might work with office centers, for example, to concentrate paper waste. You might work with service stations to do bulk recycling of motor oil and tires. You might work with retail stores to recycle cardboard. You will find that there is already competition in some of these specialty niches, so you might partner with or compete with these companies.

Here is another example. Let's say your father asks you to mow the lawn. Here are different levels at which you might think about this activity:

- My dad is making me mow the front yard.
- I am in charge of taking care of our yard. In the summer I mow, in the fall I rake and in the winter I shovel snow.
- I am the family's yard-care specialist, providing a variety of services depending on the season.
- I am a yard-care specialist and my parents are one of my clients. I give them a special rate in return for the things they provide me, such as room and board. I service the needs of six other clients in the neighborhood at my standard rate.
- I am the owner of one office of a nation-wide consortium of yard-care specialists. My parents are one of my clients, and I have six other clients in my region. Several of my friends are also members of the consortium, and each of us have our own regions. We pool money together to advertise, buy shared specialty equipment and so on.
- I am the president of a firm specializing in yard care. I have a number of employees in a number of branch offices, and I have also allied with other lawn-care firms to form a consortium. In our industry I believe it is important that...

You can see here that the highest-level vision eventually takes you to the point where you have multiple clients, multiple partners and multiple employees. All of this from mowing your front yard! Here is a final example that shows how your high-level vision can branch and thereby control your actions. Let's say there is a big dance Friday. Here is one set of levels:

- I am going to ask Suzy to the dance.
- I want to find out if I like Suzy and Suzy likes me.
- I am trying to find a person to marry by going out with different people.

Compare that to:

- I am going to ask Suzy to the dance.
- Suzy is an incredibly beautiful woman, and I want to spend time with her.
- I want to marry Suzy.

In the first case you are driving toward the general goal of marriage. In the second case you are trying to marry a specific person. The vision that you carry has a big effect on the way you approach this date. In the first case, if Suzy says "No" you can call someone else. In the second case if Suzy says "No" you might not go.

Consciously asking yourself the question "What is my goal?" can help you come up to a higher level. Once you ask the question, you can begin to understand your own motives as well as your options (see Chapter 24).

The level of your vision controls the opportunities available to you. By moving to a higher level you can see more. You may not initially be able to do anything at your higher level of vision because you lack resources, but it gives you a way to set goals and priorities.

SPEAKING AT A HIGH LEVEL

Related to the act of *thinking* at a high level is the act of *speaking* at a high level. Speaking at a high level allows you to present your ideas and goals in a way that shows you have a plan.

Here is an example. Let's say you walk up to a teenage bag boy in a grocery store and you ask, "How do you like your job?" In response you hear:

I hate this job. Any monkey can do it, but my parents forced me to get a job this summer.

Compare that to the following:

> I am learning a lot from this job. My goal is to eventually work in a retail environment, and I like the grocery business. Food has a certain fundamental connection to life that is lacking in other retail channels. My goal is to understand each position in a grocery store so that I can become a manager. Right now I am a bag boy. Next I will do stocking so I can learn about inventory and item movement in the store. Then I will try cashiering. Once I have experienced all of the jobs, I will be much better equipped for a management role.

Note that in the first response the teenager clearly does not care one bit for the job. In the second response the teenager clearly is enjoying the job, seeing it as a learning process and positioning it as one step in a set of steps leading to a much higher goal. The second teenager has clearly risen above his current situation and placed it within a larger context. As an employer, who would you rather be talking to and promoting? It's not a hard choice. The person with the high-level vision always wins.

Let me give you another example. Say you walk into an office and sit down next to a data entry clerk at a computer. The clerk is a

> *The person with the high-level vision always wins*

teenager and you ask, "What do you do here?" The teenager replies with the following:

> I take these crappy little cards that come in the mail and type the data off them. It is boring as hell.

You ask the teenager next to him the same question and get the following response:

> I am a data entry specialist. My job is to accurately transcribe the data from cards mailed in by our clients. This data is used to create a customer database that we use for advertising and sales purposes. Our direct marketing effort, for example, makes extensive use of the data I enter.

Note here the second teenager's clear presentation of not only what she does but how her role fits into the department's overall function in the company. She sees herself at a much higher level. If you are a manager looking to promote someone, you will obviously promote the second teenager.

I once worked with a person who, when asked his position, said, "I help hold the carpet down." After working with him, the high-level description of his position changed to this:

I am currently a software developer on a project team, and I am training to become a project leader. My specialties include GUI design using MFC and entity modeling. My goal right now is to learn the management skills required to be successful in a project lead role.

The point here is simple: If you describe yourself as a bag boy who hates what he is doing or as a flunky whose main attribute is his weight, *then that is exactly what people are going to think about you.* If you describe yourself at a higher level, then they will think that instead. It is a fact of life that people who speak at a high level always win. Also, by bringing your description of yourself up a level, you often gain a much clearer understanding of what you are doing, why you are doing it and what you hope to accomplish in the future.

Another place to apply high-level concepts is in your verbal interactions with other people. For example, let's say that you don't like the way your boyfriend is treating you. One end of the response spectrum might be, "I HATE YOU!!! DON'T DO THAT!!!!" The other end of the spectrum is, "I am a bit concerned about the way you are treating me at the moment. Would you mind if we discussed it?" There are all sorts of levels in between. Notice how the first response almost certainly invites an angry reply and an ensuing argument, while the second response is completely flat and invites discussion.

Let's say that you believe that you and your friend have agreed to meet at the mall at 3:00. However, your friend arrives a half-hour late. One response is, "WHY THE HELL WEREN'T YOU HERE AT 3:00??!!" At the other end of the spectrum is, "It is possible there has been a miscommunication. I was under the impression we were meeting

Your High-Level Future

One way to move your description of yourself to a higher level is to think of where you will be in the future rather than where you are today. If I were to ask you to describe yourself today you might say, "I am a student at XYZ High School." That is true but not very useful. A better way to describe yourself might be to say, "I want to be an astronaut. I have researched this career and am planning to get a degree in mechanical engineering so that I can help with the space station. I am planning to go to ABC University to get my degree, where I will join the Air Force ROTC program and gain flight experience. Currently, I am a student at XYZ High School preparing for college. I am taking pilot lessons at a local airport."

See how different those two descriptions are? The second one is extremely high and shows the person's drive, intention and plan.

at 3:00 today." Note how the second response makes no assumption of guilt on either party's part and allows open discussion of the situation.

Let's say that your parents have made a decision that causes you to miss the big dance Friday. One response is "YOU ARE BOTH STUPID IDIOTS!!! I HATE YOU!!!!" An alternative is, "Would it be possible for us to analyze this situation at a higher level to understand the fundamental issues?" Imagine how differently your parents will react to these two modes of conversation. In the first case they will either roll their eyes or scream back at you. In the

Clean Communication

High-level communication is *clean* communication. This means that it is not *dirty*.

You can instantly recognize dirty communication because it has tonal problems. For example, it insults the receiver or puts him down rather than focusing on the facts. For example, "You are an idiot for thinking that..." is a typical piece of dirty communication. The tone it sets is very negative, and it immediately puts the receiver on the defensive. It ends the possibility of effective communication. By removing the offensive part and sticking with the facts you allow other people to hear what you say.

second case you might be able to have a discussion.

Perhaps a friend comes up to you screaming at the top of her lungs, obviously upset about something. One way to handle it is to scream back. A better response might be, "I am wondering if we might be able to calmly discuss the cause of your anger. Tell me what you are feeling."

Adults use these techniques all the time to help diffuse situations or avoid angering people when offering constructive criticism. One word for this activity is *diplomacy*. It sometimes seems like a lot of work, but it is almost always worth the effort. It is a fact of life that if you say certain things in certain ways it is guaranteed that no one will listen, while if you say *exactly the same thing* using different words people will hear you. For example, replace "Are you an idiot?! You can't do that!!!" with "I wonder if there might be any value in considering some alternatives?" and you will get a totally different reaction from your audience. Watch how successful adults talk to each other, or how they talk to you, and you will notice this. Successful adults learn that certain modes of communication shut people down or infuriate them. Other modes allow people to discuss things rationally rather than escalating to anger and confrontation all the time.

Speaking at a high level allows you to show that you have an understanding of how the world works and how people work within that world. High-level speech can open a lot of doors and help you understand what is going on around you. Start practicing, and within several months you will notice the difference it makes. See also the chapter on anger, because you must control anger in order to work at a high level.

CHAPTER 23

Goals Guide Your Success

I f you were to try to identify the most important things that distinguish successful people from those who are not, you would have to pick *goals and dreams*. Goals and dreams directly control your success. They also give meaning to life. You are applying goals whenever you hear yourself asking questions like these:

- What am I trying to accomplish here?
- What am I going to do tomorrow?
- What do I want to be when I grow up?
- What do I want to do with my life?
- What is the meaning of life?
- What am I doing here?

The funny thing is many teenagers never ask questions like these in their conscious minds. If you miss these questions, life occurs randomly and you forfeit a huge number of opportunities. There are two sayings that you may have heard before and that bear repeating here:

- "You cannot make a dream come true unless you have a dream."
- "Failing to plan means planning to fail."

Both of those sayings tell you something obvious, but both are commonly ignored.

THE ROLE OF GOALS

Let me give you a simple example to show you how a goal can change your life. Imagine that, as a teenager, you have a job. You drive 10 miles each way to get to your job, and you work there 5 days a week. On your way to and from work your path happens to take you past a small municipal airport—the kind of airport where people fly private airplanes. There is a big sign out front that says "LEARN TO FLY!" Every time you go past that airport you think, "Wow, it sure would be

157

Satisfaction

In his short story entitled *The Pearl*, John Steinbeck offers this perspective on goals:

"For it is said that humans are never satisfied, that you give them one thing and they want something more. And this is said in disparagement, whereas it is one of the greatest talents the species has and one that has made it superior to animals that are satisfied with what they have."

nice to know how to fly one day." If that is how you live your life you will *never* learn how to fly. You will simply drive back and forth past the airport five days a week for the rest of your life. The phrase "it sure would be nice..." simply does not accomplish anything.

Let's say you change your way of thinking about flying. You get home one day and you sit on your bed and you think, "I want to learn how to fly. That is my dream. I am going to set a goal and I am going to make this dream a reality." You get out an index card. You look at today's date, which happens to be April 2, 1998. On the index card you write:

I WILL HAVE MY PILOT LICENSE ON APRIL 2, 1999

You put that card on your dresser so you see it every day.

That little card changes a lot of things. If you are truly going to have your pilot license in one year, there are lots of things you need to do. The first thing you need to do is find out what the heck you need to do to get a pilot license. So you decide to drive over to the airport and ask. You learn that you are old enough to get a license and all you have to do is sign up for lessons. It takes about 50 to 60 hours of flying time to get your license, and you have to pass a long, written test. The only catch is that it's pretty expensive. However, it is not *that* expensive. You find that you can easily afford one lesson a week using the money you make at your job.

So what do you do? You sign up! There is nothing to stop you, so why not? It seems incredibly easy. Every week you take a lesson. During the week you study all the books they give you, and you learn everything you need to learn to pass the test. And sure enough, on April 2, 1999 you solo and you earn your license. It is as simple as that!

What's the point? *The point is that you can accomplish nearly anything you can imagine just that easily if you simply decide to do it*. It is the setting of the goal that makes it happen. Prior to setting the goal there really is nothing motivating you in a particular direction. Once the goal is set, things proceed down a path until you accomplish the goal.

Think about your own life. In your life there are dreams floating in your head. There are all sorts of "things you would like to do one day." By simply making those things priorities—by setting concrete, specific goals—you can actually start to make them happen today. A good friend of mine has a saying: "Beginning is half done." And that is exactly the case. If you start to do something you often make its completion a foregone conclusion. The act of setting a goal and moving yourself in its direction causes the goal to be accomplished. A dream begins to come true the minute you take concrete action toward realizing the dream, rather than just dreaming.

There are three types of goals. It is important to recognize the difference because you handle them differently:

1. Simple goals—Simple goals are goals that you can complete simply by starting. A pilot license is a good example of a simple goal. Once you decide you want a pilot license, the steps to achieving the goal are straightforward. You have to raise the money, allocate the time, show up and do the work until the job is done and reap the reward. There are a huge number of goals that work this way:

    *   "I want a red Corvette." All that you have to do is earn enough money to buy a Corvette and you can have one. In some cases it may not even be necessary to earn the money. All you have to do is find a job that generates enough income and you can lease the Corvette tomorrow.

    *   "I want a college degree." All that you have to do is apply to a college, get accepted, come up with the money for tuition and pass the classes.

    *   "I want a nice house." You need to raise the money for a down payment and meet the conditions for a mortgage. Then you pick out your house and buy it.

    *   "I want to contribute $1,000 to the church's world hunger drive." You need to raise or collect the money that will be contributed and then send it in.

    *   "I want a good job." You need to find a job that you enjoy and that pays well, learn the skills necessary to get that job and apply.

    *   "I want to have my own business." You need to learn about different businesses, pick one that you would like to own, raise the money to purchase the business and buy it. In the meantime, you can work for someone else who runs the same type of business in order to learn the necessary skills.

- "I want to take a trip to France." You need to raise the money and buy your ticket. Off you go! See also Situation 3 in Chapter 24.
- "I want to understand how computers work." You need to get a book or take a course that explains how computers work.
- "I want to start a charitable organization that helps children with AIDS." You need to learn about the steps necessary to start such an organization, find other people who are interested and start the organization.
- "I want to be able to bench press X pounds." You need to allocate the time each day to do your training. Each day you get stronger and soon you have reached your goal.
- And so on.

2. Goals that require perseverance—Simple goals are nice because they are simple. There is a clear path from where you are to where you want to be. Goals that require perseverance are different because the path is not obvious, and you are going to have to try multiple paths before you find the one that takes you to your dream. That means that you will fail along the way, but at each failure you will learn something or gain a skill that makes it possible to achieve the goal. Here are some goals that require perseverence:
   - "I want to be a best-selling author."
   - "I want to be a famous actress."
   - "I want to be the President of the United States."
   - "I want to win an Olympic medal."

3. Goals that are impossible—Some goals simply cannot be achieved. For example: "I want to run a marathon in one millisecond." To reach that goal you would have to be able to run at a speed of 93,600,000 miles per hour. That's 5,000 times faster than the space shuttle. You could rephrase the goal, however, and it becomes a goal that requires perseverance. For example, you could say, "I want to set a world record time in the marathon." You might state a nearer-term goal as well, such as, "I want to finish a marathon."

Look at the simple goals listed above. If you decided today to set one of these as an important personal goal, any of these dreams could become a reality. There may be things standing in your way at this moment. For example, you might ask your parents to let you go to France and they might say "No." That does not, however, stop you from stating a goal that you achieve when you reach 18 or 21.

Look at any of the perseverance goals listed above. It is unclear how you will arrive at these goals (if it is clear, then it becomes a simple goal), but you definitely will never get there unless you start. You need to set the goal and work every day to achieve it.

THE EFFECT OF GOALS

Goals have an extremely interesting effect on your life. They completely change how you look at things on a day-to-day basis. Here is a very simple example to show you the difference. Take the question "What am I going to do tomorrow?" If you do not have a goal, then the answer to that question is difficult. What ends up happening is that you lie on the sofa all day watching TV. One more day of your life slips past with nothing accomplished.

If you *do* have a goal, then the answer to the question is extremely easy. As soon as you set a goal, especially a simple goal, you can begin to create a plan to get there. If you want a pilot license, for example, and set that as your goal, the path becomes immediately obvious. You have to get a job to earn the money to take the lessons to get the license. Therefore, the answer to "What am I going to do tomorrow?" can be found as the next step on your path. Either you need to go to work to get a paycheck, you need to go take a lesson or you need to study for the written exam. The path materializes out of thin air as soon as you set the goal. You can determine all of the steps needed to get where you are going.

I spent a good part of my life teaching in a university. I met all kinds of students in the classes I taught. It was always easy to tell the difference between the students who "want to be in college because it is a personal goal" and those who "happen to be in college because their parents made them go" or those who "went to college because they could think of nothing better to do." Goals make college relevant; if you have a goal that requires a college degree, then sitting through four years of college makes sense. You see each class you take as a step toward your goal. Otherwise, the classes seem pointless.

DREAMING

What is your dream? How do you set goals in your own life so that you can achieve your dreams? The important thing to recognize is that *there really are no limits to your dreams*. Let me give you an example of how far your dreams can go:

- I want to live in a colony on the moon.
- I want to be President of the United States.
- I want to win an Academy Award.
- I want to be on the New York Times best seller list.
- I want to win a gold medal at the Olympics.
- I want to be on an NFL football team.

- I want to be a millionaire.
- I want to end poverty world wide.
- I want to have a house in Malibu.

What, exactly, stops you from dreaming these dreams and working toward them? Nothing but your own mind. Thirty years from now *someone* is going to be President of the United States. Why can't it be you? Many people will win Academy Awards. Why can't you get one of them? The only way for it to be a possibility is if you set a goal and move in that direction now. Things may happen down the line that cause you not to get an Academy Award, but by the same token things might happen down the line that make it certain you will receive one. *At this point in your life, your chances of getting an Academy Award are just as good as anyone else's!* You simply need to start working in that direction.

SETTING GOALS

Quite often when you go on a job interview the question will be asked, "What are your one-year, five-year and ten-year goals?" Why is it that most people cannot possibly answer that question? Why do employers prefer people with goals? Employers are interested in knowing your goals because people with goals are going somewhere. People with goals are going to be successful, especially if they have thought through their goals well enough to be able to articulate them in an interview. Goals show that you have a plan, and that means you will have a plan in your job as well. Goals indicate management potential, they show good organizational skills and they reveal what you think you are capable of accomplishing.

If you ever interview a bunch of people and ask that question, you find that the vast majority of people have no goals. They never ask themselves questions about the future, set goals or make plans. That means that on any given day the things they do are completely random. If they have a job they go in to work because they "have to," they do their work, they leave, and they come back the next day and repeat it. In

Twenty years from now many people will win Academy Awards. Why can't you get one of them? The only way for it to be a possibility is for you to set a goal and move in that direction now. Your chances of getting an Academy Award are just as good as anyone else's!

the absence of a long range plan it is all meaningless because there is no reason or direction.

In your own life, the question becomes "What are my goals?" What would you like to accomplish? This can be a very difficult question to answer if you have never thought about it. A good way to start is to take out a sheet of paper (or a computer spreadsheet; it makes sorting easier) and do a brain dump. Sit and think, perhaps over the course of several days, about all of the things you might want to accomplish "one day." Think also about the big dreams you have—things like winning an Academy Award. Ask yourself questions like these:

- What do I want to accomplish?
- What would be really cool if I were able to do it?
- What have I always wanted to do but seems so far away it is impossible?
- What kind of person do I want to become?
- What might I like my job to be one day, if I could choose any job in the world?
- And so on.

Make up the list. Once you get rolling you will discover all kinds of hidden things about yourself—things you vaguely knew but never wrote down. Things like:

- I want to travel around the world.
- I want to have a nice house in the woods.
- I want a happy spouse and 10 kids.
- I want to learn to ski.
- I want to become a doctor.
- I want to solve inner-city poverty.
- I want to run a big corporation.
- I don't want to be shy anymore.
- I want to drive a fancy sports car.

List them all out. Anything you can think of, whether it would take you 2 days or 20 years to accomplish it.

Good Books

A good book to read for more information is *Seeds of Greatness* by Dennis Waitley. See the references section for more information.

Once you have a big list you can do two things. First, you can put time estimates next to everything. Things like "1 week," "1 year," "5 years," "20 years," etc. You can also prioritize them to some extent. You can put big stars next to the ones that are really important to you.

One question you might find yourself asking is "Is this list valid? Can I really do these things?" Why not? The only thing that stops you is you. You can set the biggest goal you want; You have as good a chance of reaching it as anyone else. Another question you will find yourself asking on a lot of them is, "How can I accomplish these things?" In many cases the goal is easy to state but the path to it is not. For example, let's say one of your goals is, "I want to race Indy cars." It's a good goal. Someone has to drive the cars in the Indianapolis 500 and other races like it. But what are the stepping stones? If you hunt around and do some research, you will discover that there are racing schools (for example, Skip Barber has a number of schools). You can go there to learn the basics, begin racing yourself and move all the way up if you are so inclined. You will also find it is fairly expensive, so that will lead you to find ways to get money. Which will lead you to find ways of getting a good job, or finding a mentor or sponsor. That might lead you to jobs in the racing industry... Do you get the idea? If you set a goal and then research how to achieve it, all sorts of other sub-goals open up. The sub-goals are often as interesting as the main goals.

Once you have your list and have researched and planned how to achieve some of your goals, you can actually set reasonable goals. A goal:

- should be extremely clear
- should have a specific deadline
- if large, should have a plan with its own sub-goals and sub-deadlines

The reason you set a deadline is because the deadline helps you to discover when you are faltering. For example, say you have a goal to learn how to play the banjo in a year. That breaks down into sub-goals that include buying a banjo, finding a teacher, earning enough money to take lessons and taking the lessons. If you set a one month deadline on buying the banjo and one month later find you haven't even looked at banjos, then you know it is time to recalibrate your deadlines, get your act together or drop the goal. The deadline helps you detect problems and keep things on schedule.

SITUATIONAL GOALS

In any given situation or problem that you face, you can often come to a much better solution if at some point in the process you ask yourself three different questions:

WHAT ARE MY GOALS?
WHAT AM I TRYING TO ACCOMPLISH?
WHAT ARE MY OPTIONS?

By asking yourself, "What are my goals?" and, "What am I trying to accomplish?" you allow yourself to come up to a higher level (see Chapter 22) and bring the problem into your conscious mind rather than simply reacting to the situation. By asking yourself, "What are my options?" you allow yourself to see a number of possibilities rather than just one. The next chapter will help you to understand the concept of *options* and *options analysis*.

CHAPTER 24
You Have Options

I n order to reach your goals and be successful, you have to become an expert in finding options and picking the best one for each situation. Finding options involves research and creativity. Selecting the best option involves optimization and rational decision-making.

Successful people are excellent at both of these activities. They get excellent at these activities through practice. Think about people you admire or heroes that you remember for their brave acts. They often are admired for their ability to choose the best option among many possibilities, especially in the face of adversity:

- A star quarterback is admired for his ability the "read" down field and successfully choose the best option in milliseconds under the tremendous pressure of oncoming defensive linemen.
- A successful president is able to look at a critical situation or long-term problem and solve it by choosing a "perfect" or creative solution.
- A thriving businessperson is successful because he or she is able to creatively solve complex problems that face the business.
- The astronauts and ground control specialists involved in Apollo 13 are admired because they evaluated thousands of options to hundreds of problems and chose exactly the right ones to bring the astronauts home safely.

The problems that most people face on a daily basis are normally much more mundane than these, but they can be just as important. Your success is determined by your ability to gather options and choose among them.

Let me give you an example that drove this point home to me. There was a point in my life where I needed to drain a rather large hole. The details of why this particular hole needed to be drained are better left

166

unsaid, but suffice it to say that I had a hole approximately 30 feet long, 20 feet wide and 4 feet deep that was full of water and needed to be empty. At the time I did not have a lot of excess cash, but it was important enough that I would have been willing to spend perhaps $200 to drain the hole.

One option was to use a bucket. If you think about it, however, that option is not a particularly good one. A hole 20 by 30 by 4 feet holds something on the order of 15,000 gallons of water. With a 5-gallon bucket that is 3,000 trips. At a minute a trip that's 50 hours of emptying, provided it does not rain between the time you start and the time you finish. I also thought of siphoning, but the position of the hole did not lend itself to a siphon.

Being a teenager I did not have a very good option space in my head. I knew of a friend who had a pump you could attach to an electric drill and I knew he had gotten it at Wal-Mart, so I went to Wal-Mart to investigate. Wal-Mart did indeed have a drill-type pump, but its capacity was very low. However, they had one other kind of pump called a sump pump, which is used to drain basements. It claimed the ability to handle almost 1,000 gallons an hour. I bought one of these for $80. Once I got it home I realized it had several problems. First, it did not handle mud very well and this hole was full of mud, so I had to build a sort of filter for it. Second, it could not possibly pump even a 100 gallons an hour through a normal garden hose because of the diameter of the hose. So I built a manifold and bought several hoses to discharge the water. Even so, the pump never did better than about 100 gallons an hour. It took a number of days for this pump to do its job and empty the hole. It was extremely frustrating.

Common Sense

When someone says, "You have no common sense!" they mean one of two things. Say I tell you a story about a person who buys a new car. He drives it for 20,000 miles and then his engine blows up. It turns out when the mechanic looks at the engine that the guy never changed the oil. A typical comment from someone hearing that story would be, "The guy has no common sense!" What is meant is that he lacks common knowledge ("change your oil every 3,000 miles") that everyone is expected to know.

The other kind of common sense is found in how people react to a situation. If you choose to do something without considering your options, or if you look at options and consistently choose a bad one, you will quickly pick up the "no common sense" label. In this case, you do not understand how to weigh the advantages and disadvantages of your options; therefore, you cannot determine the consequences of what you do.

It was not until about a year later that I happened to walk into a good farm supply store. I was amazed to find a whole *wall* of pumping options. Hand pumps, electric pumps, gas-powered pumps, tractor mounted pumps, wind mills and so on. The selection was unbelievable! If I had known about this place I could have spent $150 and drained the hole in about an hour! The problem I had, as a teenager, was that:

1. I did not know there were hundreds of options available, and
2. It never occurred to me to ask!

If I had just done a more complete options analysis, called around a little, asked a few people and so on, someone would have pointed out that there are places where hundreds of pumps are available.

What I have noticed, in this situation and many others like it, is a simple fact of life:

*ANY PROBLEM YOU HAVE—AND I MEAN **ANY** PROBLEM—HAS LIKELY BEEN FACED BY THOUSANDS OF PEOPLE BEFORE YOU, AND THEY HAVE ALREADY WORKED OUT HUNDREDS OF GREAT SOLUTIONS!*

You can buy those solutions, you can buy a book and read about those solutions or you can ask people questions about what they have tried and seen. Most problems have already been looked at before. All you have to do is look for the options people have already developed and evaluate them in your own situation. In addition, you can come up with new and creative solutions of your own. One key to success is learning this simple fact and applying it to your own life.

COMING UP WITH OPTIONS

In many situations you can come up with plenty of options simply by sitting down and thinking about the problem. In other situations it can be helpful to ask others and/or do some research. The key is asking yourself the question, "What is my goal?" and answering that question by coming up with a set of options to reach the goal.

Let's look at four situations and some of the options that are available in those situations.

Situation 1

Imagine that you have been going out with your girlfriend/boyfriend for a year. One day you notice that you are fighting a lot and there is distance growing between you that you do not understand. Several weeks later your girlfriend/boyfriend asks to stop seeing you, and you discover he or she is going out with someone else. Your girlfriend/boyfriend has dumped you for another man/woman! When you ask yourself, "What is my goal?" your mind answers, "To die!" It hurts so bad you cannot stand it. You feel like you have been betrayed, you know you have been completely rejected and humiliated and you do not understand how someone you were so in love with could do this to you. However, after thinking about it for several days, you realize your goal is, "To get past this and get on with my life." What are some of your options?

1. You can commit suicide.
2. You can find a handgun and plot to kill your boyfriend/girlfriend.
3. You can be incredibly depressed and droopy and hide for three months.
4. You can harass your old girlfriend/boyfriend with 700 phone calls a day pleading with her/him to take you back.
5. You can walk away from her/him and forget about it. There are, after all, other fish in the sea, and one day you will find someone better. You can also learn quite a bit from the experience.

The first two options are obviously useless and absurd, but it is interesting to lay them out as options so that you can reject them. The disadvantages associated with these two options are so huge that they are discarded immediately. Why would you want to screw up the rest of your life over this girl/guy? That is silly. The third option certainly is easy but has no benefits (see Chapter 15). The fourth one is common but pathetic. The fifth one has the most potential. What if you could actually do that? It would require a good bit of maturity and discipline. For the first week or two it might be very hard, but it is possible. If you could pull it off it would have a lot of benefits and no significant disadvantages. The question then becomes, "What can I do to help myself get past this and not wallow in self-pity?" There are a number of good options listed at the end of Chapter 40. You might also try talking with someone who has had a similar problem. They could give you advice and insight, and they can also help you gain perspective.

Situation 2

Let's say that you take the advice in Chapter 6 and decide that you need a video camera to make your own movies. When you ask yourself, "What is my goal?" you get two answers. Either:

- Accumulate enough money to buy a video camera, or
- Find a video camera someone has and borrow it.

Here are some of the options available to you:
- You could rob a convenience store or gas station to get the money (see the next section for some cautions).
- You could get a job to earn the money and buy one.
- You could ask for a camera as a Christmas present.
- You could borrow the money from your parents and repay them.
- You could borrow the money from a bank (see Chapter 44).
- You could get three or four friends together and pool your money to buy a camera.
- You could borrow a camera from a relative.
- You could see if the media center at school has a camera they will let you check out on weekends.
- You could get a job or volunteer for an activity that uses video equipment and see if you can borrow equipment on weekends.
- You could work at a store that sells video equipment and try to buy one at a discount as an employee.
- You could go to a junk store, a flea market or pawn shop and see if you can find a used camera cheap.
- You could look in the classified ads for a used camera. Perhaps you could barter with the owner.
- You could forget about shooting live-action film and turn to hand drawn or computer-generated animation instead.
- You could see if a local community college offers courses in film and take the course.
- You could go to the library and read all of the books that they have on film making while waiting to get enough money to buy a camera.

If you sat and thought about it you could probably come up with that many options again on your own. Out of that huge pool of options, surely one of them is going to work for you. The point is that at first glance getting a video camera seems impossible. By brainstorming options you find that there are easy ways to achieve your goal.

Situation 3

Let's say that for whatever reason you are obsessed with going to France (or Hawaii or wherever) this summer. For whatever reason you really, really want to travel to France. However, your parents won't let you go alone. What are your options?
- You can moan and sulk and curse your parents, making both yourself and your parents miserable.
- You can go down to the local Army recruiting office and see if they have any slots available in France.

- You could find a tour group going to France through a travel agent and see if your parents would let you go that way.
- You could organize a group of students at school and get a teacher (or your parents) to be chaperone, raise the money and go that way.
- You can convince your parents that they would like to go to France with you and take a family vacation there.
- You can wait until you get to college and go with a college tour group.
- You can find four friends who want to go to France and convince all parents involved that you are mature enough to go together.

Situation 4

In Chapter 40 there is a story about a boy being teased about his weight so mercilessly that he eventually hung himself. What were some of his other options?

- He could ignore his peers and not let them get to him.
- He could talk with a teacher or the principal about the problem and see what might be done to remedy it.
- He could join a peer group of other overweight teens.
- He could lose weight.
- He could transfer to another school.
- He could ask his parents about home-schooling.
- He could talk with his parents about it every day to try to relieve the stress of rejection. In doing this he would know that they understand and love him.
- He could get a video camera and create an award-winning documentary film about his problem and the way society treats him. He could then build from that a career in film. Similarly, he could write a book or a magazine article.
- He could spend his time with adults, who will accept him, rather than his peers.

The point is, in any situation you have options. It is extremely useful to list them and look at them. If you cannot think of options ask a friend, your parents or a teacher and see what they suggest. There are always options available for any problem. By listing your options and carefully thinking through them you greatly increase the probability of success.

OPTIONS HAVE ADVANTAGES AND DISADVANTAGES

Once you have collected a set of options you need some way to evaluate them so that you can choose one (or a combination of several) as your course of action. The key to this process is to understand that every option has both advantages and disadvantages. Probably the easiest thing to do when considering options is to list the advantages and disadvantages of all of the options together so that you can compare them.

Let's look at some of the video camera options discussed in the previous section and discuss advantages and disadvantages. The first option listed is:

- You could rob a convenience store or gas station to get the money.

This truly is an option. It has one advantage: you can get the money you need very quickly and with little work this way. If there were no counterbalancing disadvantages this would clearly be the way to go. The problem with this option is that it has several disadvantages and they are rather serious. The disadvantages include:

- You could get shot by the store owner.
- You will likely get arrested, and when you do it will affect you for the rest of your life. You will end up in jail and then have a criminal record (see Chapter 21).
- It is against the law, and therefore wrong (see Chapter 18).
- There is no future in it. What do you do the next time you need money? Rob another store? And then what? The most you will get from a convenience store robbery is $100 or $200. If you instead got a good job you could make that much or more every day in a completely legal way.

If you went down the rest of the list looking at advantages and

It Depends

Think about these two sayings:

- Haste makes waste.
- He who hesitates is lost.

Both are true. Both are options. The question I had as a teenager was, "Which one is right?" The answer: It depends on the particular situation. In the same way, you will often get *conflicting* information when you ask multiple people for advice. How do you decide on a path when both paths have advocates?

To make a choice, the best thing to do is list the advantages and disadvantages of both possibilities. If you are asking other people for advise, ask them for recommendations for your list of advantages and disadvantages. In many cases the proper thing to do will become obvious. But sometimes you can't make a decision. It will be a "six of one, half-dozen of the other" sort of situation. In that case, go with your gut feeling.

disadvantages for each option, it is likely that you would find one or two options that seem "obvious" and "easy." They have a good set of advantages and no significant disadvantages. Choose one of them.

CREATIVITY

In many cases creating an option list is not easy. This is where *creativity* is important. People are admired for their ability to find creative solutions to problems. In fact, you can make an entire career of finding creative solutions to problems that seem unsolvable.

As an example, let's say that you have a personal dislike of automobiles because they produce so much pollution. The pollution produced by automobiles, in your mind, comes both from the direct emissions of the internal combustion engine as well as from the toxic effects of oil spills. You would like to figure out a better way to propel vehicles.

 A good book to read for more information is *A Whack on the Side of the Head* by Roger von Oech. See the references section for more information.

While we are on this subject, have you ever stopped to wonder why 99.9% of all of the cars in America use an internal combustion engine that burns gasoline? Surely there are other ways to propel a car. The reason the internal combustion engine is so popular at the moment is because it currently has significant advantages and no overwhelming disadvantages when compared with the alternatives. That is the only reason. As soon as an option comes along that costs less or eliminates one or more of the major disadvantages of the gasoline engine, there will be no more gasoline engines.

To understand what alternatives might be available, you can come up a level and ask, "What is gasoline and the internal combustion engine doing?" At the highest level you can think of gasoline as a way to store energy, and you can think of the internal combustion engine as a way to release that energy in the form of motion. If you think of it that way there are lots of other options to look at. To propel a car:

- You could burn natural gas, which is far less polluting.
- You could burn hydrogen, which creates no pollution.
- You could use a giant spring and "wind up" the car before going for a drive.
- You could store energy in a flywheel.
- You could use batteries and an electric motor.
- You could use solar cells to convert sunlight to electricity.

- You could use hydrogen and oxygen in a fuel cell to generate electricity.
- You could use a small nuclear reactor to produce heat or electricity.
- You could make a car light enough that the driver can pedal it like a bicycle.
- And so on.

> *A successful person can use creativity to give birth to completely new options that solve a problem or fit a situation perfectly.*

The problem with all of these options, at this moment in time, is that none of them have advantages that outweigh gasoline. If we ran out of oil tomorrow, that would change everything. But since we have plenty of oil and society (the group of people currently living in America) does not seem to mind air pollution, greenhouse gases or oil spills, gasoline "wins."

The creative part of all this is the fact that there may be another option that no one has invented yet. This option would have significant advantages over gasoline and no significant disadvantages. If you could invent that option and bring it to market you would be rich beyond your wildest dreams.

There are many places in your life where you will be faced with a problem that is "hard" or "unsolvable" and you will come to a point of extreme discomfort. Then all of a sudden you will create a new option out of thin air that has lots of advantages and no significant disadvantages. It will be "clean" and "obvious" and "elegant" and you will ask, "Why didn't I think of this before?!" A successful person is someone who can do that consistently. A successful person can use creativity to give birth to completely new options that solve the problem or fit the situation perfectly.

CHAPTER 25
Everything Takes Time

E verything takes time. That is a hard fact for many teenagers to swallow. Nonetheless, by understanding and accepting this fact of life you can gain a much clearer understanding of what you are doing now, why you are doing it and what might happen to you in the future.

Let me give you an example. Let's say that you are 15 and there is a 40-year-old businessman in your neighborhood that you admire. He has a great house, a great car, a great family and so on. You look at that person and you think, "I want to be just like that person," but then you realize it is impossible. You cannot do anything but earn minimum wage. What you are missing is that this person you admire started off *just like you.* The difference is that he has been working for *25 years* to get where he is today. For you to get there it will likely take you 25 years of effort as well. Let's look at some of the steps this person went through to get where he is today:

- Age 17: He gets a great summer job and learns that he really enjoys mechanical engineering.
- Age 18: He enters college and works toward a mechanical engineering degree.
- Age 20: He meets the girl of his dreams.
- Age 22: He graduates Magna cum laude from college.
- Age 22: Upon graduation he is immediately offered a job at a large aircraft company. He gets his first apartment and his first real car.
- Age 23: He gets engaged. He sets a wedding date.
- Age 24: In the same year, he gets dumped by his fiancée and loses his job in an economic downturn. Total despair. No job prospects. He moves back in with his parents when his financial situation becomes impossible. He gets a job as clerk rather than sitting home all day.

175

- Age 26: He lands a new automotive design job. He moves to Detroit and gets a new apartment.
- Age 27: He gets a big promotion for innovative design work.
- Age 28: He finishes saving enough money for the down payment on a tiny, two-bedroom house.
- Age 29: He falls in love with the Realtor who sold him the house.
- Age 30: He marries the Realtor.
- Age 32: Their first child is born.
- Age 33: He gets a management position with the firm. Good pay increase but longer hours.
- Age 34: Their second child is born. The family outgrows the house and has enough money to buy a nice new house in the suburbs.
- Age 36: His company provides a company car to all managers.

Now, you meet this person at age 40. What you are missing is the incredible amount of work that went in to getting where he got. You are also missing all the down times. You missed him losing everything at age 24 and having to start over. You missed the broken engagement, the year of heartache and the five years he went through without a girlfriend. You missed the part where he lived with a crying baby in a tiny, two-bedroom house. All you see is the final result, and it looks great and easy.

Teenagers, because they have been observing the world for so little time, tend to miss the transformations that occur over the course of years. They see everything immediately and expect immediate results from everything. Adults see the world differently. They have seen things go through a number of cycles, and they understand those cycles. They understand that time can cause very small actions to get amplified. Teenagers want to leave home and immediately have a great house, a great car, a great wardrobe, a great spouse and so on. All of these things take time and effort. Many of them take years and years to achieve. Adults tend to understand that if you put in a little effort every day and do it over a long stretch of time you can accomplish great things. Little or nothing happens overnight.

If you can understand the *value of time* you can take advantage of its effects. Let me give you several examples:

- Wealth takes time—If you want to accumulate wealth, one way to do it is by saving small amounts of money over long periods of time (see Chapter 29). People do this in many different ways, but one way is by purchasing a house (see Chapter 32). You have to live somewhere. Either you will rent or own. By renting you are throwing the money away. By owning you are building "equity" (value) in a property. So each month you are able to add a little bit to your equity. Looked at on a scale of one or two months the amount of money you accumulate is small. But you will be alive for decades, and over decades the equity can add up to huge sums. You can get this same effect by depositing just a few dollars in a mutual fund account each day. Over the period of a month or two the amount accumulated is very small. But over a period of years you can create a huge pile of money.

- Skills take time—Any skill takes time and practice. If you practice consistently over a period of months and years you get better and better at what you are doing. On any one day you learn just one or two little bits of the skill. But there are 365 days in a year, so those few bits a day add together over time to create a huge pile of skill. This is what makes a great athlete. Great athletes practice every day so they get better and better, stronger and stronger over time. If you want to be good at any skill—piano playing, woodworking, rock climbing, computer programming—it takes time. The sooner you start the better. Remember these three things when learning any skill: 1) You must start at the beginning, 2) you must take things one step at a time, and 3) you must learn to walk before you can run. Words to live by! Do not be discouraged because, on the first day you try playing the piano, you cannot play Beethoven and Mozart. It takes time to become an expert. That is normal.

- Knowledge takes time—Knowledge is accumulated a little bit at a time. On any given day you can learn a certain number of things. Over time the knowledge you gain accumulates into a huge storehouse of information.

- Trees take time—This is extremely easy to miss as a teenager but becomes obvious to you as an adult. I live on a farm in North Carolina. If I let a field lie untouched it will grow weeds the first year. The second year, a few pine seedlings will sprout. The next

Differing Perspectives

This section about trees brings up a good point about the differences in perspective that two people might have. Let's say you come to my farm and look at my trees. I see them as "a bunch of trees that sprouted one year because I was too busy to mow the back field." You see them for the first time and what you see is "established forest." Same piece of land, same trees but a totally different perspective. Because of my perspective I might cut down the trees and sell them off without a qualm, while you might find that act sacrilegious. The difference in perspective comes from our different time lines. I know the complete history of the trees, and I can distinctly remember when they were a weedy field. You have none of that history, so you see things from a completely different point of view.

year more seedlings will sprout and the first year's trees will be about 6 inches tall. The next year the trees will be about a foot tall. And so on. On any given day you can go out and look at the field and it appears that nothing has changed. But one day you walk out to the field and it suddenly dawns on you that the trees are taller than you are. Ten years later the field begins to look like a forest. Twenty years later you could consider cutting all the tress down to pay for your child's college education. In doing that you know that the next year a few seedlings will sprout...

- Opinions take time—Many of your opinions will change throughout life as you encounter new experiences, make more money and meet new challenges (see Chapter 38).

- Credit takes time—When I was 19 I got my first credit card, and it had a $500 limit. Compared to the limits most adults have, that is a pittance. The reason adults have much higher credit lines is because they have earned them by demonstrating responsible behavior over time. For example, if you handle a credit card responsibly, then every year the credit card company will raise your limit. For example, if they raise your limit $500 each year, by the time you are 40 you will have a $10,000 or $12,000 credit line.

- Possessions take time—One difference you will notice between your parents' house and the house or apartment of anyone under 20 is the fact that your parents have a lot more "stuff." That is to be expected. When your parents started out they did not have any stuff either. Most people, when they move into their first apartment, can fit everything they own into the trunk of their car. Then they buy a sofa. The next year they save up enough extra money to buy a nice kitchen table. Then one year they buy a nice TV and VCR. Another year they buy a nice desk. Then a washer and dryer, then a nice bedroom set, and so on. Your parents didn't get to the point where they have a house full of stuff all at once. Instead, they bought things one at a time over 20 years and accumulated all the things they own. You will go through that same progression.

- Jobs take time—You always go through a progression from "gofer" up when you enter the job market. You start at the bottom. You learn a set of skills. You get a promotion. You learn more skills. You change positions. You get a promotion. And so on. No one starts at age 18 as the CEO of a gigantic corporation. You have to learn starting at the bottom and working your way up like everyone else. Or you have to start your own company and build it up.

- Weight takes time—A funny thing that most people don't realize until it is too late is that your body puts on weight through this same mechanism. Let's say that you consume just 30 extra calories per day of your life. That is certainly not that many calories. It's the equivalent of perhaps 2 ounces of soda per day. At that rate of intake you will gain about 2 pounds a year. After 20 years you will be 40 pounds overweight. After 40 years you will be 80 pounds overweight. That is why so many older people are overweight. They are just over-consuming by a few calories per day over a long period of time and it adds up. On any given day the difference is absolutely unnoticeable.

Once you have been through a few cycles, things begin to make a lot more sense. For a person who first puts money in the stock market, a stock market crash is devastating. Someone with a lot of stock market experience, however, knows that every crash is followed by a rise. Anyone who has been through the death of a good friend knows that it is incredibly painful, but the pain subsides over time. Death is no easier to take knowing this, but the pain of it is more understandable.

Adults understand the cyclic nature of things and the fact that things take time. They use that understanding to their advantage.

A TYPICAL TIMELINE

One of the funny things about being a teenager is that you cannot imagine ever being an "adult with two kids" or a "grandparent." It just seems so far off that it is impossible to comprehend. However, every human being on the planet starts life as an infant, then moves to childhood, then becomes a teenager and then an adult in a very natural, daily progression. The following timeline will help you to understand the natural progression a "normal, middle-class professional" person would go through.

13-19	• You are a "teenager." • You go on your first date. • You give your first kiss. • You get your first job. • You start shaving or using make up. • You graduate from high school. • You get your driver's license. • You get your first traffic ticket. • You apply to colleges and get accepted. • You go to your senior prom. • You start college.

	• You start smoking if you are going to smoke (No one starts smoking after they become an "adult"—only teenagers pick up the habit, and once they do they get addicted). • You become eligible to vote. • You think, "If only I had $100 or $500, I could…" and what you could do is buy your own TV for your room, or better speakers, or a new jacket you really want, or some special shoes or whatever.
20s	• You are a "college student" or "just out of college." • You graduate from college. • Your body stops growing and "fills out." If you looked like a "bean pole" as a teenager this is where you start to look "normal." In your mid to late 20s your metabolism slows (one cause: lowering growth hormone levels) and you get a beer belly, love handles or other signs of weight gain if you do not actively prevent it. • You get your first "real" job. • You get your first "real" car paid for by you and in your own name. • You shop for and buy your first real furniture. • When you get out of college you get your first apartment. • In your mid to late 20s it becomes possible to consider buying your first house. • Once you buy your first house you buy your first lawn mower. • You get your first mortgage. • You have your first car wreck (not required, but many people do). • You get engaged. • You get married. • You have children. • For most men, you can actually grow a respectable beard in your 20s. • If you are going to lose your hair, it happens in mid to later 20s. • Minor wrinkles, crow's feet, smile lines are noticed for the first time • Life insurance becomes important. • You think, "If only I had $1,000 or $5,000, I could…" and what you could do is use it as a down payment on a car, or buy an engagement ring, or get a new bedroom set or whatever.
30s	• You are an "adult." • You attend PTA meetings. • You start to call teenagers "kids." • You get your first management position or major promotion, putting you into a position of direct responsibility. • A "real" house becomes feasible. You have been through one or two mortgage cycles, so you understand the process. • You actually finish buying a complete set of furniture and

	appliances. You then begin buying second TVs and some "nice" furniture. • You advance to a riding lawn mower. • Since you are half-way there, you begin to worry about retirement. • Pop music that you hear on the radio sounds "noisy" and "bad." You don't really care about it any more. You listen to the news instead because you care about what is happening in the world and how it will affect you and your family. • You begin to have money for investment purposes. • Your own kids become teenagers. • Cars with four doors begin to look good. Midsize cars, mini vans, etc. • Voting begins to matter. • First significant wrinkles begin. • You begin to feel like you understand how the world works. • You think, "If only I had $10,000 or $50,000, I could..." and what you could do is use it as a down payment on a house, or get a really nice car or whatever.
40s	• You are a "mature adult." • Upper management positions become possible. • Gray hair starts, if you have any hair. • Menopause starts for women in mid to late 40's. • Since your house is full of furniture you begin replacing all of it with "nice" furniture. • Your own children leave home and go to college. • Reading glasses become necessary. • First age spots form. • If you have a "mid-life crisis" it often happens here. • The music you like is "oldies" on the radio. • You think, "If only I had $100,000 or $500,000, I could..." and what you could do is send your kids to college, or pay off the mortgage, or start seriously saving for retirement or buy a vacation home.
50s	• You are a "mature adult" or a "grandparent." • With the kids gone and a good high-paying job, massive saving for retirement begins. • Luxury trips to Europe, etc. become possible. More travel in general is possible, more "enjoying of life" because you have the money and the kids are gone. • Large luxury cars begin to look attractive. • Your first grandchildren are born. • Heart attack age starts. • Lung cancer, emphysema start in here if you smoke.

- Serious estate planning begins.
- Annuities begin to look attractive.
- You think, "If only I had $1,000,000 or $5,000,000, I could..." and what you could do is retire early.

In looking at this timeline there is something important that you should notice: a *lot* of really big things happen in your 20s. As you make the move from teenager to adult you will graduate from college, get your first real job, move out on your own, buy a car, buy a house, start paying taxes, get married, have kids and so on. If you are 15 years old now it is extremely likely that you will be a completely different person in 10 years. You will think about the world differently and you will care about different things. That is the reason why, for example, young marriages (people who get married at age 18) don't last. The two people who get married at age 18 are completely different people by age 25 and they no longer have anything in common. Try to keep this simple fact in mind as you are making decisions as a teenager:

YOU WILL BE A COMPLETELY DIFFERENT PERSON IN 10 YEARS

Because of that fact, you should try to avoid making big decisions, like marriage, that lock you in to anything permanently.

CHAPTER 26
You Can Control Your Anger

A nger is a tough one. You can be going along at age 10 or 11 doing just fine without a care in the world. Then puberty comes and completely changes your personality. A lot of teenagers end up having a problem with anger as a result. As a two-year old you got angry. You had all sorts of screaming tantrums, but it was impossible for you to control your anger because you lacked the ability to think and reason. As a teenager it is different, because presumably you are able to think as a teenager. One consistent trait of all truly successful people is that they learn to control their anger and use it productively.

an·ger (ăng′ger) *noun*
A strong feeling of displeasure or hostility.
[Source: *The American Heritage Dictionary*]

The problem with anger is that it is almost always destructive. TV and movies teach you that anger is normal, common and useful. In real life it just doesn't work that way. Anger is destructive rather than creative. It tears people down rather than building them up. There are many sayings that express anger's low value in solving problems. Here are just a few:

- "Nine strong horses cannot bring back angry words once they are spoken." [Chinese proverb]
- "Be not hasty in thy spirit to be angry: for anger resteth in the bosom of fools." [Hebrew Bible. Ecclesiastes 7:9]
- "Anger is a brief lunacy." [Horace]
- "When angry, count ten, before you speak; if very angry, an hundred." [Thomas Jefferson]

- "Let not the sun go down upon your wrath." [Bible: New Testament. Ephesians 4:26]
- "Anger is one of the sinews of the soul; he that wants it hath a maimed mind." [Thomas Fuller]

You can also look at words frequently associated with anger and find that none of them are useful or complimentary:

- Anger
- Rage
- Hatred
- Revenge
- Grudge
- Fury
- Wrath
- Resentment
- Indignation
- Berserk
- Violent
- Aggressive
- Tantrum

However, anger does have a place:

"We praise a man who feels angry on the right grounds and against the right persons and also in the right manner at the right moment and for the right length of time."   -Aristotle

Why can anger be such a dangerous emotion? Where does it come from? How can it be used productively? These are important questions.

UNDERSTANDING ANGER

Anger is an emotion common to all animals. Mice, dogs and chimps all get angry just like people do, and often for the same reasons. There are some classic events that may trigger anger in animals and humans alike:

- A physical threat requiring a defensive response.
- The need to protect an important resource like food, water or a mate.
- An annoyance. For example, a dog overwhelmed by a group of playful puppies will respond angrily when he has had enough. Similarly, if a puppy accidentally bites too hard in its play it will be dealt with through anger.

As a human being you respond in a similar manner unless you learn to control your anger. You have the ability to control two aspects of your brain's anger engine: the level at which anger is triggered and the level and timing of your response. Both of these levels change naturally as you get older, and you can additionally apply control to them with your conscious mind at any age.

Your anger's trigger point changes throughout life and throughout the day. In general the trigger point rises as you get older. A two-year old will have tantrums at the slightest provocation, and some teenagers are nearly as bad. Most grandparents, however, are fairly slow to anger. You may have also noticed that stress and fatigue

Understanding Your Anger

One interesting thing you can do to understand your own anger is to sit down and make a list of things that you know anger you. Such a list can be educational. If you find you are unable to create this list, watch yourself over the next several days and notice the things that trigger an angry response. Your parents or friends treating you in particular ways might make you angry. The actions of strangers or society, traffic, insults and so on can also lead to anger. Make a list of specific events that you notice, and then try to find some patterns.

make anger easier. For example, if you are late for an appointment a red light can spark a furious response. On the other hand, if you are on a date with a person whose company you enjoy, a red light might actually make you happy.

You can think of the trigger point for anger as the point at which a frustration or event finally causes you to explode. Throughout the day things happen to you, and each thing has some "annoyance level" for you. So a light turning red has an annoyance level, someone telling you that you are stupid has another annoyance level, someone standing you up for an appointment has another and so on. You could chart events and their annoyance levels throughout the day, as shown in this diagram:

Anger and Jealousy

Jealousy is a part of the coupling mechanism. It is stronger in some people than in others. It is tied directly to the anger portion of your brain.

You can think about jealousy this way: Jealousy is a way for the brain to recognize that the other half of the couple might be straying. It is the brain's way of defending the couple. Imagine a couple in the wild. Man A is coupled with a woman and they have a child. Man B begins making advances on man A's mate. Man A responds with jealousy, which manifests itself as anger in the form of yelling/hitting/killing. It probably worked great 20,000 years ago. It has a lot of problems now if it is not controlled to some degree.

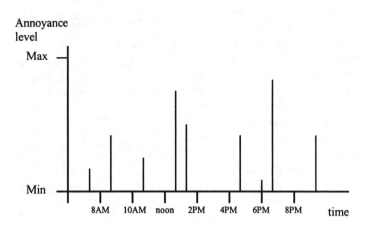

This graph shows the "annoyance level" for the events of the day. At 7:15 you burned your toast. At 8:30 you got cut off in traffic. At 12:20 your lunch date stood you up. And so on. You can lay your trigger level over this graph to see how many times you explode in a day:

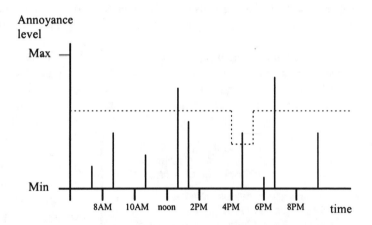

The dashed line is the trigger level. This graph shows that on this particular day the chain of annoying events you saw would have normally caused you to explode twice, but you were rushing to a 4:30 meeting and that lowered your trigger point so you actually exploded three times during the day. This, of course, is an idealized way of looking at the events of the day, but it does give you a perspective on things. If you are an easily-angered person, then your trigger point is very low and the smallest provocation causes an angry response. On the other hand a calm and collected person has a very high trigger point and is very slow to anger.

The *level* of your response is also under your control. Certain things make everyone angry, but we all respond to the stimuli differently. Some people fly off the handle in a violent rage. Others respond completely diplomatically. The difference is control.

If you look around you and watch how different people deal with different events, you will notice certain patterns. Mature adults can express their opinions without yelling, even when they are angry. They may get angry, but they do not respond with overt action. There is no such thing as a successful person who cannot control his or her anger. Everyone understands that angry displays imply immaturity and a lack of control.

You will notice that anger is a special issue for couples. Couples fight when they both happen to be in a bad mood or if they are in conflict already. It would be nearly impossible for two people to live together constantly and not get on one another's nerves occasionally. The thing to watch is what they do after a fight. A strong couple will be able to forgive and forget the incident because they both know it was meaningless. They release the anger, forgive and move on. Married people who are working well together can totally forget a fight and move in a completely different direction once it is over. Those who are not hold grudges and snipe at one another for days afterward. There is a funny saying that is applicable here: "It takes two people to start an argument, but only one to stop it."

CONTROLLING YOUR ANGER

Learning to control your anger is a long, uphill slog for most people.

It Just Doesn't Matter

If you keep a journal of all the things you get angry about—even if you only do it for a week—one thing you will notice is that a lot of the things *just do not matter* in the grand scheme of things. Think of some of the things that make you angry:

- You want to wear a certain shirt to school, but it is not clean.
- Your mother does not get home exactly when she said she would.
- Your sister listens to one of your CDs.
- Your favorite TV show is preempted by a football game.

Who cares? What difference does it make? It isn't worth wasting the time to be angry because these things are irrelevant.

It is hard. And yet it is rewarding because anger accomplishes nothing and is always destructive. By learning to control anger you remove a major impediment to your success.

Imagine that your parents do something that truly angers and upsets you. You can respond in anger by screaming, "I DID NOT ASK TO BE BORN!!! I HATE YOU!!!" You can stomp and slam your door and fume for days. But think about it. How, exactly, is a parent supposed to respond to that? It is totally useless behavior. It accomplishes absolutely nothing.

Here are three things to try as you attempt to gain control of your anger:

- Wait an hour or, better yet, a day or two, before responding to something that makes you angry. Keep your mouth shut and think. You will be *amazed* at how trivial a lot of things look a day later. You will also be amazed at how your brain can come up with good, rational solutions to any problem if you give it time.
- Rise above the anger. See that you are becoming angry and say to yourself, "I am better than this. I am a mature adult. What is the mature response to this situation?"
- Respond rationally rather than angrily. Analyze the situation rationally and respond appropriately.

Something else to try is to keep a journal. Record the things that make you angry each day, and also record your response to each event, even if it was a bad response. What you will notice, over time, is certain patterns. What you will also notice is that nothing good ever comes from an angry response. By keeping a journal you will be able to see physical proof of that, and it will teach you something.

What you want to strive for in controlling your anger is the ability to respond in a productive way, rather than a violent way, to the stimuli. Look at the thing that is making you angry and ask, "Why is this event making me angry? What would I rather have happening?" For example, if your brother takes one of your CDs without asking, decide what it is that makes you angry. Then, rather than exploding at him, try talking to him about it instead. Will he listen? Maybe or maybe not. He might tell you that you are an idiot (especially if you are younger). Let's say he does that. In that case here is something to try. There *will* come a point in the future where he needs something from you. At that point you can say, "Remember how I politely asked you to stop taking my CDs? I will do what you are asking now in return for an agreement on that issue." At that point, he will listen. It is a very interesting way to accomplish things, and it is a very common technique for successful people to use in resolving disputes.

Understanding Your State of Mind

Every successful adult has a keen understanding of his or her own state of mind. Adults monitor their state as they are listening to people. Often in a conversation they will disclose their state of mind to help the other person understand context. For example, an adult can feel when he or she is starting to become angry, uncomfortable, intimidated, confused and so on. An adult also understands that mental states change. For example, an adult might say, "I am feeling intimidated by what you say, and I am not yet sure I understand your motive. Let me give you my immediate reaction now and then we can discuss it again after I have had time to think about it." Notice how much information has been disclosed. First, we can see how the person is feeling about the conversation: It is intimidating. The person states confusion about motive, which tells the speaker he is not communicating clearly. The person also understands that he has not thought through everything yet, so he is "reacting." Later he will be able to respond intelligently.

Another thing to notice is the disconnection most successful adults create between *emotions* and *actions*. When a child "gets angry" he responds instantly and physically with anger. Anger is directly connected to action in a child. An adult can "feel" anger but disconnect it from action to allow time to think. Here is an example to help you understand the difference. If you were to touch a hot stove right now, you would immediately jerk your hand away. The "stimulus" (heat) and the "response" (jerking your hand) are directly connected, and your conscious mind is not involved in the action. But what if you could feel the pain, register it in your conscious mind, and then *think*, "What is the best response to this pain signal?" so you could react accordingly. That is what an adult is able to do with anger. Successful adults can sense when they are getting angry and then think about an appropriate response to the anger rather than lashing out immediately. This level of control is the mark of mature adulthood. It allows those around you to rely on you and your emotions.

CHAPTER 27

You Learn by
Listening

I can distinctly remember that as a teenager I had a
tendency to want to TALK so that I could to be
HEARD because I KNEW EVERYHTING and the
world should LISTEN. It certainly wasn't as extreme as all that in reality,
but there certainly was a tendency in that direction. Perhaps you feel this
way sometimes. You feel like you MUST say something or people will
forget you are there or think you are stupid. Or perhaps you find yourself
talking constantly but saying little or nothing.

Earth is a planet full of people, many of whom have excellent ideas
and interesting things to say. Those ideas are available simply by
listening. All that I have to do is keep my mouth shut and listen to the
ideas and thoughts of other people and I can learn a great deal from them.
It wasn't until I was an adult that I found I can learn from people who are
more experienced and wiser than I am, especially when they have already
been down a path that I am considering taking. By listening you can save
yourself a lot of trouble.

A lot of people want to talk to you about problems. Either they have
problems *with* you, or they have problems of their own that they want to
talk to you *about*. Problems can be hard to discuss, and they require a
special form of listening. They are especially hard to discuss when the
problem is a complaint or criticism. Like all people, I do not like to find
out that I am wrong or stupid. It is hard to listen in these cases.

There is an interesting quote from the *Encyclopaedia Britannica* that
is relevant here:

> Just as the infant is preoccupied with his physical self in a world
> of new stimuli, so the adolescent (teenager) may be preoccupied
> with his own thinking in a world of new ideas. Such
> preoccupation often leads to a kind of egocentrism, which can
> manifest itself in two ways: First, the individual may presume that
> his own concerns, values, and preoccupations are equally

important to everyone else; second, the urgency of this new thinking may paradoxically give rise to an overestimation of one's uniqueness, often resulting in feelings of alienation or of being misunderstood. Although the formal-operational stage is the last stage of cognitive development in Piaget's theory, the egocentrism of this stage diminishes over the course of the person's life, largely as a consequence of interactions with peers and elders and—most importantly—with the assumption of adult roles and responsibilities."

[Source: "The Development of Human Behaviour: Cognition," *Britannica CD*, Version 97, Encyclopaedia Britannica, Inc., 1997.]

One important sentence in this paragraph is, "The individual may presume that his own concerns, values, and preoccupations are equally important to everyone else." Once you wade through all the jargon, one thing that sentence says is, "Teenagers talk too much." Another thing the paragraph says is that the feelings of egocentrism that accompany most teenagers tend to diminish, over time, through listening.

Having said all of this, you can see that listening has several important advantages:

- You can learn a lot.
- You can discover new ideas or new approaches to problems.
- You can realize that you are not the center of the universe.
- You can develop a sense of respect for others.
- You can find out what other people want.
- You can avoid putting your foot in your mouth.

It is that last one that is especially important to your success in the real world.

UNDERSTANDING LISTENING

Listening *seems* easy. All that you have to do is hear what someone says. Right? Let's talk about two different types of non-listening in order to understand that there are different levels:

- Let's say you are in a room with another person. You are speaking and the other person is "listening." If the other person is dead, is that person listening? No. If the other person is deaf, is that person listening? No. If the other person does not understand English, is that person listening? No. If the other person is alive and can hear you but is thinking about her date last Saturday, is that person listening? No. You can see from this that there is a difference between *being in the same room* and *listening*.
- Let's say you are in a room with another person. You are speaking and the other person is "listening." If the other person cannot understand what you are saying (for example, you are talking

about computers but the other person has never seen a computer), is the other person listening? No. Or let's imagine that you say something that you believe is totally innocuous and suddenly the person begins screaming at you. For example, you say, "I like your cat," but the person thinks you have said, "I think you are fat." Is the other person listening? No. You can see from this that there is a difference between *hearing* and *listening*.

To listen means that you hear, understand and are able to respond to what was said in an appropriate way. Effective listening requires five steps:

1. Receiving the information
2. Understanding the information
3. Understanding what the speaker is trying to accomplish with the information
4. Deciding what you think about the information and the speaker
5. Responding appropriately to the information

Often, when you are engaged in an important conversation, you have to accomplish all five steps in just one or two seconds. It can take a great deal of practice to be able to listen effectively in such a situation. Let's look at all the steps.

Step one should be easy. When someone speaks to you, you receive the information by turning on your brain and focusing your attention on what the speaker is saying. That way you accurately and completely hear the speaker.

Step two requires work. To understand you have process the information and find its meaning. You can often make communication more effective by confirming that you understand the meaning. For example, after someone speaks to you, you can say, "If I am understanding you correctly, what you said is..." In other words, you paraphrase back to the speaker what you think he or she means in order to confirm the meaning.

Step three requires that you listen "between the lines" to decide what the speaker is trying to accomplish. The speaker might be:

- Trying to entertain you with a story
- Trying to fill time
- Trying to keep you from leaving
- Trying to teach you something
- Trying to scare you
- Trying to make you feel bad
- Trying to make you feel good
- Trying to make small talk
- Trying to express his or her feelings
- Trying to persuade you to do something

- Trying to make you uncertain of your own thinking
- Trying to offer constructive or destructive criticism
- Trying to insult you
- Trying to get to know you better
- Trying to test you
- And so on.

In the same way you can clarify meaning, you can also clarify the speakers' intent if you are unsure by asking for confirmation. Paraphrase the intent and ask about it.

Step four requires that you make a decision. You have to decide what you think about what you have heard. Or not. It is possible to realize that you cannot decide without thinking about it over a period of an hour or a day. In that case you can ask for time to make a decision.

Once you decide what you think, you can choose a response. The response is often the hard part, especially for a teenager. A teenager, due to lack of experience, does not have as broad a range of responses as an adult. In addition, many teenagers tend to act impulsively rather than thinking. Impulses often lead to inappropriate responses. There are a wide range of responses possible. Here are three examples:

- If someone says, "I see you have three green horns growing from your head," it is possible that an appropriate response is to ignore the speaker because what he is saying, at least on the surface of it, is absurd. You may want to ask for clarification prior to ignoring the speaker, but if there is no deeper meaning ignoring the speaker is likely the best response.
- If someone says, constructively, "You are naïve," you have several possible options. One response would be to ignore the speaker as in the previous case. Another might be to respond with an angry outburst. However, it might truly be the case that you are naïve, as described in Chapter 2. Therefore, you potentially have something to learn from listening. Your response might be one that indicates you are open for learning.
- If someone says, destructively, "You are a total idiot!" things are more complicated. You need to respond and you may also need to protect yourself. In this case you need to understand the speaker's intent and work to change it.

As you can see, the act of listening can require a great deal of effort and concentration. However, people who listen well are generally much better positioned for success because they communicate and respond effectively in all situations.

See also the section on "Speaking at a High Level" in Chapter 22.

INTERACTING WITH GROUPS THROUGH LISTENING

Let's say that you are meeting a new group of people. The group might be made up of adults or teenagers. You might join the group at work, at church or at school. It might be something important or something frivolous. One way to make your interaction with the group go more smoothly is to spend some time listening before speaking. This is especially true if you are the "new guy" coming into an existing group.

In any group of human beings, there are some pretty standard interactions. For example, you may notice some or all of the following at a meeting:

- The group will generally have a leader. The leader may have a formal title or may be a de facto leader.
- The other members of the group may or may not accept the leader. If they do not accept the leader, they may express that overtly or subtly.
- Different people will say things and you will agree or disagree with their statements. You will find that you generally tend to agree or disagree with different people once you have heard a number of statements from them. You come to "like" certain people in the group and "dislike" others.
- There may be certain "hot button" topics that are difficult for the group to discuss. Each group has a history, and these difficult issues may have a long record within the group.
- Each member has a personality. Some are loud and talk a lot. Some are quiet. Some speak suddenly and without thinking, while others do not speak until they understand what they want to say. Some are inflammatory and some are soothing. And so on.
- The group may be working toward a consensus or may be deeply divided.
- The group might be highly organized with a strict agenda, or the group might be completely loose and disorganized. Or it might be somewhere in between.
- The group may or may not like you being there, or may not care.

By listening to the group for one or more sessions, you can discover all sorts of things. You can discover what is important to the group and what the group is trying to accomplish. You can then help the process.

There is nothing that requires you to speak. But if someone asks you a direct question before you have anything meaningful to say you can:

- Say something like, "I am still too new to the group to understand all of the issues. Let's continue, and I will let you know when I have come to a point where I have an opinion to offer."

Consultants

Last year I visited with a friend of mine in California. He had told me about a computer game his 10-year-old daughter had been playing for about a month. While we waited for dinner I sat down with her so she could show me the game.

The idea behind this game is interesting: You are a person living in the 1800s and you are trying to organize a wagon train to California. The game starts with your arrival in a small Midwestern town. You have a certain amount of money in your pocket. Your goal is to go around to all of the different stores in town and buy your wagon, your animals, and all of your equipment and supplies. Then during the rest of the game you make your way to California experiencing (vicariously) all the events and hardships a real wagon train might have experienced.

The game starts and I "walk around" the town. Here are some of the questions I have:

- How big a wagon do I need?

- Is it best to power my wagon with horses, oxen or mules?

- How long will it take me to get to California?

- Given the answer to the previous question, how much food do I have to buy considering I am having to buy 1800's kinds of things, like "50 pounds of flour," "10 pounds salt pork" and "a barrel of crackers"?

- How many guns and how much ammunition do I need? Will I be hunting or defending myself?

- What "other things" do I need that I might not know about (salt is one good example)?

The pharmacy was the most interesting place. There you could buy all sorts of chemicals, none of which I had ever heard of before. Which ones would I need? What could they do? When would I use them? What is the proper dose? I knew none of this.

However, my 10-year-old friend did. Apparently she had played the game about 100 times. She took me to each store and told me exactly what I had to buy and why. All of this knowledge she had gained through *experience*. She was acting as my *consultant*. All I had to do was *listen* and my chances of success rose significantly.

In your life there are consultants standing all around you in the form of adults. Before you go down any path, it is wise to talk with someone who has been down that path to see what you can learn. Your potential for success will rise significantly when you learn to do this.

- Ask a clarifying question on a recent topic rather than stating an opinion.
- Try to summarize what you have heard so far and bring it up to a higher level (see Chapter 22).

Of course, if you are ready you can also offer your opinion. What is important in many cases is to simply not say anything until you have something important to say. By listening you can understand what is important. You can also understand how best to deliver your message so that the people in the group will actually hear what you have to say. By thinking before you speak you can ensure what you have to say is worthwhile and meaningful in the context of what you have heard.

CHAPTER 28

Success is Your Responsibility

A successful person stripped of all worldly possessions might temporarily be without a home, but he or she would never be "homeless." A successful person knows how the world works and has a set of important skills and knowledge that are intrinsically valuable. A successful person is able to use that knowledge to become successful again.

This book has discussed a number of specific attributes that help a person achieve success. As you search for success in your own life, you can strive toward improving these attributes and making them work for you. The following sections summarize several of the keys to success.

CONTROL

In this book we have discussed many of the different parts of your brain that you are able to control through conscious action. These areas have a direct effect on your success. They include:

- Your Teenage Illusion Module (TIM) discussed in Chapter 2
- Your anger, discussed in Chapter 26
- Love and sexuality, discussed in Chapter 9
- Your ability to look at yourself and evaluate your own actions, discussed in Chapter 22
- Your happiness, discussed in Chapter 15
- Your confidence, discussed in Chapter 14
- Your ability to listen to others, discussed in Chapter 27
- Your ability to set goals and evaluate options, discussed in Chapters 23 and 24
- Your ethics and values, discussed in Chapter 18

These abilities, taken together, reflect your *maturity*. A mature person is someone who is "in control" at all times and who is able to make good decisions and carry them out. An immature person is someone who does not have that level of control and who is scattered and inconsistent.

PERSEVERANCE AND DISCIPLINE

Successful people always have perseverance and discipline. While it is possible to set a course toward the general goal of "success" and be lucky enough to reach it on your first try, that is generally not the way the world works. For example, your goal might be to become a successful actor. While it is possible that you will land a lead role in a major motion picture on your first audition, it is extremely unlikely. You will need the perseverance and discipline to attend many auditions, to face many rejections, to hone your skills and to become a great actor.

For 99.999% of the people on this planet success is a gradual process that requires the perseverance, hard work and discipline needed to move toward success every day for years at a time. A part of this perseverance is a basic optimism (see Chapters 14 and 15) that helps you see the possibilities in every situation. But the other part is plain old hard work. It is hard work to sit and do your homework in high school when your friends might be out partying, but good grades get you in to college. It is hard work to slog through four or six years of college acquiring the knowledge you need to get a good job, but that knowledge does let you get the job of your dreams. It is hard work doing all parts of a job well, even those parts of a job that you do not particularly enjoy. But it is the consistency and discipline you show that gets you a promotion. Perseverance and discipline make it possible for you to be successful.

RISK TAKING

To be successful you must take risks and be willing to accept that those risks might not pay off. In other words, you must be willing to fail. Having failed, you must be willing to get up, make the best of it, learn from the mistake and take a risk again. It is a fact of life that many of the most successful people failed spectacularly (and often many times) before they became successful.

KNOWLEDGE

The thing that allows a successful person to be stripped of wealth and then bounce back is what that person carries in his or her head. Knowledge is what makes you valuable. What is amazing is that knowledge is free and available to everyone. You can go down to any public library and begin absorbing knowledge in *any* field that excites you, and you can do that today. As discussed in Chapter 6, you can make yourself valuable by becoming an expert in any area you choose. Once you have that knowledge, no one can take it away from you. It is yours forever.

LUCK

Successful people are lucky, but they are lucky in an interesting way. There is a saying by Louis Pasteur (a famous 19th century scientist): "Chance favors only a prepared mind." That is the sort of luck successful people have. Every day every person is presented with a set of accidental opportunities. Some are small opportunities and some are large ones. A successful person is someone who can take an accidental opportunity, see that it is an opportunity and apply the effort necessary to make something out of it. This happens all the time in science, and it is important to understand the process. Let me give you two examples:

- Let's say you are working in a laboratory, and you are working with bacteria in petri dishes. One day as you are throwing away old dishes you notice a bit of mold has accidentally grown on one. The bit of mold is surrounded by dead bacteria. You culture the mold, prepare an extract and find that it is able to cure certain bacterial diseases in animals. This is exactly how the first antibiotics were discovered. What is interesting is that a number of people had noticed the effect prior to Alexander Fleming's particular chance discovery. He simply applied the effort necessary to get it noticed.
- Let's say you are working in a laboratory, and you are doing experiments wherein you inject chickens with bacterial cultures. One day you inject the chickens with a certain culture. You expect them to die, but instead they get sick and then recover. You go back and discover that the bacteria you gave them was old. When you inject the chickens again with active bacteria, you find they do not get sick at all. Louis Pasteur experienced this particular chance occurrence and was able to build the foundation of immunology upon it.

There are thousands of well-documented accidents like this in science. X-rays were discovered by accident. The role of the pancreas in diabetes was discovered by accident. Pulsars were discovered by accident. And so on.

The mark of a successful person is the ability to take an opportunity that presents itself by accident, see that it is an opportunity, apply the work and resources to make it into something worthwhile and reap the rewards. We call the chance discovery "luck," but it really is a very special kind of luck because it is available to everyone.

GOALS

As discussed in Chapter 23, successful people have goals and they work toward those goals actively and daily. *They do not sit on the couch all day watching television!*

GOOD DECISIONS

The ability to list your options, evaluate your options in relation to your goals and then make good decisions from your evaluations is important to success (see Chapter 24). Successful people are consistently good at making the correct decisions in the situations they face

PUTTING IT ALL TOGETHER

If you take the time to read the biographies and autobiographies of successful people (several are listed in the references section at the end of this book), you will find a great deal of commonality. Most start young and apply all of the keys to success described above.

Take, as an example, Bill Gates. As President of Microsoft he is one of the richest people in the world today. If you read his book "The Road Ahead" you will find that he started as a teenager just like you. He was fascinated with computers, so he started programming as a teenager in school. He showed perseverance and discipline by creating a extremely small and efficient BASIC interpreter while still a teenager. He took a risk by quitting college to start his company. He set goals and achieved them. He has a history of making extremely good decisions in the areas of technology and software. Of course, there was some luck thrown in, but the key is that at each point where opportunity arrived he was able to take advantage of it.

There is nothing that stops you from achieving success in this same way. Your chances are just as good as anyone else's. However, success is your responsibility—you will have to do something active to make it happen, and that activity requires a certain amount of effort. The key is to start and to apply a set of principles that have worked for nearly every successful person who has come before you.

PART 6

The Facts About Money

Money is incredibly important in American society. You learned exactly how important it is in Chapter 1. You learned that money really matters and that money and jobs are facts of life.

Once you have money, *money management* becomes important. By *managing* your money you can accumulate wealth and accomplish your goals much more quickly. This section shows you the fundamental facts of money management so you learn the basic vocabulary and concepts. If you find this material interesting, you will want to supplement it with any number of books you can find at the library or your local book store.

CHAPTER 29

You Can Control
Your Finances

The "world of personal finance" is a huge space with hundreds of options and its own peculiar vocabulary. Most teenagers therefore have no idea what *personal finance* is or what it means to *control your finances*. That lack of knowledge can severely limit your chances for success. If you take it step by step, however, you actually can penetrate this field and completely understand it. In this chapter we will start at the beginning and see how the most basic things in life directly affect you and your finances.

If you are an adult and are like most normal folks, *you have a job.* You saw in Chapter 1 that you really don't have a choice in the matter. You go to your job every day. Every two weeks or every month you get a paycheck for some amount. For the sake of example let's imagine a fictitious person named Bob, a 24-year-old computer programmer out of college two years. Bob is paid $3,000 each month, or $36,000 per year (1997).

Because you have a job *you have taxes.* There is no way around it. The government, in an effort to make your life easier, politely lifts something like a third of your paycheck without you having to do a thing. Poof, it's gone—you never even get to touch it. The federal government takes perhaps 23%. The state government takes perhaps 7%, depending on the state. The social security administration (FICA) and Medicare take another 7.5% or so. Bob's $3,000 paycheck diminishes to perhaps $1,850 by the time he sees it:

The amount subtracted depends on whether Bob is married (and if so whether his wife works), whether he owns a house, what state he lives in

```
    $3,000 gross income
-   $   690 Federal income tax (23% of gross)
-   $   210 Typical state income tax (7% of gross)
-   $   250 FICA, Medicare, and other withholdings
    ------
    $1,850 Bob's net take-home pay
```

203

and so on.

As you live your life it costs money. Therefore, *you have expenses.* A normal person in America has some pretty typical monthly expenses. Bob is a single guy, and his monthly expenses look like this (1997):

- Rent: $700
- Car payment: $300
- Car maintenance (gas, insurance, repairs, etc.): $200
- Power: $80
- Phone and Long distance: $50
- Cable TV: $50
- Cell Phone: $50
- Groceries: $120
- Entertainment, eating out, etc.: $300

For many people it would mark a major financial milestone if they could create a simple, clear monthly vision of their expenditures like this one.

The total expenditures shown here are $1,850 per month. If that were all there were to life, Bob would be set to some degree because in this example expenses exactly match income. Unfortunately in life there are three other things.

1. *You have problems.* For example, you get a speeding ticket one day. The court fines you $60 to begin with, and your insurance goes up $30 per month. Or your car blows a gasket and it costs $500 to repair. Or you meet a "special friend" and feel compelled to take him or her out to dinner 14 times in one month, tripling your entertainment budget. Or you lose your job.

2. *You have desires.* All humans do, some more than others. You might desire new living room furniture, a new TV or stereo, a nice gift for your mother or spouse at Christmas, a special piece of jewelry, new clothes, whatever. You may desire all of it all at once. Occasionally you cannot control yourself and one of your desires is filled. Perhaps one month Bob buys a $400 TV without realizing it.

3. Therefore, *you have debt.* Debt makes up the difference between income and expense. For most people day-to-day debt goes on a credit card, and large items like cars and houses are handled with more formal loans. Debt itself is not bad. The problem arises when debt accumulates for no apparent reason. In Bob's case, problems and desires would push his credit card balance upward each month because there is no other source for the money. Since his expenses match income in a normal month, any abnormal spending will go on the credit card.

Let's say someone waved a magic wand and doubled Bob's salary. Wouldn't that be nice? It would indeed, except that 99% of us (Bob included) would feel an irresistible urge to double our expenses at the same time. In fact, it is likely that if you told 100 people that their salary would double in six months, 99 of them would begin doubling their expenditures immediately, *in anticipation of the actual funds.* They would immediately move to a nicer place, drive a nicer car, buy more stuff and so on until they got in exactly the same expenditures-are-greater-than-income position again. That is how Bob got where he is today. Clearly, making more money is not going to solve this problem because humans seem to have a natural tendency to spend what they earn in the same way that they eat everything on their plate and fill all available closet space. It is a normal fact of life. The vast majority (90% or 95% of the people in the U.S.) live their lives just this way. Those who have control of their financial lives figure out a way to get into a different mode of living.

THE BASIC TOOLS OF FINANCIAL LIFE

Most adults, no matter what their financial position in life, use three basic tools to control their finances. These tools are:
- A checking account
- A credit card
- Insurance

Most teenagers feel comfortable with a checking account. In a checking account you deposit money at the bank. You can then withdraw that money by writing *checks*. If you happen to write checks for an amount greater than the amount in the account, the check *bounces*. A bounced check is considered by all adults to be a flagrant financial sin. It goes on your permanent credit record and will be used against you when you try to get loans or other accounts. Because bouncing is bad, you try to keep a record of exactly how much money is in the account each time you deposit money or write a check. You *balance* your checking account each time you get a statement from the bank to make sure you have made no mistakes.

Most teenagers also feel comfortable with a credit card. With a credit card you can buy things using money you do not have. The bank issuing the card makes you a loan, which you are expected to repay. In return for the loan you pay *interest,* usually at an outrageously high rate ranging between 15% and 25% annually. Each month you get a bill from the credit card company that itemizes your purchases and interest and tells you how much money you owe for the month. You do not have to pay the full amount, but you do have to pay some minimum every month. If

Financial Instruments

A *financial Instrument* is a place where you can park or invest money. A checking account is a financial instrument that has its own particular advantages and disadvantages. As you get older, other financial instruments become relevant because you have more money that you want to save and invest. These instruments include things like savings accounts, certificates of deposit, stocks, bonds and mutual funds. See Chapter 31 for details.

you fail to make a monthly payment, it is considered by all adults to be a flagrant financial sin. It goes on your permanent credit record and will be used against you when you try to get loans or other accounts.

Most teenagers do not understand insurance. There are many different kinds:

- Automobile insurance
- Home owners or renters insurance
- Life insurance
- Health insurance
- Disability insurance

Most adults carry at least three of these at any given time in their lives. Many adults have all five kinds continuously.

The idea behind insurance is to spread *risk* across a group of people. For example, imagine a small town of 1,000 houses with an average price of $100,000. Let's say that, on average, one house burns down a year. No one knows whose house it will be. Therefore, everyone could pay $100 a year into a pool and the poor soul whose house burns down in any given year could use the pool to rebuild. Insurance starts from that simple community idea and builds on it. Because house fires are relatively rare, house insurance is fairly inexpensive. You can insure a $100,000 house for $300 to $500 (1997). Because car wrecks are relatively common, car insurance is much more expensive. You can insure a $15,000 car for perhaps $800 per year if you are over 25 and have a good driving record (1997, North Carolina). It gets much more expensive as you get younger because young drivers, on average, have far more wrecks than adults. Most states require drivers to have car insurance because car wrecks are so common.

FINANCIAL STABILITY

There is a concept called "financial stability" that is important to your household once you are living independently. Let us imagine that you were to hire a professional financial analyst to come to your apartment and look over your finances. What the person will say to you will vary depending on your situation, but in general you will hear at least the following:

- You should have a clear set of financial goals that you are working toward.
- You should make more money than you spend, not just on a monthly basis but across the year.
- You should build a good credit history.
- You should be carrying no credit card debt.
- You should have a three- to six-month "safety net"—financial reserves that let you weather unexpected financial storms.
- You should be saving for retirement. The earlier you start, the better.
- You should have a will.
- You should have life insurance if other people (spouse, children) depend on your income.

These are the fundamental elements of stable financial life. If you are going to "control your finances," this is where you begin. Most people have none of these when they get started.

These elements are important because without them you live a life of financial randomness. You lack control or even a basic understanding of where your money is going. If something goes wrong you have no reserves to fall back on. The following sections explain each of these elements of financial stability.

Financial Goals

Financial goals give you something to shoot for. Rather than spending your money randomly, you can save it to achieve one of your goals. The section below entitled "Getting Started" discusses the advantages of setting financial goals and shows you how to get started.

Income vs. Expenses

It is important that you gain enough control of your finances so that you can make sure that you spend no more than you make. Income must exceed expenses on an annual basis, not just month by month. Unexpected bills like car insurance and property taxes, which happen only once or twice a year, can blow your budget if you forget to plan for them.

Credit History

As a teenager you are in a perfect position to begin building your *credit history*. Your credit history tracks your bank accounts, your loans, your credit cards and your payment and balance histories. Several large companies in America keep track of credit histories. It is important that your history shows the successful acceptance and repayment of loans, as well appropriate use of things like credit cards and checking accounts.

Your credit history is important because it is used to decide things like acceptance for mortgages (see Chapter 32). As a teenager you can begin to build your credit history by opening a checking account, getting a credit card and taking out and repaying small loans. The idea is to start building a good reputation early so that it is easy to get larger loans as you progress through life.

Credit Card Debt

It is very easy, upon getting a credit card, to quickly run up a large balance. The problem is that credit card debt is wasteful and unnecessary. This is important: Credit cards tend to have very high interest rates. If you have a $2,000 balance on a credit card, you are paying something like $30 per month in interest alone ($360 per year). That's a lot of money. That's $360 that could be going toward your financial goals instead. You want your financial plan to demonstrate a clear reduction in credit card debt, and you want to stop using your card on "random purchases." It is the random purchases that prevent you from getting the things you truly want and need.

Building a Credit History

You can actively build a credit history by applying for and repaying successively larger loans. At the same time you can build a personal relationship with a bank loan officer (see also Chapter 44). Start a credit history by opening a normal savings account at the bank where you want to build your relationship. Put, for example, $500 in a savings account. Now go to the loan officer and say, "I am trying to build a credit history. Can I apply for a secured $500 loan using my savings account as collateral?" There is no reason for the bank to deny you this loan because it is guaranteed. Take the money from the loan, deposit it, and pay the loan back over four to six months. Each time you make a payment, do it in person during non-busy hours and take the time to get to know the people at the bank. Once the loan is paid back, apply for another that is larger. Work toward the point where the bank trusts you to hold an *unsecured loan*—a loan that has no collateral. If you did this at two or three banks, you would move yourself to a position, prior to age 20, where you would have an excellent credit record and a true financial resource.

Safety Nets

Experts tend to recommend a safety net of three to six months of your salary. As you recall, Bob brings home about $1,850 per month. Therefore, he would want to have a safety net of $6,000 to $11,000 dollars sitting in a savings or money market account to use in case of an emergency like loss of his job.

Retirement

Retirement savings may seem totally and absolutely irrelevant to you right now, especially as a teenager. Chapter 30 will attempt to convince you otherwise. Please read it with an open mind. Retirement savings are a great way to accumulate wealth, and the earlier you start, the better.

Life Insurance

As a teenager you do not need life insurance, but you may need it later in life. See Chapter 33 for more information on this topic.

GETTING STARTED

One of the hardest things about "controlling your finances" is getting started down the path. During high school and college, and even after college for most people, finances are mysterious and maddening. There is never enough money. Financial control gives you the ability to understand where your money is going.

One way to start down the path of control is to give yourself some sort of incentive to do so. If you feel that you are getting something from controlling your finances, then it is much more likely that you will do it. Different incentives work for different people. Let's try two approaches that might encourage you to start to controlling things better.

Approach 1: Becoming a Millionaire

Many people find it hard to believe, but becoming a millionaire is fairly easy. Becoming a millionaire overnight is more difficult, but doing it over time is a reachable goal for every American citizen who is 25 years old.

Here is how you can become a millionaire. Start at age 15 and simply deposit $20 every week in an account that earns 12% interest. Twenty dollars is not a lot of money. If you smoke, it is the amount of money you are probably spending on cigarettes each week. If you go out for lunch every day, it is less than what you are probably spending on your lunches.

It is less than $3 a day. Every American—even people begging at a New York subway stop—can put together $3 each day.

If you added $20 per week to an interest bearing account earning 12%, and you did that starting at age 15, then by age 55 you would have a million dollars.

Here is another way to think about it. You were born 15 or 20 years ago. Imagine that, on the day of your birth, your parents opened an account earning 12% and deposited just $20 per week in that account. They did it every week of your life. If they did that, then at age 20 they would be able to write you a check for about $80,000. Hard to believe but true. Small amounts of money, accumulated consistently and earning interest over a long period of time, really add up.

You probably have three questions:

- What, are you kidding? That is all I have to do?
- Why didn't anyone tell me when I was 5?
- Why didn't my parents do this for me when I was born? I sure could use $80,000!

It may be that your parents did do this when you were born. If so, that is how they are planning to pay for your college education.

The point is, with just a little discipline over time you can accumulate huge amounts of money. That is what "control" is all about.

Approach 2: Getting Something You Really Want

Let's say that the thought of a million dollars in 40 years doesn't do anything for you. You want something *now*. Here is another way to think about your finances.

Television is a funny thing. The technology behind it is simple and seemingly harmless: Television transmits moving pictures to your home. What could be the problem with that? The weird thing about television is that if the proper images are transmitted to your home they can change the way you think. In particular, they can increase your desires. Take, for example, the Salad Shooter. Would it have ever sold without the mind-bending influence of TV? No. At the same time, television tends to encourage you to satisfy all of your desires immediately. That is why, two weeks after you have purchased a brand new car, commercials can make you believe that you need another one.

Let's try to imagine an alternate and parallel universe without television. In this universe, a person who wants something stops and says, "In order for me to have that something, I need to save up enough money to buy it first. Then I will purchase it." Would this work? No, it would not in some cases. For example, is it worthwhile to wait 30 years until you save up enough money to buy a house, and then buy one? No (see

Chapter 32 for a discussion of this particular purchase). Is it worthwhile to save money for 5 years before you buy a car? Not necessarily, mainly because you have to have a car to survive in most American environments.

But let's say that on all other desires in your life you were to follow a "save first, buy later" rule. What would happen? Two things. First, you would notice that your desires might suddenly change dramatically. Second, you would have to find a way to accumulate money over time and hold it so you could realize your desires.

It is this simple but fundamental change of thinking—the "save first, buy later" rule—that can lead to the concepts of "controlling your finances" and "accumulating wealth." If you can make that change it will cause you to modify your thinking so much that in a short period of time things like stocks, bonds, CDs and all the rest suddenly become interesting and relevant.

In order to organize your life in this "save first, buy later" way you have to determine your *financial priorities*. To determine your financial priorities, the first thing you have to do is think of the things you would like to have in the future and then organize them. Therefore, I would like you to try taking 15 minutes to come up with a list of "things you would like to have one day." Simply take out a sheet of paper and list as many of your desires as possible. It may take a few minutes to get started; if you find yourself staring at a blank sheet of paper here are some thoughts to help you get started:

- Do you want or need a car?
- Do you want to start your own business?
- Do you want a house or apartment?
- Some furniture?
- A computer?
- A new spring wardrobe?
- A college education?
- A trip to Paris?
- An engagement ring for your girl friend?

Just start imagining all the things you would love to have one day, and write as many of them as you can think of down on the sheet of paper. For most folks, if you think about all of the things you want to have, both short- and long-term, you end up with a pretty long list. If you have a spouse create the list together.

Now you have a list. Take another five minutes and write down prices next to everything. If you don't know the exact number, write down an approximate number. If you don't know an approximate number, just guess and then double that number.

Now take your list and find the one thing on that list that you REALLY want. The thing that would make you happiest or solve the most problems or bring the most joy to you or a friend. On that list there is one thing that brings the biggest smile to your face when you think about it. Put a big star next to it and focus your attention on it.

Now here is an important fact: You can have that thing. It will take some work, but you can have it. And you will have it if you can gain control your finances.

Let's go back to Bob from the previous chapter. He made his list. He put prices next to everything. Then he took about half an hour to think about everything on the list and discovered the one thing that he really wants, more than anything, is a pilot license (see also Chapter 23 on goals). Bob wants to learn how to fly. He can't exactly explain why. He just wants to get his license and he has wanted it since age 13. He called a local airport, and it costs about $4,000 for a person to get a private pilot license. So what Bob needs is $4,000. And his question is this: "This is great. Now I know exactly what I want, and I can taste it I want it so bad. But where in the world am I going to get $4,000???"

"Where in the world am I going to get that kind of money???" is the central question for anyone who wants to gain control of his or her finances. It is the one question that can trigger the transformation from random money management to controlled money management. It can compel you to get a job. Similarly, it can compel you to try to get a good job so you can get there faster. The reason you made a list of all of your desires and then picked the one thing you really want is simple: If you really want that one thing, you may be willing to put in some extra effort, and perhaps endure a little pain, to get it. It will also force you to control your other spending in order to accumulate money for the thing you really want.

Read Chapter 23 on setting goals. Then make this one thing you really want an important goal in your life. You might be surprised by how quickly you can reach your goal if you put your mind to it.

CHAPTER 30

Retirement Accounts Build Wealth

As a teenager, retirement is probably the *last* thing on your mind. While you are under 30 you may think that saving for retirement is totally irrelevant. However, retirement is a fact of life and adults are highly concerned about it. When you hear adults talk about 401(k) accounts and IRA accounts and annuities, what they are talking about is retirement. The goal here is to help you to understand what they are talking about and why they think it is so important. It turns out that if you can get money into a retirement account at a very early age, like 15, it can have significant long-term advantages for you. Retirement saving is central to the whole concept of "financial security" and "accumulating wealth," and retirement savings under a 401(k) plan or IRA can have amazing short- and long-term benefits.

Why are your parents always talking about their 401(k) plan? Because retirement is a big deal. It takes an incredible amount of money to retire comfortably in America. Let's say your parents bring home $50,000 a year now (1997). When they retire, if they plan to have a lifestyle similar to the one they have now, they will need about $40,000 per year in today's dollars. Since they are going to retire at age 65 and might live to be 90, that means they need 25 years worth of $40,000 per year. A quick calculation might make you think that means they need to save $1,000,000. Unfortunately, inflation increases the cost of everything over time, so they need to actually accumulate something more like $3,500,000 if the inflation rate is 4%. That's a lot of money. It may seem like an impossibly large quantity of money, and that is why so many people "worry" about retirement.

Here is a funny thing about retirement: It helps if you start saving early. It helps a whole lot. Let's say that you, at age 15, were to start saving for retirement. If you saved just $50 a week in an account earning 10% (typical of mutual funds), you would have $3,500,000 at age 65.

213

Fifty dollars a week might seem like a lot to you now, but it will be peanuts once you have a real job. By comparison, if your parents are age 45 and they start saving for retirement today, they would have to put aside over $1,000 a week (about $55,000 a year) to accumulate the same $3,500,000. That is clearly impossible since they only make $50,000 a year in this example. The reason why you can do it with so little money per week at age 15 is called the "time value of money." Little bits of money accumulated in an account with a good interest rate over long periods of time reap huge rewards. As you can see, if you wait too long it can be nearly impossible to save for retirement, but by starting early it is easy.

Tax Consequences

Adults spend a lot of time talking and thinking about the "tax consequences" of the things they do. As a teenager that seemed ridiculous to me. My thought was, "Who cares?"

Things change after you get a real job and you set some financial priorities for yourself. Let's say you graduate from college and get a good job that pays you $30,000 a year (1997). Federal and state taxes will take at least 30%, or about $10,000 of that $30,000, away from you. *That is a lot of money!* You earned it, but you never see it and someone else is spending it. That *really* starts to bug you after awhile, especially when you consider what you could be buying with that money.

There are two easy ways to cut down the amount of money that the government takes from you: retirement savings (IRAs, 401Ks, etc.) and home mortgage payments. If you deposit $2,000 in an IRA it will not be taxed, so you "make" a free $600 or so. $600 is a lot of money! The same thing happens if you pay a $800 mortgage payment every month. That mortgage payment might mean an extra $1,500 in your pocket at the end of the year because mortgage interest is tax deductible. $1,500 is a lot of money! That is why adults are always considering the tax consequences of everything they do. It is free money.

The other thing that is important to building retirement wealth is called "tax-sheltered compounding." If you put money in a normal savings account and earn interest on it, you have to pay a tax each year on the interest. But in an account like a 401(k) or an IRA, the money compounds tax-free. This causes it to grow at a faster rate. Remember from Chapter 1 how big a bite taxes take out of a paycheck. Retirement accounts let you avoid the tax until you retire.

So, what is a 401(k) plan? It is a "defined contribution employee benefit plan" that allows tax-deferred retirement savings. 401(k) plans are made possible by a paragraph in the IRS tax code numbered 401(k), hence the name. The words "defined contribution" imply that employees contribute their own money to the plan, normally through a payroll deduction. The money in a 401(k) plan is "tax deferred," which means that you do not pay taxes on the money when you contribute it but instead when you withdraw and actually use the money during retirement. There are limits to the amount of money you can channel into a 401(k) account, currently 15% of income or a maximum of $9,500 (1997) per year per person. If you are married, both you and your spouse can each open separate accounts with your respective employers and these individual limits remain in effect individually.

As a savings vehicle, 401(k) plans have a number of distinct advantages:

- The money is withheld directly from your paycheck, just like taxes, so you never really see it or have a chance to spend it.
- You do not pay taxes on the money when it is withheld, so it lowers your net tax bill.
- The money in the account can be invested in a number of mutual funds, giving you the opportunity to earn a good yield and help the money grow faster. The interest you earn on the money is also tax deferred until you withdraw the money. This allows the interest to compound much more rapidly than you would expect.
- It is in your employer's best interest to get as many employees to invest as much money in the 401(k) plan as possible, so many employers will match your contribution in some way. For example, for each $100 you contribute to the plan your employer might kick in an extra $20 for free, as an incentive. Often this money is tied to some sort of "vesting schedule," which means that you need to stay at the company some period of time (for example, three years) before the matching funds actually land in your account. However, they do land there just as though you had been getting the money all along, and so at the three-year point your account balance suddenly jumps in value. This is free money that your employer is giving away—people are stupid not to take it.
- If you leave the company, the money in the 401(k) account is truly yours, and you can take it with you to your new employer or "roll it over" into a personal IRA account so it can continue earning money tax deferred.
- Many 401(k) plans let you take a loan against your balance, typically at an interest rate like 8.5%. However, when you pay the money back, you are the one who gets the interest. The interest you pay goes directly into your account. You are truly borrowing the money from yourself. The only cost of the loan is normally a minor processing fee of $50.

It is the loan provision that makes 401(k) plans particularly interesting. It means that you can actually use your money before you retire with no tax penalties. You can use the funds you accumulate in your 401(k) plan as a safety net, or you can accumulate funds in your 401(k) plan and then use them to make a down payment on a house. The IRS and your employer will impose certain restrictions (for example, you cannot borrow more than 50% of the account value). Because it is your money, however, 401(k) loan policies are generally lenient.

There are no significant disadvantages to 401(k) plans. However, be aware of the fact that money contributed to a 401(k) plan or IRA cannot be withdrawn until age 59.5 without a penalty (the penalty is that you must pay taxes on the money withdrawn, plus you pay a 10% fine to the IRS). The loan provision makes the age limit on withdrawals a moot point for most people.

CHAPTER 31

You Have a lot of Financial Options

I f you are new to "financial management" and "investing," one of the hardest things to figure out is the answer to what should be an easy question: "Where should I invest my money?" The reason that the answer to this question is not simple is because there are so many options, and each option has so many variables attached to it. These options are a fact of life. If you can learn about all of the options available you can make much smarter financial decisions.

Let's say that you have $1,000 in your hands right now and you would like to *invest* it so that it will earn a reasonable rate of return and grow over the next 10 years. Perhaps this $1,000 is a gift you received from your grandparents that is intended to help you buy a new house when you graduate from college. Here is a list of possible investing options—certainly not an exhaustively complete list, but a list of the most common options:

- Your checking account
- A normal "passbook savings account" at a bank
- A money market account
- A CD
- A U.S. Savings Bond
- A corporate or municipal bond
- A bond mutual fund
- Stock in some company (a large established one like IBM, a new one no one has ever heard of or something in between)
- A stock mutual fund

That is a lot of options. If you are just starting out, it is a "bewildering array of options." The following sections describe, in English, the attributes, advantages and disadvantages of each of these investments. As I write this it is early 1997. All of the numbers I quote are based on the rates available today.

217

YOUR CHECKING ACCOUNT

Even if none of the other options feel comfortable to you right now, you should have a reasonable understanding of how your checking account works. You know that you could deposit the $1,000 into your checking account and leave it there for 10 years. You also know the advantages and disadvantages of doing this. The advantage is that the money is incredibly easy to access. It is, in other words, *liquid*. You can instantly withdraw the money by writing a check or by visiting an ATM. In many cases the extreme liquidity of a checking account is important. For example, when you pay a bill you want extreme liquidity. However, the disadvantage of this sort of liquidity is that, on most checking accounts, you earn nothing in return. In fact, you may actually lose money over time because of fees. Therefore, a checking account is probably not an appropriate place to place your $1000.

A NORMAL "PASSBOOK SAVINGS ACCOUNT" AT A BANK

A normal bank savings account is almost as good as a checking account in terms of liquidity (for example, you can normally withdraw the money at an ATM), but almost as bad as a checking account in terms of return. Today bank savings accounts average a 2.7% return. Therefore, your $1,000 will earn $27 in a year. Unfortunately, inflation is running at perhaps 3.3% right now, so you are actually losing money. A year from now it will cost $1,033 to buy what it costs $1,000 to buy today if the rate of inflation is 3.3%. Knowing that, you can see why having only $1,027 in your savings account a year from now is actually losing money. In addition, you have to pay income taxes on the $27 earned, so it is really worth only $20 or so (depending on your tax bracket).

A savings account might be a good place to park money that you wish to accumulate over a very short period of time. For example, you might accumulate cash to cover your "hidden expenses" in a savings account simply because it is easy to transfer money between a savings and checking account (and because some interest income is better than none). However, it is not a good place to put money that you are planning to hold for 10 years.

A MONEY MARKET ACCOUNT

A money market account at most banks works approximately like a savings account, but it gets a better rate of return. In addition there might be a few restrictions on a money market account, like a minimum balance or a maximum number of withdrawals per year. A money market account has the same advantages and disadvantages of a savings account. Current money market rates average 4%. For money that you plan to hold for a short period of time (three months to a year) and that needs to be liquid, a money market account is probably your best bet.

A CD

A CD, or "Certificate of Deposit," is a bank account that earns a better rate in return for a fixed time commitment on your part. You deposit money into the account and receive a "certificate" that allows you to withdraw the money at some later date. You can get six month CDs, one year CDs, five year CDs and so on. The rate normally rises with the length of the time commitment. If for some reason you need to withdraw the money early, the bank officer will look at you sternly and generally penalize you by withhold all or part of the interest you would have earned.

Certificates of deposit have several advantages. First and foremost, they are absolutely secure if they are held by an FDIC-insured bank and the account balance falls within the $100,000 limit. It is impossible to lose the money. However, there are two disadvantages. First, CDs are not very liquid, so they are not good for money that you may need to use on a moment's notice. Also, they represent only a "holding action"—you generally do not make any money off a CD. Here's why: let's say that the current rate of return is 5% and the inflation rate is 3.3%. Therefore, the real return rate is 1.7%. However, you must pay taxes on the money that the CD earns each year. The taxes essentially nullify the 1.7%. Therefore, the real rate of return from a CD is zero, and this is almost always true. If you are absolutely certain that you cannot afford to lose the money then a CD may be the best place to put it. However, the money will not grow.

A U.S. Savings Bond

A U.S. Savings Bonds has many of the same attributes as a CD. You deposit the money for a fixed period of time and earn a rate of return that is on the order of 4.5%. The most typical bond—a "series EE bond"— must be held for at least five years to earn this rate.

A Savings Bond has one advantage over a CD; you do not have to pay state income taxes on the interest. Also, if used to pay college tuition, you may not have to pay any federal taxes on the interest either (see your bank for details or call 1-800-USBONDS). Savings Bonds are also absolutely secure, like a CD. They share the same disadvantages as a CD as well: low liquidity, penalties for early withdrawal and a relatively low rate of return.

A CORPORATE OR MUNICIPAL BOND

A corporate or municipal bond represents a loan. The corporation or municipality needs money for some project—a new factory, a new school, whatever—and issues bonds to raise the money. The corporation or municipality then pays interest on the money over time at some rate. The rate of interest depends on the prevailing interest rates at the time of issue as well as the stability of the entity issuing the bond. A bond issued by IBM, for example, will have a lower interest rate than a bond issued by a two-year-old small company. You may have heard the term "junk bond"; it refers to bonds issued by riskier corporations.

Municipal bonds generally have some sort of tax advantage. For example, you may not have to pay state or federal taxes on municipal bond interest. Therefore, municipal bond rates are generally lower to reflect this advantage.

You could use your $1,000 to purchase a 10-year corporate or municipal bond. The advantage (and the only reason you would buy this sort of bond as opposed to a U.S. Savings Bond, given a choice) would be a higher rate of return. However, be sure that you take the tax consequences into account when calculating the return on a bond. If you are spending the $1,000 on college tuition, then a U.S. Savings Bond may have a better rate of return. Ask your bank (or call 1-800-USBONDS) for details. The disadvantages of corporate and municipal bonds make them less suitable for small investors. The disadvantages include:

- Risk—If the corporation or municipality has problems, then the bond may become worthless. Most municipal bonds are considered to be "safe," but then Orange County, CA, had its problems and put at risk thousands of bond holders. Corporations can also have problems.
- Lack of liquidity—A bond has a fixed time period attached to it. If you want your money prior to the end of that time period, your only choice is to sell the bond to someone else on the "bond market." You will have to pay a broker a commission to do this. Also, your bond will return more or less than it is worth depending on the change in interest rates. If interest rates have gone down since you purchased your bond, you will make money. If rates have gone up you will lose money. Here is an example to help you understand why. Let's say that you buy a bond for $1,000 from your county, and the bond is written such that it promises to pay you $2,000 at the end of 10 years in one lump sum. At the time you purchase the bond CD interest rates are at 8%. After 5 years, CD interest rates have fallen to 6% and you try to sell your bond. Someone might be willing to pay you $1,600

for the bond (which is more than you would expect). The person knows that in five more years the bond will pay out $2,000 and if the $1,600 were invested in a CD today it would only return 6% (as opposed to the 8% rate that was in effect when the bond was written). A bond therefore acts like a time machine, allowing investors to move back in time to a different interest rate.

A 10-year bond issued by a stable company or municipality might not be a bad way to invest $1,000, but the liquidity problem can make things difficult. Also, if you expect interest rates to rise over time a bond might not be the best place to put the money.

A BOND MUTUAL FUND

A bond mutual fund is simply a collection of bonds (generally of a certain type, like low-risk corporate bonds or NY municipal bonds) owned by a pool of people. The fund lowers risk by holding a collection of bonds. If one company goes bad, it will have a low effect on the overall pool of bonds held by the fund. A bond fund will generally pay interest every month. Also, the value of fund shares will rise and fall each day depending on the rise and fall of interest rates.

Bond funds have the advantage of liquidity. You can sell your shares any time and get out. However, your share value will change every day—share value goes up when interest rates fall and down when rates rise. Therefore, if you think interest rates are going to rise over 10 years, you may want to take that fact into account before purchasing a bond fund.

STOCK IN A COMPANY, LIKE IBM OR GM

Stock represents ownership of a company, and that is all that it is. It is easiest to understand how stock works and what it means by looking at a simple example.

Let's say that you decide you want to start a business (see Chapter 44), and you decide to open a restaurant. You buy a building, buy all the kitchen equipment, tables and chairs that you need, buy your supplies and hire a cook, waitresses, bus boys, etc. You advertise and open your doors. Let's say that you spend $300,000 on the building and the equipment, and that every year you spend $100,000 on supplies and pay roll. At the end of your first year you have paid out the $100,000 for expenses but actually earned $125,000. Your net profit is $25,000. However, at the end of the second year you bring in $140,000, for a net profit of $40,000. At this point you decide that you want to sell the business. What is it worth?

One way to look at it is to say that the business is "worth" $300,000. You could sell the building, the equipment, etc. and get $300,000. This is a simplification, of course; the building probably went up in value and the equipment went down because it is now used. Say things balance out to $300,000. This is the "asset value" of the business—the value of all of the business assets if you sold them outright today.

However, this business is a "going concern." That is, if you keep it going it will probably make at least $40,000 this year. Therefore, you can think of the restaurant as an investment that will pay out $40,000 in "interest" every year. Looking at it that way, I might be willing to pay $400,000 for it. A $40,000 return per year on a $400,000 investment represents a 10% rate of return. I might even be willing to pay $500,000, which represents an 8% rate of return, or even more if I thought that the restaurant's client base will grow and increase earnings over time at a rate faster than the rate of inflation.

If I am the restaurant's owner, I set my price accordingly. What if 10 people come to me and say, "Wow, I would like to buy your restaurant, but I don't have $500,000." Then I might sell *shares* in the restaurant. That is, I might divide ownership of the restaurant into 10 pieces, or shares, and sell one share to each person for $50,000. Then each person would receive one-tenth of the profits at the end of the year and have 1 out of 10 votes in any business decisions. Or I might divide ownership into 1,000 shares and sell each one for $500. Or I might divide ownership into 2,000 shares, keep 1,000 for myself and sell the remaining shares for $250 each. That way I retain a majority of the shares and retain control of the restaurant, while sharing the profit with other people. In the meantime, I get to put $250,000 in the bank when I sell the 1,000 shares to other people.

That is all stock is. It represents ownership of a company's assets and profits. A dividend on a share of stock represents that share's portion of the company's profits, generally dispersed quarterly or yearly. A large company like IBM has millions of shares of stock outstanding (540 million in 1997, to be exact). One measure of the value of the company, at least to investors, is the product of the number of outstanding shares multiplied by the share price.

Stocks are bought and sold at a "stock market" like the New York Stock Exchange. The NYSE can be thought of as a big room where everyone who wants to buy and sell shares of stocks can go to do their buying and selling. The exchange makes buying and selling easy. If the exchange did not exist, you would have to place a classified ad in the paper, wait for a call, haggle on a price, etc. whenever you wanted to sell stock. With an exchange in place you can buy and sell shares instantly.

The exchange has an interesting side effect. It allows the price of a stock to be fixed every second of the day. Therefore, the price fluctuates based on news from the company, media reports, national economic news, etc. Buyers and sellers take all of these factors into account each day. So, for example, when the FAA shut down ValuJet for a month in June 1996, the value of the stock plummeted. Investors could not be sure that the airline represented a "going concern" and began selling, driving the price down. The asset value of the company usually acts as a floor on the share price. The price of the stock also reflects the dividend that the stock pays, the projected earnings of the company in the future, the price of tea in china (especially a tea company's stock) and so on.

Should you invest your $1,000 in an individual stock? Probably not, for two reasons:

- You have to pay a commission when you buy and sell a stock on the exchange. The commission might be $50 at both ends. That $100 represents 10% of the $1,000, and therefore is probably too high. However, if you know a stock will go up 200% over 10 years, you might be willing to take the 10% hit.

- Stocks carry risk. If the company has problems you can lose part or all of the money you invest. You can eliminate some of the risk by investing in "blue chip" companies like IBM, GM, Disney, etc.—companies with long, successful track records. However, IBM is a good example of what can go wrong. Several years ago its share price fell by more than half when the company had problems. Later it came back. But if you had purchased IBM stock when it was high and needed to sell it when it was low, you would have lost a lot of money.

Stocks have several advantages over other investments, especially if you buy stock in more than one company (a collection of stocks purchased from several companies is called a *portfolio*). Portfolios lower risk by spreading your money over a number of companies. Also, you pay taxes on stocks only when you sell them. If you buy a stock, hold it 10-years, and it goes up 100% in that time, you will pay tax on that *capital gain* only once. The capital gain represents the money you made on the difference in the buy and sell price. You do not have to pay taxes on that capital gain each year, only in the year that you sell the stock. This is different from a savings account or a CD. In these accounts you pay taxes every year on the interest you earn. So imagine a savings account earns, say, $27 in a year. You pay the tax and net only $20. Next year, you earn interest on $1,020 instead of $1,027. That sounds like small potatoes, but if you multiply the numbers by 10 or 100 and then do it for 10 or 20 years, the difference that tax-deferred compounding can make is startling. Capital gains on stocks represent a form of tax-deferred compounding.

A STOCK MUTUAL FUND

If you are just getting into investing and have a small amount of money to invest (like $1,000), then stock mutual funds represent a good place to put money being invested for more than 5 years. A stock mutual fund is simply a pool of stocks owned by a group of investors. A big mutual fund might have 100,000 investors and might own stock in 100 different companies. The risk is lower because of the large portfolio of stocks, and the transaction fees are no longer a concern of the individual investors.

Stock mutual funds have the same disadvantages as stocks. If the economy has a problem and you need to liquidate your shares, then you can lose money. However, if the economy does well the returns can be relatively high. Many studies have shown that, on average, the stock market returns an average of 10% or so per year if you leave money in it for long periods of time. That 10% return includes market crashes. Even when the market crashes, if you can leave the money alone it will, over time, earn roughly 10%. The problem is that you may have to leave the money alone for many years, say 10 or 20, to get the 10% return.

This is why stocks are said to be "less liquid" than other investments. If the stock market is rising, then money in the stock market is very

Good Books

A good book to read for more information is *The Wealthy Barber* by David Chilton. See the references section for more information.

liquid. You can sell your stocks at any time and make a profit. But when the market falls you want to leave your money in the market so it can recover. This makes your money unliquid. Since you cannot predict the rising and falling of the market, you cannot count on the liquidity of your investment. You can sell your shares at any time on the exchange, but you will lose money if you are forced to sell when the market is low.

Thus, stocks and stock mutual funds are thought to represent a great place to put retirement money because this money is being invested for long periods of time. Stocks are probably a bad place to put money that you need a year from now because you simply do not know what the market will do over that short a time frame.

Stock mutual funds come in two forms: *load* and *no load*. Load funds charge a fee when you purchase shares of the fund. No loads do not. For a beginning investor you will probably want to choose no load funds to avoid the fees.

Stock mutual funds also invest their money differently, depending on their charter. You can discover the exact investment mix by looking at the *prospectus* of the fund. The prospectus will tell you what types of companies the fund invests in, what its rate of return has been through the years and exactly what stocks it holds at the moment. There are many general categories of stock mutual funds. For example:

- Income funds—These funds invest generally in larger, safer companies that pay dividends regularly. Therefore, you can rely on the dividend income each year.

- Growth funds—These funds invest in companies that the fund manager expects will grow, in terms of share price, over the years.

- Aggressive Growth funds—These funds invest in smaller companies. When a small company succeeds its share price has the potential of growing rapidly. However, small companies have a higher potential for failure. Therefore, aggressive growth funds tend to be more volatile (their share prices rise and fall more frequently and drastically than other funds). However, the returns over the long haul should be greater if the economy in general is doing well.

- Index funds—These funds invest in some fixed set of stocks and do not "play the market." For example, a fund might be tied to the stocks represented by the S&P 500 or the companies in the Dow Jones Industrial Average. The DJIA is made up of 30 large companies. Each day the share prices of these 30 stocks are processed to produce a single number. As that number rises and falls each day, it tells you something about the market in general. The S&P 500 is made up of 500 large companies, which are also averaged to produce a single number. An index fund invests in the stocks of a particular index, so that the fund value rises and falls in exact correspondence with the index. Usually index funds have lower fees, and you know exactly where they stand each day because indexes are widely publicized on the radio and TV.

- Foreign funds—These funds invest in stocks in foreign stock markets.

Funds are broken up into *fund families*. For example, Vanguard is a large fund family with many different mutual funds that it manages. Each fund in the family has a different personality because it invests in different types of companies. Vanguard funds are generally no load. Fidelity is a large, load fund family.

MAKING INVESTMENT DECISIONS

So, let's return to the original question. Where should you invest $1,000 that is needed 10 years from now? The answer to this question will depend on your risk tolerance. If you want a guaranteed rate of return and you will lose sleep at night if, 10 years from now, you lost part of the $1,000, then a good place to put the money is in a CD or a U.S. Savings Bond. Choose whichever one will have a better rate of return after taking the tax consequences into account.

If you are willing to take a risk that you might lose money in return for the possibility of a much better rate of return, then you should consider putting the money into a no-load stock mutual fund. Stock mutual funds have the following advantages:

- They are easy to buy.
- They have the potential of a relatively high rate of return, since the value of stocks has risen at an average rate of 10% per year over the last 50 years (although this tells you nothing specific about the future).
- They are easy to sell when you need the money and can be sold at any time.

They also have some disadvantages:

- If the market falls, you could lose money if you happen to need to sell at the time of the fall.
- You generally have to wait several days or a week to get your money out.
- Mutual funds require thought. With a savings bond you simply go down to the bank, buy the bond, put it in a drawer and forget about it. With a mutual fund you have to research and pick the fund, send in the money and watch the fund to see how it performs.

Before you invest money in a mutual fund, you have to decide if the potential benefit of an increased rate of return outweighs the disadvantages. The advanced rate of return can be important, however. For example, if you invest $1,000 in a 5% CD for 10 years, then at the end of 10 years you will have $1,640 (not counting taxes). If you invest $1,000 in a stock mutual fund that does indeed earn an average of 10% per year over 10 years, then you will have $2,710. That is, you make over $1,000 more with the higher rate of return. If the fund happens to earn an average of 15% per year over 10 years (as an aggressive growth fund might), you would have $4,460 after 10 years. That is a big difference. That is why people consider stock mutual funds over CDs for long-term (greater than 5 years) investments.

CHAPTER 32

You Will Buy a
House One Day

Home ownership is an important part of the "American Dream" and is a significant way for a person or family to express its individuality and independence. For many people home ownership marks an "arrival" in the same way that graduation or a first child does. It marks a major step toward adulthood.

There are significant financial advantages to owning a home. However, the purchase of a home is normally the most complicated financial transaction in which a person participates during a normal lifetime. The first time you undertake a home purchase, the complexity of the transaction can be particularly frustrating because there are a number of unknown rules and procedures that you are generally forced to learn through "the school of hard knocks." Many people simply give up the first time they try to buy a house because too many unexpected things happen during the process. They end up waiting perhaps six months or a year, and then they start over again. It can be that difficult.

The goal here is to help you to understand the home buying process so that you can approach it from a position of understanding rather than confusion. By understanding the process as a teenager, you can position yourself to buy a home earlier so you can reap the rewards faster. In this chapter will learn about the different types of homes available, the financial limits that banks apply to you when you try to get a home mortgage (and which control the type or size of house you can afford), the extra and often unexpected costs that you will incur during the closing process and some of the hazards to watch for as you go through the transaction. Once you have finished this chapter you will be prepared to go forth and do battle with the banks, Realtors, lawyers and loan officers who stand between you and the home of your dreams. You may need to wait a few years until you have the money necessary for a down payment, but at least you will understand the process.

THE BASICS

Imagine that you would like to buy a new television. In America just about anyone can drive down to the local discount store, pick out a TV and purchase it with a credit card in about 10 minutes. The process is easy, well understood and accepted by everyone.

Now imagine that you want to buy a new car. This transaction is a bit more complicated but still relatively straightforward. If you have the cash for a car in the bank then you can:

- Drive to the dealer
- Pick out the car
- Haggle on the price
- Sign a contract
- Write a check
- Call your insurance agent to bind coverage

You can drive the car off the lot the same day. If you have to get a loan for the car, then it might take a day or two to contact a bank and arrange for the loan (provided that your credit history is good), but you can still drive the car away with relative ease.

Now imagine that you want to buy a house. In general the process is going to take at a very minimum a month, and more typically between three and six months. There is also a fairly good probability (perhaps 25% depending on your situation) that, once you find a home you like and wish to purchase, you will be unable to buy that particular home and will have to start over again. A typical question for the first time buyer to ask at this point is, "What do you mean that I may not be able to buy the house that I pick out?" As you go through this section, you will begin to understand that there are a number of things that can go wrong if you are not prepared (and sometimes even if you are). There are three fundamental things that complicate the home buying process:

- Each home is a large, distinct, immovable, one-of-a-kind object with a distinct one-of-a-kind seller who happens to live in it. This fact means that human emotions and personalities play a much larger role than they do in most other financial transactions.
- No normal person has enough cash to buy a home, so you are forced to go to a bank and ask for a loan whose size may be measured in the hundreds of thousands of dollars. No bank is going to undertake a loan of this size lightly.
- All homes rest on a piece of land, and with that land is associated a certain amount of government red tape, including the deed for the property and sizable taxes on the home. The process of transferring ownership of a home is not nearly as simple as it is for other objects that we commonly purchase.

Having said all of this, you can expect that any home purchase will involve at least the following steps, provided that everything goes smoothly:

1. Make the decision to purchase a house.
2. Get your financial affairs in order.
3. Decide on the type of house, the location and the price range you can afford.
4. Talk to a Realtor and start looking at houses.
5. Find a house that you like.
6. Make an offer on the house.
7. Negotiate a price.
8. Shop for and select a mortgage company.
9. Apply for a mortgage.
10. Wait for approval on the mortgage.
11. Wait for the closing.
12. Attend the closing and sign all the paperwork.
13. Move in to your new home.

We will discuss each of these steps in the following sections.

STEP 1: MAKE THE DECISION TO PURCHASE A HOME

The decision to purchase a home is not a small one and involves a number of variables. Some of the considerations that you should keep in mind are listed below:

- Are you able to commit to a specific location for a period of several years? If your job or lifestyle requires you to change location frequently, then you should not purchase a home. There are two reasons for this. First, a home is not very liquid. It can take months or years to sell a home when you need to move. Second, when you sell your home a Realtor will charge you a 7% commission. That means that in many locations you will have to hold the home for several years so it can appreciate in value. Otherwise, you will lose money when you resell it.
- Are you qualified to obtain a mortgage? Step 2 will help you determine whether you are currently qualified for a mortgage. If not, you can begin the process of becoming qualified by getting a good job, saving for the down payment, improving your credit history and paying down existing debt.
- Are you financially, physically and emotionally prepared to maintain the home? Owning a home is different from living in an apartment. In an apartment complex the grass is mowed, the buildings are repainted and appliances are fixed by the owner of the complex. When you own your own home, you have to do

these things yourself or pay someone else to do them. If you are not interested in painting, mowing and fixing, then a house if not for you (although a town house or condo might be—see Step 3). You will also have to pay significant property taxes and insurance premiums once you own a home.

Keep all three of these considerations in mind as you are deciding whether to buy a home. On the other hand, you should also keep the following advantages in mind:

- A house offers you a way to accumulate wealth. When you pay rent on an apartment, that money buys you nothing but living space. By spending about the same amount of money each month to pay the monthly payment on a mortgage, you instead build wealth. If you have a 15-year mortgage, then after 15 years of payments you have accumulated an amount of money equal to the value of your house. In addition, the value of your home will normally appreciate at some rate, with the minimum rate often being equal to inflation. Therefore, if you buy a home for $100,000, then after 15 years you will have accumulated $100,000 through your mortgage payments, and in addition the home will have a value of perhaps $150,000. Instead of accumulating nothing by paying apartment rent for 15 years, you accumulate $150,000.

- A house offers two significant tax advantages. First, interest paid on a mortgage is tax deductible. This means that the effective interest rate on the loan is reduced by your income tax rate. In addition, when you sell a home you are allowed to roll the money generated from the sale into a new home without paying any taxes on the appreciated value (i.e., capital gains) of the home. A home is the only investment that works in this way under current tax laws.

- A fixed rate mortgage stops the "rent increases" that you would see at an apartment complex. Your monthly payment will remain the same until the loan is paid off.

- The price per square foot for a house is sometimes lower than the price per square foot for an apartment, depending on the area.

- A house lets you express your individuality. When you live in an apartment you take what you get. You generally cannot repaint or renovate an apartment. When you own a home you can do whatever you want.

- A house offers privacy. Your home is your castle, so you don't have to worry about people running overhead or playing their stereos at 3:00 A.M.

As you can see, home ownership has important advantages and disadvantages, and the decision to purchase a home should not be made lightly.

STEP 2: GET YOUR FINANCIAL AFFAIRS IN ORDER

Before most people can purchase a home they must get a loan. The most common form of loan used to purchase a home is called a *mortgage*. In a mortgage, the borrower pledges to repay the loan as specified, and the lender is given the right to seize the property should payments ever be interrupted. A mortgage deed, issued by the lender and recorded at the county tax office, contains an accurate description of the property and the payment terms of the loan.

Because a mortgage is usually for $100,000 or more, banks tend to be fairly particular about the people to whom they grant a mortgage. In general a bank will require you to demonstrate five things before giving a mortgage to you:

1. You must have cash on hand for a down payment. Generally an amount equal to 10% of the home's purchase price must be available. In addition, you need to have enough cash on hand to cover *closing costs* as well. Closing costs are the fees you must pay to all of the people involved in the purchase of a home.

2. You must have a job with a reputable employer that pays a steady annual income.

3. You must show that the amount you are borrowing will not overburden you financially. In order to confirm this banks use two standard tests. The first test, which could be called the allowable monthly housing cost test, ensures that your monthly mortgage payments will not exceed 28% of your gross annual income. The second test, which could be called the allowable total monthly debt payment test, ensures that your total monthly payments for all debt including your mortgage payments do not exceed 36%. These ratios are good things because they help people to avoid overextending themselves. For example, if you bring home $2,000 per month and had to make a $1,800 mortgage payment each month, it is virtually guaranteed that you would either starve to death or default on your loan. The first test tries to prevent this from happening. In the same way, if you have a number of outstanding loans for cars, boats, furniture, etc. and tried to load another large loan on top of the pile, then it is also likely that you would eventually default. Test 2 guards against this problem.

4. You must have a clean and strong credit history.

5. You must have an acceptable balance sheet and net worth.

It is possible to obtain certain government-backed mortgages that bend some of these rules. For example, an FHA mortgage (a mortgage backed by the federal government) will lower the down payment requirement. In general, however, you can expect any mortgage company or bank to follow these rules fairly closely.

You meet the first requirement by saving money over time. There is no other way to do it. If you want a house you should be able to define home ownership as "important," establish it as a financial priority and begin a savings program to accumulate a down payment.

You meet the second requirement by having a steady job with a predictable income. You will need to be able to get confirmation of employment from your employer when it is requested by the bank. You will also have to supply tax returns for three preceding years to show your income history.

You meet the third requirement by looking at your current financial situation and figuring out the maximum amount of money you can borrow based on the tests. If you find that you are way off base when you look at the ratios, then you can do two things. You can plan on accumulating a larger down payment or buying a less expensive home, and you can reduce existing debt.

You meet the fourth requirement in two ways. You build a clean credit history by paying your bills on time. You obtain a strong credit history by obtaining and repaying other loans, like credit cards, car loans, etc. If you have never obtained and repaid a loan prior to attempting to get a mortgage, it is likely that the bank will frown on this fact. It is therefore important to build a credit history by obtaining and using credit cards, obtaining and repaying a car loan, etc. (see Chapter 29).

A bank will check your credit history by obtaining a credit report for you from a credit reporting company like TRW. You can and should obtain your own copy of your credit history ahead of time and make sure

Pre-approved Loans

As you are getting your finances in order, you may wish to talk with your bank or a mortgage company and get an opinion on your financial health. This will save you the embarrassment and frustration of applying for a mortgage and being rejected after spending a significant amount of time finding a home you like. Many mortgage companies will pre-approve you for a certain mortgage amount, and going through this process can be very beneficial. Once you are pre-approved, you will know exactly how much money you can spend on a new home. You will also save yourself the hassle of getting approved once you find a home you like.

that the report you receive is accurate and contains no errors. If you know that you have a spotty or poor credit history, you should work to repair the damage. The best way to do this is to talk with a credit counselor. The Fannie Mae Foundation (a private company chartered by Congress) can provide you with help finding credit counselors and other mortgage information. Call 1-800-699-HOME for further information and assistance.

You meet the fifth requirement by presenting to the bank a net worth statement. The bank is primarily interested in your existing assets (to demonstrate financial strength) and your existing debts.

STEP 3: DECIDE ON THE TYPE OF HOUSE, THE LOCATION AND THE PRICE RANGE

There are at least six different types of housing you can purchase in most markets:

- A house—A house is a detached, single-family dwelling. It stands by itself on its own piece of land, and you own and maintain both the house and the land. This is what most people think of when they think of "buying a house." It is the most common type of property on which to obtain a mortgage.
- A Duplex (triplex, etc.)—A duplex is a detached multi-family dwelling. In a duplex there are two units (in a tri-plex three, and so on) that share a wall and the same piece of land. You purchase the entire duplex and the land it sits on in the same way that you purchase a house. Then you can live in one half and rent the other. The rental income can go a long way toward paying the monthly mortgage payment.
- A town house—A townhouse is normally part of a row of connected units. You own the portion of the building you live in and its slice of land. However, each owner becomes associated with some sort of collective or management company that maintains the grounds and the exterior of the buildings much like an apartment complex would. You pay a monthly fee for this service. The advantage and intent of this arrangement is that the exterior appearance of all units is maintained.
- A condominium—In a condominium you own an apartment-like unit but not the land underneath it. A management company owns the land and the building your condo exists within. You pay a monthly fee to the management company to maintain the building and the grounds.
- A co-op—In a co-op you purchase shares in a corporation that owns the building and land. Ownership of these shares gives you

the right to live in an apartment in the building. Because all owners own shares in the corporation, they act as a board that can lightly or severely restrict the freedom of individual owners. Presumably, this is done for the benefit of the majority. For example, in a co-op you may not be able to rent your unit, there may be pet restrictions and when you sell your shares the sale will be subject to board approval of the buyer.

• Manufactured housing—Also known as mobile homes, double-wides, etc., manufactured housing is treated by the marketplace more like a car than it is like a house. Mobile homes depreciate in value over time like cars do (rather than appreciating like a house), so you generally obtain a standard loan (like a car loan) rather than a mortgage. Manufactured housing is not the subject of this article.

You can choose to live in any type of housing. In general, the topics addressed in this article focus on the purchase of a house.

STEP 4: TALK TO A REALTOR AND START LOOKING AT HOUSES

There are two ways for you to search for a house. You can either look in the paper or in magazines advertising houses for sale by owner, or you can purchase a house directly from the owner. This route has the potential to be less expensive because an owner who sells his or her house does not have to pay a 7% Realtor commission. The disadvantage of this approach is the fact that it can be harder to find a home that you like because of a more limited selection and the difficulty in scheduling visits to each home.

The more common way to search for a house is to use a Realtor. Realtors have the following advantages:

• Access to a large selection of houses
• Entry to those houses at any time with a pass key
• Experience with neighborhoods
• Understanding of price distributions, taxes, problems, etc. across localities

Use whichever technique feels more comfortable. If you use a Realtor, take time to shop around and find someone whose style and market niche matches your own. One good way to do this is to seek recommendations from friends at work. Since you have a choice, choose a Realtor with extensive experience, and do not allow the Realtor to rush you.

STEP 5: FIND A HOUSE THAT YOU LIKE

After searching for a period of time, you will presumably find a house that you like in a reasonable location with a price that you can afford. It may take several months of searching to find such a house. At the moment you find it, make an offer immediately. It is not uncommon for a good house at a good price to be purchased by someone else if you hesitate for too long. This is the most common way to lose a house that you really like.

STEP 6: MAKE AN OFFER ON THE HOUSE

You make an offer to purchase a home by signing an *offer to purchase* form and writing a check. The check acts as a deposit and represents your commitment to follow through with the purchase should the offer be accepted. This money is normally referred to as *earnest money*. The check will be cashed, and the money will be placed in *escrow*. An escrow account is simply a bank account managed by a neutral third party, generally the Realtor or a lawyer. Should you be unable to follow through on your commitment to purchase, you will lose your earnest money. Should the offer not be accepted, the money will be returned to you. The amount of earnest money you will be asked to give varies, but it generally is 1% of the purchase price. This money is applied to the purchase price at the closing if the deal is successful.

A standard offer to purchase is a single sheet of paper. On one side are a number of blanks where you fill in your name and address, the offer price, the amount of earnest money and any conditions or contingencies on the offer. On the back are a number of standard condition paragraphs. For example, many localities require a termite inspection or bond on any house that is sold. There will be a standard paragraph covering this condition. Should the house fail to pass a termite inspection, the offer will

Buyer's Remorse

There is a funny thing that happens to many people once they make the offer. It is commonly known as *buyer's remorse*. It is the feeling that you have just done something extremely stupid and often occurs right after you sign your name and hand over the deposit check. Buyer's remorse is a natural human emotion. You can combat it to some extent by making up a written list of advantages and disadvantages for the house as part of your decision-making process. If this list is sound and true, when buyer's remorse kicks in you can refer to the list and reassure yourself that you did the right thing. Or maybe not. Just be aware that the phenomena is common and be prepared for it.

be nullified and your earnest money will be returned to you.

You can also add your own conditions and contingencies. One common condition added by most buyers is "subject to loan approval." That way, if you are denied a mortgage you get your earnest money back. Another common condition is "subject to a satisfactory home inspection by a licensed inspector." You, as the buyer, will have to pay for the inspection ($100 to $500), but you can use the results of the inspection to request repairs to the house prior to purchase. The seller pays for these repairs. You can stipulate that the seller will pay certain closing costs. This is important because it can save you a lot of money—see Step 12. You can, in fact, add any conditions that you like (contingent upon sale of an existing home, contingent upon repair of the roof, contingent upon removal of dead trees in the yard, etc.), but at the same time the seller has the option of rejecting them.

The most important part of the offer to purchase is the offer price. The seller places the house on the market with an *asking price*. You have the option to offer the asking price, or more, or less. If you know that you have three competitors and you really love the house, you may have an incentive to offer more than the asking price, but generally you will offer less. The amount that you offer depends on your personality and your negotiating strategy. Most houses sell within 90% to 95% of their asking price, but there are lots of exceptions.

STEP 7: NEGOTIATE A PRICE

The seller will either accept your offer, reject it or make a counter offer. If you receive a counter offer, you have the right to accept it or make a counter counter offer. At this point you negotiate with the seller until you reach a price and terms that are agreeable to both parties. If you do not reach agreement, the offer is eventually rejected, your earnest money is returned to you and you get to start over again. This is the second way that you can lose a house that you like.

STEP 8: SHOP FOR AND SELECT A MORTGAGE COMPANY

There are a number of good reasons to talk to a mortgage company prior to searching for a home (see Step 2). If you do not, then at this point you must start the process. Search for a company that has good rates and that seems to understand you and your financial situation. Ask several different banks or mortgage companies for quotes—the rate differences can be amazing. Your local paper will often publish a list of banks with the lowest rates in the area.

STEP 9: APPLY FOR A MORTGAGE

There are two different types of mortgages: fixed-rate and adjustable-rate (also known as ARMs). Fixed-rate mortgages come in 15-year and 30-year formats. Adjustable rate mortgages come in many different forms, but the most common form starts at some rate and adjusts itself every six months or year depending on changes in the prime rate.

Adjustable-rate mortgages generally start with a lower interest rate but carry the sometimes significant risk that your monthly payment will rise if interest rates rise. Fixed-rate mortgages are guaranteed to maintain the same monthly payment over the life of the loan.

Once you have chosen a mortgage company and a mortgage type, apply for the loan by filling out the appropriate paperwork and supplying all of the requested information.

STEP 10: WAIT FOR APPROVAL ON THE MORTGAGE

Approval may take several days or weeks, depending on the mortgage company. You may be asked to supply additional information during the process.

As discussed in Step 2, much of the nail-biting that accompanies the mortgage-approval process can be eliminated by getting your mortgage pre-approved. See Step 2 for more information, and talk to your mortgage company before starting your search for a house.

STEP 11: WAIT FOR THE CLOSING

At the time your offer is accepted by the seller, you and the seller will negotiate a closing date. With the mortgage approved, all that you can do is wait for the closing date, prepare to move and hope that nothing goes wrong.

STEP 12: ATTEND THE CLOSING AND SIGN ALL OF THE PAPERWORK

Finally, the closing day arrives. This should be a day of rejoicing because on this day you will become the proud owner of a new home. Unfortunately, this day is usually one of frustration and myriad small details unraveling. It is not exactly clear why this unraveling is so common, but it is definitely the case.

The closing normally occurs at the office of a lawyer. At the closing you will be required to pay quite a few fees, so bring your checkbook and make sure you have plenty of money in your account. The lawyer will normally provide you with a total closing cost prior to closing day, but be sure to have at least $1,000 over and above that cost available just in case.

The costs that you may be expected to pay at the closing may include the following, depending on how closing cost payments are negotiated when you make your offer to the seller:

- Loan origination and/or processing fees
- Points on the loan. Points are a front-end interest charge assessed by the lender. The more points you pay, the lower your monthly payment because you are paying your interest early. Each point represents 1% of the mortgage's value. It is not unusual for a lender to require you to pay two to three points at closing, and it is preferable for tax reasons to pay them yourself with a check rather than wrapping them into the mortgage.
- Up to one month's worth of mortgage payment, depending on the closing date
- The amount of the down payment (perhaps 10% of the home's purchase price)
- Lawyer fees
- City and county taxes
- Homeowners' fees (for townhouses, condos, etc.)
- Title search and title insurance fees
- Surveying fees
- Deed registration or filing fees
- Homeowners insurance fees (paid either prior to or at closing)
- And so on.

The total figure can add up to thousands of dollars. Some banks will let you roll these fees into the mortgage, but many will not. In that case you will have to have the cash available. You will also sign at least 15 pieces of paper.

STEP 13: MOVE IN TO YOUR NEW HOME

Presumably, this part is easy, and once you have moved in you can sit down on your couch and congratulate yourself. After several months or years of hard work you have successfully bought your part of the American Dream!

CHAPTER 33
Life Insurance

As a teenager, life insurance is something you do not need. However, at some point in your life you will be approached by life insurance salespeople. This encounter may happen as you enroll in college or just after exiting college. It is possible for an agent to pressure you in to buying a lot of life insurance that you do not need. This chapter will help prepare you for the encounter.

Life insurance is a form of insurance that pays a beneficiary in the event of someone's demise. Life insurance is a funny thing for three reasons:

1. You are never going to use a life insurance policy that you buy on your own life. After all, you will be dead when the policy pays out. Life insurance is therefore a gift that you give to someone else.

2. The chances of you dying "before your time" (say, before age 65) are pretty slim in this day and age. Therefore, the chances of a life insurance policy ever paying out at a time when it is really needed (for example, at age 40 when you have a spouse and two teenage daughters depending on your income) are slim as well.

3. However, it is guaranteed that you will die at some point, and there is a fair amount of emotion around this particular fact of life.

These three facts make life insurance work like no other insurance policy ever will. The emotional component attached to death is, in and of itself, enough the alter the entire sales process and the types of conversation that happen during the sale. If you do not know what life insurance is and why you might need it, there are two things that can happen should a life insurance salesperson happen to call:

1. You can be "guilted" in to purchasing insurance that you do not need.

2. You can be sold other components that are ancillary to life insurance at inflated prices.

The following sections give you a brief introduction to life insurance and how to purchase it rationally.

WHAT IS LIFE INSURANCE?

As mentioned at the beginning of the article, life insurance is a form of insurance that pays a beneficiary in the event of someone's demise. You purchase a specific death benefit when you purchase the policy. You might buy a $100,000 life insurance policy, for example. You then assign that $100,000 benefit to a specific beneficiary, like your spouse. Should you die during the term of the insurance, your spouse will receive $100,000.

TYPES OF LIFE INSURANCE

There are two types of life insurance: term life insurance and everything else. Term life insurance is pure, unadulterated life insurance. "Everything else" is term life insurance bonded to some sort of savings component. It is called various things by various companies: "whole life," "universal life," and so on.

Let's say that you would like to buy $100,000 worth of life insurance. If you bought that as a term policy you might pay $15 per month. If you bought it as whole life, you might pay $100 per month. Depending on the company selling the policy, you will be assured that the difference ($85 per month) will act as an investment that will "pay off the life insurance" and/or pay you a cash value at age 65.

The problem with everything besides term insurance is that the savings part is often inefficient. Also, it is only as secure as the company issuing the policy. You would potentially be much better off buying term insurance and depositing the $85 in a stock mutual fund each month. You might, over time, make much more money that way.

There is now also a growing "mini-life" industry. This industry tries to attach special-purpose life insurance policies to car loans, mortgages, etc. These policies are *dramatically* overpriced. If you feel that insurance to cover your mortgage is important, then comparison shop a normal term policy of the same value against the policy being offered by the mortgage company. You will be amazed at the price difference. Never buy mini-life policies until you comparison shop.

WHO NEEDS LIFE INSURANCE?

Some people truly need life insurance. For others it is a waste of money. Let's look at some scenarios to see who needs a policy. Let's say that you are a teenager living with your parents or you are a single man or woman living alone in an apartment. Do you need life insurance? No. Who, exactly, would be the beneficiary? There is no one in your life who is dependent on your income. The only reason you might buy life insurance is the same reason you would buy a lottery ticket—you might win. You might, after all, die young. And if you had a life insurance policy and died young, you could make someone very happy. Or you might buy a small policy to pay your funeral expenses at death. In that case $10,000 is all that you would need, and that would be one nice funeral. There are probably better things to do with your money while you are alive.

Let's say that you are a single man or woman living alone in a house with a $100,000 mortgage. Do you need life insurance? Maybe. The reason you might buy life insurance is to save your parents (or whomever else you have willed the house to) the problem of disposing of your estate. For example, imagine that you die. Your parents (or whomever) inherit the house. Now they want to dispose of the house, but it sits on the market for two years before selling. During that time they are having to pay the mortgage payments, and that might be a hardship. Therefore, you might buy a policy to cover the expected payments over (for example) two years, or the entire mortgage. The beneficiary would be the person to whom the house is willed.

Let's say that you are a married man or woman living with your spouse in an apartment or a house. Do you need life insurance? If your spouse does not work and you want to provide for your spouse should you die, then yes. If your spouse works but could not possibly support his or her current lifestyle should you die (for example, could not possibly pay the house payments), then yes. Otherwise, probably not. Having life insurance would be a nice remembrance if you were to die, but it is not essential.

What if you have kids and you provide income that they depend on? Then yes almost certainly you need life insurance unless you are rich enough to be "self insured." You need enough coverage to allow your spouse and children to live a comfortable life in the absence of your income. A life insurance professional or any number of freely available calculators on the World Wide Web can help you determine the appropriate coverage. See http://www.bygpub.com.

CHAPTER 34

Frugality Saves Money

F or most adults some form of frugality is a fact of life. For example, buying items on sale and using coupons are marks of frugality. Perhaps a better, more modern way to talk about frugality would be to call it *creative saving*. That's all it is. Frugality is the attempt to save money when you can, rather than spending it.

Why might you want to be frugal? As discussed in Chapter 29, most people start down the road of frugality because there is something they would like to have. They have set a financial priority or goal, and they are willing to save in other areas so they can reach the financial goal faster. The goal might be something as immediate as a new bedroom set or as long-term as early retirement. After you start reading this section,

---

fru'-gal, a. [OFr. frugal, from L. frugalis, economical, temperate] economical; not spending freely or unnecessarily; saving; sparing; not profuse or lavish.
[Source: *Webster's Ninth New Collegiate Dictionary*]

---

you may notice that your parents are using a lot of frugality techniques in their own lives. They are doing this so they have money to spend on other, more important or interesting things. Many of those things are things *you* want.

Other people begin down the road to frugality when they realize that Ben Franklin was wrong; a penny saved is not a penny earned. In fact, a penny saved in today's highly taxed environment is something like 1.4 pennies earned. Here is an example. Let's say that you want to buy a canoe that costs $1,000. If you earn the money to buy it by taking on an extra weekend job, you are actually going to have to earn something like $1,400 to buy the canoe. The extra $400 covers federal, state and FICA taxes. If you buy that same canoe by saving in other areas, then you only have to save $1,000 because you have already paid the taxes on that money. In addition, your weekends remain free for relaxation. Frugality is a great way to "earn" money.

In many cases it is easier to save money than it is to make more. For example, if you are home taking care of three young children while your husband is at work, it is probably not economical for you to get a job. The cost of child care and commuting can burn off all of the extra money a second wage-earner generates. In many cases a spouse's job actually costs a family money. Plus it can add an incredible amount of stress to your family life. In that case, instead of earning money focus on *saving* money. Make meals from scratch rather than buying prepared foods. Cut coupons. Grow a garden. You may find that you can "make" just as much money with savings as you would with a job and enjoy life more in the process.

There are five different classes of frugality. By reading the list below you can determine where you are on the frugality scale, and you can get some new saving ideas from the lists in each category. Here are the categories:

- Non-frugality—No attempt is made to save money.
- Obvious frugality—When a method of frugality is obvious to the casual observer, it is called obvious frugality.
- Serious frugality—Serious frugality involves the use of special knowledge or research that is perhaps not widely available to save money.
- Aggressive frugality—Aggressive frugality involves extra effort and creativity.
- Obsessive frugality—Obsessive frugality occurs when the frugal one begins to go outside the bounds of normal behavior to be frugal.

The sections below give you examples of each of these types of frugality.

NON-FRUGALITY

A non-frugal person is someone who lives his or her life without regard to prices. When a non-frugal person wants something he buys it, and that is the end of the story. There are very few people in America (besides teenagers) who are strictly non-frugal, but probably half of the population lives a majority of their lives in this way.

OBVIOUS FRUGALITY

Obvious frugality involves very little effort. You simply pay minor attention to the advertising messages swirling all around you, and you become aware that many of the messages are offering you opportunities to be frugal. The most common examples of obvious frugality include the following:

- Sales—If you are looking for a new chain saw and a store is offering a 20% sale on the one you want, why pay full price?
- Coupons—Most Sunday papers are full of coupons. Using one 20-cents coupon can seem pointless, but if you have ten 20-cents coupons and five 50-cents coupons and two 1-dollar coupons, you are saving $5.50. Do that every week and it adds up to almost $300 in a year.
- Calling in off-peak hours—Everyone knows that you pay less for a long distance phone call at night. Call your long distance carrier and find out when the rates change.
- Special credit cards—Many credit cards now give you free incentives. Discover® cards pay you money for each dollar you spend. Ford and GM give you discounts on new cars. Some gas stations give you free gas. Shop around and find a rebate card that suits your lifestyle.

SERIOUS FRUGALITY

Serious frugality requires extra effort on your part. You have to go out of your way or think long-term to earn these discounts, but the savings can be impressive.

- Comparison shopping—Any time you buy something significant (anything over $50), call around and see who has the best price. Many stores (especially discount appliance and electronics stores) have a "Lowest Price Guarantee." By pitting one retailer against another you can get the price even lower.
- Power discounts—Many power companies support programs to reduce peak demand. For example, our power company (Carolina Power and Light) has a "Time of Use" program; CP&L installs a special meter that can record two different types of power usage: on-peak and off-peak. Surprisingly, you can move a large percentage of your power consumption to off-peak hours if you are willing to pay attention to your consumption patterns, and you can save a lot of money as a result.
- Discount airline tickets—By calling 30 days in advance you can get massive discounts on airfare. Call a travel agent for details.

- Extra bonuses—Many companies will waive fees or give you extra bonuses if you ask nicely. For example, many credit card companies will waive the annual fee if you ask them. If you call your long distance carrier and threaten to switch, they may give you something to stay. It can't hurt to ask!
- Stock up—When something you need comes on sale, stock up. For example, say you have a dog. When its favorite dog food comes on sale, buy a month's supply (or more). You know that you will use it eventually. Do the same thing with any item that you use regularly and that has a long shelf life: breakfast cereals, Kleenex, soft drinks and so on.
- Make your lunch each day and avoid eating out—Eating out is expensive. You can make a meal for about a quarter of the cost of buying a meal in a restaurant. If you are trying to save big money, restaurant meals should be the first thing to go.
- Grow a garden—If you have the time, the space and the right personality, you can save a lot of money with a garden.
- Exercise with friends—Health clubs are expensive. Many cost over $300 per year. Instead of paying to exercise, organize a group of friends and run or ride your bicycles as a group.

AGGRESSIVE FRUGALITY

Aggressive frugality requires that you search for creative ways to save money. You will have to put in some extra effort to make use of these techniques, but if you are willing to move to a hard-core stance against spending these techniques can save you hundreds of dollars each year. These techniques can be especially useful if one spouse is at home while the other works.

Negotiating Prices

Many times a price that might seem to be fixed is actually negotiable. This phenomena is especially true on high-price items (cars, houses, etc.), one of a kind items (art, antiques, collectibles), items bought in large quantities or any item bought from a company having cash flow problems. For example, if you are going to do a lot of construction work, almost any building supply company will give you a contractor's discount. Any company in need of cash will often lower its price to get the cash needed to survive. You get a discount simply by asking for one. You might say, "What might I do to get a discount on this merchandise?" You then negotiate for terms. When you ask for a discount the answer is frequently "No," but you will be surprised how often it is "Yes" once you get in the habit of asking.

- Use a clothes line—It sounds old-fashioned. If you have an electric dryer, it probably costs you $1 or more each time you dry a load of clothes. If you run five loads a week, that's about $250 a year. You can save that money by drying most of your clothes with free sunshine.
- Shop at consignment stores and yard sales—Most large cities now have consignment stores that sell used clothing and household items at 50% to 75% discounts. If you don't mind buying something used, this can be an easy route to big savings.
- Buy no name brands or prepared products—Name brand items cost more because of advertising expenses. In addition, most prepared foods charge a premium for convenience. If you were to buy nothing but staple items like flour, sugar, salt, rice and meat and make everything yourself from scratch, you could potentially save hundreds of dollars a year.
- Put it on your Christmas list—If you want something and you know your family is searching for a Christmas gift for you, put off purchasing the item and instead ask for it for Christmas or a birthday.

CONCLUSION

This part of the book has discussed a number of financial topics and issues that are important to adults. As you can see, financial life is interesting but can be complicated. The time to start learning about this stuff is now, as a teenager. That way you understand your options and obligations before you jump into things unprepared. After reading this section, you may wish to go out and read any number of books on personal finance so that you can get ready for real life.

PART 7

The Other Facts

A wide variety of other facts will be useful to you as you work your way toward becoming an adult. This section lists a number of other important facts of life.

CHAPTER 35

Laws, Police and Lawyers

The most frustrating things in the world to many teenagers are all the rules, laws and restrictions that seem to impose limits on everybody. A teenager is faced with a wide variety of limitations:

- Speed limits
- Noise ordinances
- Minimum drinking age
- Community standards
- Curfews
- Social etiquette
- Bureaucratic rules, like those at the Department of Motor Vehicles
- Building codes
- Drug prohibitions
- Closing times
- Truancy rules
- Licenses and permits
- "No Trespassing" signs
- Helmet and seat belt laws
- Application deadlines
- Dress codes
- Parental rules and restrictions
- School regulations
- And on and on and on

It seems like every time you turn around someone else is telling you what you can and cannot do. It may also seem like a large number of these laws and rules are ridiculous and unneeded. For example, why are there building codes? If you want to build something, why can't you simply build it rather than having to read and abide by the uniform electrical code, the uniform plumbing code, etc.? Why are there seat belt laws? Why can't people play their stereos as loud as they want?

Rules, restrictions and laws are all facts of life. There is nothing that you can do about them but accept them. However, they are much easier to accept if you understand their intent and realize that they are open to change.

IT'S A LOT BETTER THAN IT USED TO BE

One thing to keep in mind is that, at least for teenagers, things are a lot less restrictive than they used to be. The following are the "Regulations for Dormitories" that were posted on every student's door at North Carolina State University in 1905:

REGULATIONS FOR DORMITORIES

Duties of Students. - To be present at all classes, exercises, formations and inspections; to observe the college regulations; to avoid whatever wastes time and money, or damages health and character; to do unto others as you would be done by.

REGULATIONS.

Study Hours. - 8:15 AM to 1:15 PM - 2:15 PM to 4:15 PM - 7 to 10:30 PM

Inspections. - PM 7:00, 9:00, 10:30; Sunday, breakfast formation; special inspections at any time.

Rooms. - Swept, tidied and bed made by 8:00 AM and kept so; doors unlocked 8:00 to 10:30 AM; each occupant responsible for room and contents.

Uniform. - Worn at all times (except during work in Barns, shops, laboratory, etc.) by all students (except winter course students and specials over 21 who room and board outside of college).

Liberty. - *For all*, Saturday PM 1:30 to 6:00; Sunday, 8:30 AM to 1:00 PM, 1:30 to 6:00 PM; 7:15 to 10:30 PM.

Juniors - Friday, 7:15 to 10:30 PM; sign liberty book (Friday night).

Seniors - Two evenings (according to choice), 7:15 to 10:30 PM; sign liberty book (nights of choice).

Vaccination. - Required of all students

Withdrawal. - Any student not employing his time profitably to himself and to the college.

Dismissal. - For cheating, falsehood, stealing, insubordination, hazing, drunkenness, gambling and other gross offenses.

DEMERITS.

1 demerit for tardy, loafing in study hours, delaying to send in excuse.

2, absent dinner or supper formation, untidy room.

3, absent breakfast or chapel formation.

4, absent 7:00 PM or 9:00 PM inspection; not wearing uniform, not signing liberty book, lights after 10:45 PM.

10, absent 10:30 PM inspection; absent class, shop, drill; violating liberty in daytime, smoking cigarettes or having same in room or possession; playing cards or dice or having same in room or possession; having in possession or room pistol, dirk or other deadly weapon.

25, absent after 11:30 PM, violating liberty at night.

50 to 100, very disorderly or scandalous conduct; using liquor or having same in possession or in room; interference with others.

100 demerits in one year will require withdrawal.

If these were the restrictions imposed on college students at a public college, you can imagine what the restrictions for high school students must have looked like in 1905. The point is, teenagers are freer today than they have ever been in the history of the world. Whether that is a good or bad thing is a topic frequently debated by adults.

THE PURPOSE OF LAWS AND RULES

Although it may seem at times that laws and rules are nothing but obstacles to your freedom, most laws and rules have legitimate reasons for their existence. There are three reasons for a law or rule to exist:

- *A law exists because a majority of the people in this country agrees with it.* Why can't you walk down the street naked on a hot summer day? Because a majority of people in this country don't want to look at you. It's as simple as that.
- *A law exists because it promotes the health or safety of everyone in society.* Seat belt laws are enforced in all 50 states because seat belts save a lot of lives. A majority of people will normally support life-saving rules even if they infringe on personal freedoms to some extent. All building codes and health ordinances exist to protect the public in this same way.

- *A law exists because it helps society to function more smoothly.* Traffic lights are a perfect example of this sort of law. Because people obey traffic lights society works efficiently. If everyone did whatever they felt like doing at every intersection, we would have anarchy.

You can see an example of the second type of law when looking at building codes. Building codes are a classic example of rules that are put in place and enforced to protect the public health and safety. They demonstrate how changes take place over time as society learns new things. They also show why, upon your arrival on the scene, things seem like a complicated mess.

Take the building codes for plumbing. Let's say you want to put a toilet in a house. Two or three hundred years ago this was not a possibility—everyone used outhouses. If you visit the Governor's mansion in Williamsburg, VA, you will see that even England's high colonial governor used a pair of three-holer outhouses located at the back of the formal garden. Eventually, public water supplies and pressurized well systems allowed people to have indoor plumbing, and this allowed for the addition of indoor toilets. A toilet has to flush somewhere, so sewer systems evolved.

Why can't you run the sewer line from a toilet or a sink out of the side of the house so it spills on the ground? That certainly would be easy and inexpensive, but people learned fairly quickly that human waste spilled on the ground smells bad and leads to incredible disease problems. Therefore, the idea of septic tanks and sewer systems evolved. The uniform plumbing code lists hundreds of rules for septic tank installation. These rules ensure that tanks work properly over many years.

Now that you have a septic tank, you can add sewer lines from the sink or toilet to the septic tank. Say you tried this approach:

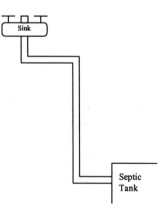

The problem with this approach is that as the septic tank fills up with stuff it produces a rather malodorous cloud of fumes. These fumes float from the septic tank up the sewer line to the sink and into the bathroom. Not good. Therefore, plumbing codes require a "P-trap" at every drain opening, as shown here:

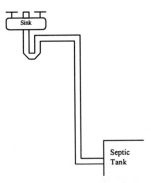

You may have wondered why you find these funny loops of pipe under every sink in your house. The idea is that water gets trapped in the "P." This water blocks the fumes from the septic tank and keeps them from entering into the bathroom. Unfortunately, a P-trap alone does not solve the problem because it turns out that the fumes in a septic tank are under pressure. The fumes simply bubble through the water in the trap and cause the same problem. Therefore, there is the concept of a *vent pipe,* which allows the pressure to escape, as shown here:

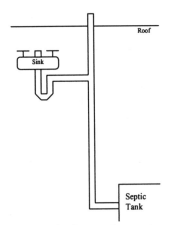

You may have wondered why houses have pipes sticking up out of the roof. They are vent pipes to relieve the pressure so that P-traps can do their jobs. It turns out vents also break vacuums so water flows down the pipes faster.

Besides covering P-traps and vent pipes, the uniform plumbing code specifies all sorts of other things:

- The required diameters for pipes
- The allowed materials for pipes
- The types of joints you can use
- The necessary supports for pipes
- The angle at which pipes must fall
- The longest distance for lateral pipes
- And on and on and on through hundreds of pages

The code seems huge and totally ridiculous when you first see it because you missed the 100 years of evolution that have brought us the code we have today. The thing you realize as an adult is that, instead of being ridiculous, all of these rules *actually work*. When plumbers follow all the rules, they are able to create extremely reliable and safe plumbing systems. Over time new rules get added as people realize funny little quirks and nuances. These new rules prevent problems in the future, and each one makes the code a little bigger and better. Our entire legal system has grown in exactly the same way over the course of several hundred years.

Although it may not seem like it to you, nearly every law or rule has a reason behind it. It either promotes health or safety, helps society to run more smoothly or supports something a majority of the people in this country believe is a good idea. If you find a law where none of these three things are true, then it is time to change the law.

LAWYERS

A lawyer is a person trained to understand our legal system. Because the legal system has grown steadily more complicated over the last several hundred years, a lawyer is almost essential whenever you need to negotiate a legal problem.

Let's say that you are unfortunate one day and are pulled over for speeding. Unless you were going 100 miles per hour, you will generally be allowed to either mail in the fine or appear in court. What should you do? You should get a lawyer and appear in court. Even though a lawyer may cost several hundred dollars, it is worth it. Here are two facts of life that you must keep in mind:

- The fine on the ticket may be only $50 or $100, but if the violation shows up as points on your car insurance your insurance will go up. A lot. That is a fact of life. It may be that you are not paying for your car insurance right now, and in fact have no idea how much car insurance costs. Therefore, you might be thinking, "What do I care?" If your parents end up paying $300 a year more for your insurance, that is $300 a year they can't spend on something else, and thus it is $300 they cannot spend on you (see Chapter 1). Or they may ask that you pay the increase, and then you really will care.

- Points on your insurance last three years in most states. Eventually you will have to pay the insurance bill, and then it really will be your problem. You will be paying $300 extra a year for no good reason. Because the rise in insurance rates greatly exceeds the fine on the ticket, your goal is to avoid the insurance penalty if possible.

When you go to court without a lawyer you will be asked to plead "innocent" or "guilty." If you were innocent you would not have been issued the ticket. Therefore, you are guilty and you might as well have mailed in the fine. With a lawyer present, however, a whole set of extra options opens up. Normally a lawyer can do a variety of things to eliminate the points. You will still pay the fine and court costs, as well as the lawyer's bill, but it will end up costing much less over time than an insurance premium increase.

Why can a lawyer get you off the hook? The legal system in this country is incredibly complex. A lawyer is a person experienced with the legal system. The lawyer knows the DA, the judge, all the options and loopholes available in the legal system and all of the areas of flexibility. You hire a lawyer to gain access to this knowledge.

Is this a fair system? Should we have a legal system so complicated that a specialist, in the form of a lawyer, is required to help a normal citizen negotiate it? Should a specialist be able to charge money for this service? Is it fair that rich people, who have the extra money to afford a lawyer, have greater access to this sort of help than other people? These are all good questions. However, it is a fact of life that the system currently works this way. If you don't want to deal with lawyers then don't break the law. It's as simple as that. Or work to change the system.

Laws and Rules Change

Look back at the "Regulations for Dormotories" shown earlier in this chapter. You may have noticed that those rules no longer apply. If you are a teenager and think those rules are dumb, you should thank all of the college students who protested in the 1960s for the elimination of most of those rules, the elimination of the concept of *in loco parentis*, the creation of such things as coed dorms and so on. It really *is* possible to change things.

Laws and rules are constantly changing. Because you are a teenager and have probably not been through a major change cycle, it may seem to you that this statement is untrue. However, rules are constantly in flux as the ideas, principles and mood of the majority changes. For example, it was illegal for a woman to vote 100 years ago. No one would consider denying women the right to vote today.

One of the most interesting changes I have noted in my lifetime has been the change in smoking rules and regulations. When I was a kid people could and did smoke anytime, anywhere, in any public place. They smoked in airplanes, restaurants, offices, movie theaters, meeting rooms and so on. There were absolutely no restrictions on smoking because a majority of adults in the United States smoked. Look at how things have changed. It is now illegal to smoke in virtually any public area. People stand outside of office buildings to smoke. It was an amazing transformation to watch. In terms of social change timelines it happened very quickly. The thing that caused this change was the fact that smokers lost their majority in the population. As people have realized how unhealthy smoking is, people have stopped smoking in record numbers. Once non-smokers held a decided majority, all the laws changed.

Let's say you find a law or rule that you think is unreasonable. To change it, all you have to do is convince a majority of voters (meaning adults) to agree with you and work toward a change through your congressman or other elected officials. It is really as simple as that.

DEALING WITH POLICE OFFICERS

Let's say you are driving down the road one night minding your own business. Suddenly, flashing lights appear behind you and you hear a siren. You are being pulled over for speeding. What should you do?

When dealing with a police officer, for whatever reason, it is important to keep two things in mind:

- It is the job of police officers to enforce the laws of society. As discussed earlier in this chapter, the laws of society are agreed to by a majority of the people who make up the society. Therefore, what the police force does is a good thing.
- Society has empowered police officers with absolute authority. That means if you give an officer a good reason to do so, he or she has the right and the power to kill you. To avoid having to resort to that level of force, police officers have other options. For example, they can handcuff you and take you to jail. This is not a minor amount of power.

- Police officers, by the nature of the job they hold, have to deal with a lot of rather difficult and often deadly people on a regular basis. When police face any armed assailant, from a drug dealer down to a drunk husband, the individual officers are risking their lives. This makes the job of a police officer different from other jobs—things are taken much more seriously. A police officer in every situation is performing an extremely intricate calculus to determine what level of response is appropriate. Into these calculations goes a healthy margin for personal safety as well as for the spouse and kids at home. If an officer is going to make a mistake, it will often be in favor of too much force rather than too little. Anything else would be suicidal for the officer.

From this discussion you can see that whenever you look at a police officer, you are looking at a person who has the power to take away your freedom or your life and who has every reason to do so immediately rather than waiting. A person with that kind of power is not someone you deal with trivially. This is the kind of person that you treat with maximum respect all of the time, even if he or she seems to be wrong at the moment. To do anything else is extremely dangerous and simply asking for trouble.

When you are pulled over for speeding, you should sit in your seat. You should get respectful very quickly. You should place both hands in clear view on the steering wheel so that it is obvious you are not armed. You should make no sudden movements. You should, in fact, do nothing unless you are specifically told to do it. And you should answer every question with "Sir" or "Ma'am." It is as simple as that. If the police officer is wrong it is probably best to simply keep your mouth shut, cooperate in every way and deal with it later in court.

There was a good story that made all the national news shows and papers in November 1996. It demonstrates why this sort of thing is important. A woman saw a police officer writing a ticket for a parked car at an expired parking meter, so she put a coin in the meter thinking she was being helpful to the person getting the ticket. It turns out that this act is illegal in many cities, and it was illegal in the city she happened to be standing in. Does it make sense that this act is illegal? It doesn't matter. This gets back to the whole idea behind laws—at some point a majority of the public, or a majority of people elected by a majority of the public, felt that this sort of law represented a good idea. Once it is a law it is a law until you change it, and that is simply how our society works.

So, what we have is a police officer standing on the street with a woman who has broken a law. It is not the officer's job to judge the validity of the law. It is the officer's job *to enforce the laws created by society*. The officer told the woman about her violation. If the woman, at that point, had simply gotten immediately respectful and apologized, it is likely the incident would have ended. However, the woman did not do that because she did not understand how the world works.

The officer asked for her ID. She refused. At that point she had committed a serious offense. The officer was forced to escalate and told her she was under arrest. He had no other choice. If the woman had gotten respectful at that point, she would have had problems but they would have been relatively minor. She did not. Instead she attempted to turn and walk away. At that point, of course, the officer had to escalate again and break out the handcuffs because she was resisting arrest. The woman started screaming. And so on. She eventually ended up in jail.

At every single point in the transaction the woman did the wrong thing and the police officer did what his job requires him to do. He simply reacted logically to the woman's actions. The point of all of this is simple: this woman wasted a tremendous amount of her time because she did not treat a police officer with the level of respect that a police officer deserves. If you have a lot of free time in your life that you want to spend in jail, you can follow in her path. In general, however, it is not worth it. Police officers act the way they do because it is their job. Understand that and respect it. It is a fact of life.

CHAPTER 36

Sports are Eternal

S ports are a fundamental element of most societies on this planet. The human obsession with sports stretches way back in time to the giant Roman coliseums built before the birth of Christ. Sports are central in many different ways.

How important are sports in American society? Just look around you:

- Look at the number of coliseums, stadiums and gymnasiums there are in America.
- Look at how many people attend major league, college and high school sporting events.
- Look at how much money advertisers pour into advertising during sporting events.
- Look how many people you know watch the Super Bowl. Of the top 25 TV shows (in terms of number of viewers) of all time, almost half of them are Super Bowls.
- Look at how many people attend and watch the Olympics.
- Look at how popular sports figures are.

Once you accept that sports are fact of life and that you cannot change this fact, a lot of other things make sense. Why do athletes get so much attention? Why do girls hang all over athletes? Why do high schools that may have really crappy libraries and no computers have really fancy football stadiums? Because sports are an immutable fact of life.

BECOMING AN ATHLETE

What if you are a scrawny, wimpy teenager like I was, and hate sports and athletes? I feel your pain. I was a scrawny, wimpy, uncoordinated teenager. I hated PE. I could not climb the rope or do chin-ups or make a basket or anything else. Let me fill you in on a secret I learned. *All of that was an illusion.* The reason I could not do those things is because I *thought* I could not do those things. There was absolutely no other reason. Let me tell you how I learned that. At about age 16 my mother gave me a 10-speed bicycle as a Christmas present. I discovered that I really liked to ride my bicycle. I can't explain why—I just liked it. Anyone can ride a bike, it is almost impossible to look uncoordinated and it felt good. It was a good way to blow off excess energy/ anger/frustration. So I started riding every day. One day I rode 10 miles. Then 15. And so on.

Eventually, I worked up to where I could ride over 100 miles in one day. This was incredibly inspiring. Imagine; a scrawny, wimpy guy had gotten himself in good enough shape to ride 100 miles in a day. No one else in my school could do that. Of course, no one cared either, but that didn't matter.

> *I was a scrawny, wimpy, uncoordinated teenager. I hated PE. I could not climb the rope or do chin-ups or make a basket or anything else. Let me fill you in on a secret I learned. All of that was an illusion.*

Once I realized I could do that, I tried to do a chin-up. I found that if I really tried, I could do one. But I did it every day and two weeks later I could do two. Eventually, there came a time when I could do 20 in a row. Then I did push-ups. Then I started running. One weekend in college a friend of mine and I rode our bikes from Albany, NY to Utica, NY (about 100 miles) and back because he wanted to impress a girl at Hamilton college. When we arrived in Utica we played a game of racquet ball with her! That's pretty good for a wimp.

By the time I got out of college I could have been an athlete. I loved exercising and sports. The question I eventually arrived at is, "Why in the world couldn't I do all of this in high school??? I could have kicked some butt!" *The ONLY reason I could not do this stuff in high school is because I had convinced myself I could not. It was all a mental illusion brought on by a lack of confidence.* It turns out that confidence in yourself is 90% of everything. See Chapter 14 for a discussion.

What should you do if you are an unathletic teenager right now? I would suggest that you try to become an athlete. Here is how I would do it. Pick a sport that you think you might like. If you like being alone, pick a lone wolf kind of sport. If you like competition, pick a competitive sport. If you like nature, pick an outdoor sport. If you like groups, pick a team sport. There's a million to choose from:

- Running
- Bike riding

- Golf
- Volleyball
- Basketball
- Football
- Baseball
- Hockey
- Figure skating
- Tennis
- Racquet ball
- Weight lifting
- Skiing
- Snow boarding
- And so on

Now start doing it, every day if you can. You will look silly when you start. You may be in terrible shape. You may lose every game. Ignore all of that. Just keep at it for several months, and one day you will notice something happening. You will actually get good enough to where you are able to do something extraordinary. Then you will be able to do two extraordinary things. And so on. The key is to keep at it, practicing every day for a long period of time. If it doesn't work out with the first sport your try, try another.

The advantage of doing this as a teenager is the fact that you have lots of free time to practice, and your high school has all of the equipment for you to use. Later in life you will be able to use your skill in whatever sport you choose, and it will be a joy to you. It will also help you keep your weight down. Here's a fun fact: If you take the time to get really good at a sport as a teenager, you will still be good at that sport when you are 50. Your body somehow remembers. Becoming good at something as

Golf

Let's say that you are interested in becoming more athletic, but you don't know which sport to pick. If you are picking a sport at random, then you might as well pick one that will have a lot of benefit later in life. Who plays football once they get out of college? No one. The sport to pick for later in life is GOLF. Let your friends laugh, and just blow them off. Become a golf expert. Here's why: More major business deals are transacted during a golf game than you can imagine in your wildest dreams. Golf is central to the American business scene. If you were to start in high school and really work at it, you would be a tremendous golfer by the time you got a real job. That single skill will be surprisingly valuable and make a big difference in your life. Take my word for it. If you don't believe me, go ask some of the successful business people you know.

a teenager pays a lifetime of rewards, and it is much easier to pick up any sport as a teenager.

Keep these things in mind:

- The only thing preventing you from being an athlete is your mind.
- The thing that makes you uncoordinated is lack of practice, and if you practice enough you can become coordinated at any sport.
- There is a lot of good that comes from sports (see the next section).
- Sports will help your physique.
- Sports are a great way to build confidence.

SPORTS AND CHARACTER

One thing you will often hear about sports is the fact that they "build character." I know when I was a teenager my question was, "What the heck does that mean?" Let me give you some examples to help you understand this concept:

- Sports build discipline—The act of practicing for a sport day in and day out—even when you don't want to, even when the weather is bad, even when you have something else you would rather be doing—teaches you discipline. It teaches you to have the self-control necessary to do things, even when you would rather not. This is an extremely important skill in many other parts of life, particularly once you start working.
- Sports build commitment—Once you commit to a sport, you have to keep at it day in and day out if you want to keep participating. For example, once you commit to the football team, you have to stay committed to the team and your training unless you want to be dropped from the team.
- Team sports build trust—When you work in a team sport, you learn to trust other people on the team and they learn to trust you. That level of trust is rare outside the area of sports for most high school students.
- Sports help you understand winning and losing and help build a positive mental attitude—When you play a sport you go through natural cycles of winning and losing. Those are the same cycles you will go through in life as you succeed and fail at the things that you try. Sports, therefore, prepare you for the natural cycles of life. Sports also teach you how to win and lose graciously.
- Sports teach you pain—One aspect of sports is pain. Being able to understand pain and work through it to win is a discipline that is extremely useful to have. The only way to understand pain and to train yourself to endure it in normal life is sports.

- Sports teach you to work on a team—Team sports show you how to interact with team members and how to work inside a team. This ability makes you much more valuable in a business environment because every business is a team.

Let's go back to a central question of all scrawny high school guys: Why do girls hang all over athletes? There is a component that cannot be denied: in general, athletes are a lot more confident than non-athletes, and people naturally gravitate toward confident people. That is a fact of life. See Chapter 14 for details.

CHAPTER 37

Life is Short

L ife is short. That is a fact of life. It is impossible to understand this simple fact as a teenager, however. As a teenager you look at senior citizens and you *know* you will never look like that. You look at people like your parents—people in their 30s and 40s—and you cannot imagine ever being that old. The thought of looking just two years down the road is probably difficult.

Most teenagers feel they are immortal. That is one of the great advantages of being a teenager (see Chapter 16). This feeling of immortality will last perhaps into your 20s, then it will vanish as reality sets in. Since it is impossible, I won't attempt to convince you that you, too, will one day be 60 or 80. Or even 30. However, let me try to give you an analogy to help you understand why you feel the way you do about life.

Let's say you are standing in a desert. You are standing next to a gigantic tank that holds 30,000 gallons of water. The tank is 11 or 12 feet in diameter and about 40 feet tall. The tank is full to the brim. This is your drinking water. Every day you drink about a gallon of water.

Let's say that someone walks up to you and says, "Hey, can I have a gallon of water?" Your response would probably be, "Sure, why not?" In fact, if someone asked you for 100 gallons of water, your reaction might be the same. You've got 30,000 gallons after all, and there is nothing for you to do with it but drink it. What do you care? If you spill a little water, it doesn't matter either.

As you go through life drinking about a gallon of water a day, you begin to notice something. Each day it doesn't seem like you are taking anything out of the tank, but over time you can see that the level in the tank is getting lower. You look in one day and the tank is only half-full. Then it is only a quarter full. Then there is only an inch in the bottom of the tank. At that point, how much would a gallon of water be worth to you? Quite a bit, because now you can see that your water is scarce: you can see the end of the supply looming in the near future. One fateful day you extract the last drop from the tank, and you realize that today is the day you will die. You are, after all, standing in a desert. And that night you die.

The number 30,000 is significant. If you assume you will live to be about 82, there are 30,000 days in your life. Right now your tank of water is full. If you are 15 you have only used about 5,500 gallons, so water seems to be plentiful. In fact, the supply of water seems to be infinite and you feel immortal. However, each day you live you drink a gallon from your tank, and there is no way to add any more once you use it.

What you often don't realize as a teenager is that there are a lot of easy ways to put holes in your tank or spill large quantities of water on the ground. As you are spilling the water you don't really care because you have so much water it seems infinite. However, you can easily spill 20 or 30 years of water as a teenager. That water will be extremely valuable later in life. When you get older there are going to be lots of important things that you will want to enjoy: your children, your

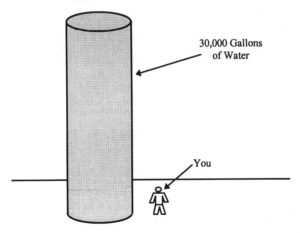

30,000 Gallons
of Water

You

grandchildren, your spouse, your friends, your retirement. At that point water will be extremely valuable to you, and you will realize how foolish you were to spill it as a teenager. But at that point there will be absolutely nothing that you can do to get it back. You will die way too early.

The following sections look at the three most common ways for people to waste life.

SMOKING IS STUPID

One of the best ways to shorten your life is to smoke. If you take up smoking as a teenager, you might spill perhaps 10,000 of your 30,000 gallons of water.

Ask any adult what they think about smoking. *Any* adult, smoker or non. If you ask non-smokers, what they will tell you is that smoking is a bad habit. If you ask smokers, they will also tell you is that smoking is a bad habit and they wish they never started. You really should try this—go to an office building where there are older smokers standing outside and ask them what they think about the habit. You will learn a lot.

Imagine that I come up to you one day at school and we have the following conversation:

Me: Hi, How's it going?
You: Fine.
Me: Hey, I've got this new thing I'd like you to try.
You: Tell me more.
Me: Well, it's a pill I think you will want to start taking.
You: What does this pill do?
Me: First of all, it is a known carcinogen. It is extremely likely you will get lung cancer due to this pill, for example. It is going to cause a lot of other short- and long-term health problems as well. It will make your breath, hair and clothes stink. It will make a mess of your car. You will take this pill about 40 times a day. This pill, by the way, is addictive. Once you start taking it, it will be extremely difficult to stop. And a supply of pills will cost about $2 to $4 a day, depending on where you buy them.
You: I have to pay for this??? Are you kidding??? This pill sounds absolutely disgusting!!! Why in the world would I want to take it???"
Me: It will make you think you are cool.
You: Oh, well, why didn't you say so? Sign me up! Where can I get some???

Two other good reasons not to smoke:

- An average smoker who starts at age 15, dies at age 60 and smokes two packs a day will consume 657,000 cigarettes. 657,000 cigarette butts is disgusting.
- Assume each cigarette costs a nickel, and assume the money wasted on cigarettes was instead deposited in a mutual fund earning 10%. The value of the money wasted on cigarettes during a lifetime is about $500,000. If you assume cigarettes cost a dime each the value exceeds $1,000,000. There *must* be a better way to spend that money.

Besides that, cigarettes can significantly shorten your life. Although you likely don't care about that now, you most certainly will in the future. That is a fact of life.

TV IS A WASTELAND

One thing you will notice about successful adults is that they watch far less TV than unsuccessful adults. A successful adult thinks, "Life is short! Who has time to waste it on TV?" There are three problems with TV that lead to this trend:

1. The rate of information transfer for TV is very low when compared to the data rate for reading. For example, the transcript for an hour-long educational show like Nova is very thin, and you can read it in 10 or 20 minutes. If you want to learn something, it is almost always faster to read about it. If you want to know what is happening in the world, read the newspaper. It is always much more detailed than the TV news and you can control exactly what you read.

> *The average American spends about 2 hours a day watching TV. Teenagers spend far more. If you stop watching TV today and use the time in a productive way, you can begin being far more successful in life.*

2. Most of the stuff on TV is incredibly mindless crap that has no value. It is either harmless but a total waste of time, or it is harmful. It is harmful when it repeatedly injects negative thoughts into your brain. For example, a typical child is exposed to 8,000 murders on television by the time he or she finishes elementary school. A typical teenager sees 200,000 acts of violence on TV by age 18. The vast majority of people in normal life are exposed to zero murders and very few violent acts. TV makes violence seem normal and acceptable. What value does that have?

3. TV transmits commercials that lead you to buy things you would neither want nor need in the absence of TV. These items are a waste. See Chapter 29 for details.

The following quote is interesting:

I invite you to sit down in front of your television set when your station goes on the air, and stay there. You will see a vast wasteland—a procession of game shows, violence, audience participation shows, formula comedies about totally unbelievable families... blood and thunder ... mayhem, violence, sadism, murder ... private eyes, more violence, and cartoons ... and, endlessly,   commercials—many   screaming,   cajoling,   and offending.

This quote was made by FCC chairman Newton N. Minow to the National Association of Broadcasters. What is funny about this quote is the fact that it was made in 1961. If anything, TV has gotten worse rather than better since then.

The average American spends about 2 hours a day watching TV. That is the equivalent of over 18 weeks of 8-hour days. This is time, and life, that is *completely wasted*. Read instead, take a walk, get a part-time job, learn to play an instrument, create a work of art, talk to other people, take up a sport (see Chapter 36) or do *anything* constructive. Eighteen weeks of 8-hour days is a gigantic amount of time, and you would be amazed at what you could accomplish if you used that time constructively. If you stop watching TV today and use the newly free time in a productive way, you can begin being far more successful in life.

The following facts are published by an organization called "TV-free America" (http://www.essential.org/tvfa/). They are enlightening:

- Number of 30-second commercials seen in a year by an average child: 20,000
- Number of minutes per week that parents spend in meaningful conversation with their children: 38.5
- Number of minutes per week that the average child watches television: 1,680
- Percentage of children ages 6-17 who have TVs in their bedrooms: 50
- Percentage of day care centers that use TV during a typical day: 70
- Hours per year the average American youth spends in school: 900 hours
- Hours per year the average American youth watches television: 1500
- Percentage of Americans that regularly watch television while eating dinner: 66
- Number of murders seen on TV by the time an average child finishes elementary school: 8,000
- Number of violent acts seen on TV by age 18: 200,000
- Percentage of Americans who believe TV violence helps precipitate real life mayhem: 79

Here is a thought experiment to try. Imagine that you had been brought up without ever watching television. Your parents then take you to a grocery store. Would you want Lucky Charms? Sugar Pops? Kellogg's Frosted Flakes? No. You would not have any preferences when you walk down the cereal aisle. You would try some cereals until you found one you that suited you. Now imagine going to a toy store. Would you want GI Joe? Barbie? Any action figure or doll? No! In fact, you would think that a lot of these things were stupid. *TV commercials make you want things that you would never want or need otherwise.* Simply stop watching television. It will be hard at first. You may not be able to comprehend life without TV, but after a few months your head will clear and you will find that you enjoy life a whole lot more. Try it and see.

DRUGS ARE WORTHLESS

And then there are drugs and drug addiction: heroin, cocaine, amphetamines and all the rest. No successful person uses drugs. That is a fact of life. Drugs make you stupid for long periods of time, and that limits your potential for success.

The promise of drugs is a "high" or a "feeling of euphoria." For example, heroin causes a euphoric "rush." I have heard it described as "better than sex." I have heard it described as "like being in heaven." All kinds of things. The problem is that the feeling always comes at a cost once the high ends. The cost is a feeling of depression of greater magnitude. You cannot have the high without the despair or depression. You can safely ignore anyone who tells you otherwise. So you are forced to either maintain the high or absorb the despair. Unfortunately, the despair lasts far longer than the high does. So what have you gained?

Drugs are a lot different from sex, and they certainly are not "better than sex." If you have a wonderful night of passion with your spouse, you will feel very good for a long time afterward. Drugs are nothing like this. With drugs you get a rush, then you crash and burn. The only way out is to take the drug again. This is why you see people on cocaine binges or week-long sessions with amphetamines. To stop means despair.

What, you might ask, is the point? If the high is *always* followed by despair, what have you gained? In fact, you have lost. The euphoria is addictive and causes you to crave it.

There simply is no value, or point, in getting started with drugs. Simply walk away from the people who tell you otherwise.

CHAPTER 38

People Have Opinions

An opinion is a position that a person takes on a particular topic. Some people are very strong and unmoving in their opinions, while others are open-minded and willing to listen to other points of view (even if they continue to disagree with them). Everyone has opinions, and the range of opinions is often amazing.

As a card-carrying member of the human race you get to form your own opinions. As a card-carrying American you have the right to express

o·pin·ion (ə-pĭn′yən) *noun*
A belief or conclusion held with confidence but not substantiated by positive knowledge or proof: *"The world is not run by thought, nor by imagination, but by opinion"* (Elizabeth Drew).
A judgment based on special knowledge and given by an expert: *a medical opinion.*
A judgment or an estimation of the merit of a person or thing: *has a low opinion of braggarts.*
The prevailing view: *public opinion.*
Law. A formal statement by a court or other adjudicative body of the legal reasons and principles for the conclusions of the court.
Synonyms: opinion, view, sentiment, feeling, belief, conviction, persuasion. These nouns signify something a person believes or accepts as being sound or true. *Opinion* is applicable to a judgment, especially a personal judgment, based on grounds insufficient to rule out the possibility of dispute.
[Source: *The American Heritage Dictionary*]

your opinions openly as part of your right to free speech. You get to be strong or subtle in how you express your opinions. That is your choice.

What a lot of teenagers seem to miss initially is that the opinions they hold are not universal, nor are they binding on the rest of the people on the planet. Note these two important points:

- Opinions are formed out of data and information that you obtain in the course of living. Therefore, different people hold different opinions based on their life experiences. Someone who grew up in poverty might have a different opinion of welfare than someone who grew up in a mansion, for example. A mother whose child dies because of a drunk driver might hold opinions on this topic that differ wildly from those of a college student at a party.

- Many of your opinions will change throughout your life as you gather more data and experiences.

Another thing teenagers often miss is that people are different. All you have to do is walk into any grocery store to see that. Why do we need 700 different kinds of potato chips? Six hundred different kinds of breakfast cereal? Forty-seven different kinds of hair coloring in 14,734 shades? Why do we need hair coloring at all for that matter? We have all of these variations because people are different. These differences have a big impact on the opinions that different people hold.

OPINIONS AND SOCIETY

At any given moment there are certain "hot button" topics which are being worked out by society. On these particular topics you will often be asked about your opinion. If you were to go back to the turn of the century, for example, one of these hot button topics was the right to vote for women. In 1900 women could not vote, but a lot of people (both men and women) felt that was wrong. Today the vast majority of people feel that women should have the right to vote. No one is currently discussing women's suffrage because no one cares today. The issue has been settled. In 1900 it was a common topic of conversation.

This changing of women's voting rights points out the role opinions play in society. We live in a democracy where the majority rules. When a majority of people hold a certain opinion, that opinion becomes law and governs everyone in society. Those people who hold the minority opinion have the right to attempt to convince the majority to change their opinion. If they are successful the law changes. That is what makes the "hot button" topics interesting. These are the topics where the opinion of society is in flux. You have the ability to participate in the process with your own opinions.

Is the system of majority rule a good system? Is it good for the majority to be able to force its will on the minority? In my opinion the answer is "Yes." I believe (and the founding fathers of the country also believed) that the vast majority of people are good, and that in groups over the long-run this fundamental goodness leads to good decisions. That is why women now have the right to vote, even though women could not vote on changing their voting rights. The goodness of the

Opinion Journals

It can be extremely interesting to write down your opinions now, then come back and look at them after 10 years. On some topics your opinions will change dramatically as you account for your life experiences.

At this moment you probably have certain opinions on marriage, children, child-raising, capital punishment, pre-marital sex, drinking ages and so on. Write down your opinions now and watch how they change as you mature. It is a very interesting process.

majority of voters gave women the right to vote because it was the right thing to do.

There are a number of hot button topics at the moment (1997). Some of these topics include abortion, gun control, welfare, the role of government and so on. A great deal of what you hear on the evening news or read in the newspaper has to do with stories that revolve around these topics. Your parents and other adults will often end up talking [or arguing (or throwing things)] about these issues amongst themselves. That is how we all participate in the process of deciding where our society is going.

In this chapter I would like to talk about two current hot button issues to show you how this process works. The topics are abortion and gun control. I am going to present to you, in an unbiased way, both sides of these two issues so that you can see them clearly and begin to understand what the points of conversation are. Then you can begin to formulate your own opinions about them and enter into meaningful discussions with adults concerning these topics. As you live your life, continue to accumulate data and experiences to refine your opinions on these and other topics.

ABORTION

An abortion, technically, is "an induced termination of pregnancy." In this country abortion is extremely common. The October 1996 issue of *Scientific American* magazine reports:

> About half of all U.S. women will opt to abort an unwanted pregnancy at some point in their life, a survey from the Alan Guttmacher Institute finds. These women, two-thirds of whom intended to have children in the future, come from every age group, race, social class and creed—including those thought to oppose abortion. Catholic women, for example, had an abortion rate that was 29% higher than that of Protestant women. Six out of 10 women having abortion used protection.

Abortion is an extremely contentious topic at the moment and one of the most volatile. It has been for quite some time and will likely continue to be well into the future.

In America today there are two opinions about abortion;

- A woman has a right to control her own body. To say it another way, she has a right to choose what happens inside her body.
- A child is itself a human being and has a right to live.

One of the things that makes abortion difficult to discuss is that both of these opinions are true. A woman does have a right to control her body. No one can deny that. And a child, like all other humans, does have a right to live. No one can deny that either. The difficulty, and the huge argument that we have in our society, comes in drawing the line. The problem in drawing the line occurs because you can approach the line from two directions. If you approach the line from one side or the other, you reach completely different conclusions. Let me show you what I mean.

We can approach the line from one side. A woman has a right to control her body. Do you agree with that? Yes. Obviously. If a woman has a tumor in her body she has the right to remove it. One way to approach abortion is to look at pregnancy in exactly the same way. The woman's body is the woman's body and that is that. If there is anything in this world that you own undeniably, it is the body that is you. You have to be able to control it and what is inside it. Even if you were to say that a pregnant woman has "another life" inside her, it is still inside her, and her right to her body overrides everything else.

We can approach the topic from the other side and reach a completely different conclusion. A five-year-old child has a right to live. Do you agree with that? Yes. Obviously. Humans have a right to live. A one-year-old child does too? Yes. And a one-day-old child also? Yes. A one-minute-old child? Yes. What about the minute before it is born? It seems logical that this is the same child that will be there a minute later. So yes, obviously, one minute prior to birth a child has a right to live. What about two minutes before birth? Yes. What about one day before? Yes. One month? Yes. Two months? Yes. From here the logic goes all the way back to conception, because it must. It can be no other way. Three months? Yes. Four months? Yes. Five months? Yes. Six months? Yes. Seven months? Yes. Eight months? Yes. Nine months? Yes. A child is a child is a child no matter what. The child has a right to live from conception on. Under this logic, the woman's right to her body ends the moment a child is conceived.

It is like an optical illusion. If you look at it from the woman's standpoint, she has rights. If you look at it from the child's standpoint, the child has rights. Both interpretations are correct. It just depends on how you look at it.

A person on the "woman's side" might argue against a person from the "child's side" as follows. Every month a woman's body releases an egg into her reproductive system and flushes it out through menstruation. Do you agree with that? Yes. Is that OK? Yes. So an egg is not a child? Yes. And a man produces billions of sperm all the time, and they often arrive in a woman's body and swim around aimlessly because there is no egg to meet, and that is OK? Yes. So sperm are not a child? Yes. Say there are sperm and egg in a fallopian tube and they do not meet. Is that OK? Yes. Say the sperm and the egg meet. One second before meeting it is not a child. Therefore, one second after meeting it is not a child either.

A person on the "child's side" would say at this point, "at the moment the sperm and egg meet, a child is created. That is how we define a child." A person on the "woman's side" would then say, "Look at your argument for the child. You said earlier that the minute before birth and a minute after birth you have the same thing—a child. What I am saying here is that the minute before sperm and egg meet and the minute after it meets is the same thing—not a child."

A person on the "woman's side" would then say, "So, following my logic a single cell is not a child. It is just one cell. The single cell divides and becomes two cells. Still, clearly not a child. Two cells become four. Still clearly not a child. We are talking about four cells here. There is no personality, no brain, nothing. It is just four simple cells." A person on the "child's side" would then say, "So when are you going to say it is a child? A two-day old infant has no personality either, but you cannot kill it. When do your 'cells' become a 'child'"? This question is open to interpretation, but society has settled on a point where 'cells' end and 'child' begins. This interpretation is presently (1997) the law in America.

As you can see both sides are "right." Our legal system had to pick one side to be "legally right" and it chose the "woman's side." That does not stop people from arguing, however. Sometimes vigorously and painfully and violently.

You will eventually form your own opinion on this topic. The above discussion shows you that there are two ways to look at it. Both of them are valid. Let me point out eight things from an adult perspective that you can add to the information that you use to create your own opinion. The first four come from the "child's side":

1. Abortion seems "easy," but it is not easy for the person who has one. It is something that is carried with you for a long time. Ask anyone who has had one.
2. As people age, their opinion of abortion often changes. This happens for two reasons. First, when you have children of your

own it changes your perception of children and your understanding of "parental love." As a non-parent now you cannot foresee those changes. Second, as discussed in Chapter 2, people become less self-centered throughout life. That tends to change opinions toward abortion throughout life.

3. From a logical standpoint, the definition of a child from the "child's side" point of view is much cleaner than the "woman's side." If you think of a new-born child as a child and carry it backwards, you arrive at a definition of "child" that starts at conception. That is much easier to argue, logically, than an arbitrary definition that is based on cell counts or "appearance."

4. There are thousands of childless couples who would love a baby as their own if they had the chance to adopt one. Therefore, adoption is an alternative to abortion. This option requires an incredible amount of pain and giving on the mother's part, but it is a way of helping another couple who are sterile. It could be thought of as one of the highest gifts possible, both for the child and the sterile couple.

These four arguments come from the "woman's side":

1. Society, in general, has no use for an unwed, teenage mother. That is a hard row to hoe. Your friends and family may totally reject you and then you are alone as an unwed, teenage mother. Your likely landing spot is welfare and poverty.

2. As an unwed, teenage mother you cut off a huge number of options in your life.

3. Marrying a man as a teenager and trying to make life work is almost as hard as remaining unwed. It would take an extremely special couple to make it through. Statistics show that success is rare.

4. The mental anguish of adoption is equal to, if not greater than, that of abortion.

GUN CONTROL

In America today guns are legal. A person has a "right to bear arms" that allows nearly any individual to purchase and possess both hand guns and long arms (rifles and shotguns) as well as ammunition. Usually some sort of permit is required, but the process of obtaining a permit is a formality.

There are perhaps three widely-held opinions about gun control in America today:

- Guns should be completely legal and freely available as they are now.

- Hand guns should be illegal, while long arms should be legal.
- All guns should be illegal.

There is a rather large debate going on at the moment (1997) over the issue of gun control, and that debate is punctuated each time a person dies at the hand of someone carrying a gun. Let's look at both sides of the debate.

On the one hand, we have people who feel that the majority of Americans are good, responsible citizens who have a legitimate need and desire to possess guns. The need arises from activities such as hunting as well as the self-defense of property. The desire arises from collectors who simply like guns and want to have them around as works of art or historical relics. People on this side of the issue see criminals who misuse guns as an aberration that should be dealt with through punishment.

On the other hand, we have people who see guns as lethal weapons able to kill people. Hand guns in particular are easily concealed and specifically designed to kill other people. No one goes hunting in the woods with a hand gun, for example, because hand guns are inaccurate. Their short barrels mean that they work only at short range. Because of this limitation, hand guns are strictly useful as weapons against other people.

A person on the "guns side" would say to a person on the "no-guns side," "If you feel afraid of people who own guns, then get a gun and learn to use it properly so you can defend yourself. An armed society is a polite society. If everyone is armed we are all equal." A person on the "no-guns side" would say to that, "Look, I don't want to have to worry about defending myself. If no one had guns then I would not have to own one or worry about it. Besides, by owning a gun I open myself up to accidents. What if my child accidentally picks up my gun and shoots himself? If I don't have a gun, I don't have to worry about that."

A person on the "guns side" would say to that, "You can make guns illegal, but it is impossible to eliminate guns from the criminal element. Criminals will always have guns. Therefore, by making guns illegal you make good, honest citizens impotent against the criminal element. Because of this simple fact of life, guns should be legal and everyone should arm themselves." A person on the "no guns" side would say to that, "By making guns legal you make it so easy to obtain guns that criminals can get them everywhere. If guns and ammunition were illegal, guns would be rare. We could essentially identify all criminals as 'people who have guns' and that would make it a lot easier to round up these criminals and put them behind bars. Also, by making guns legal, you put them into the hands of normally-good people who come unglued one day and kill in a fit of rage. Without freely available guns, this would never happen."

And so on. You can see from this discussion that again, both sides are right. They both have valid arguments and those arguments are convincing.

One thing that is interesting about gun control is that it represents a larger area of discussion that revolves around personal freedoms in general. For example, should alcohol be legal? It currently is, and millions upon millions of people use it safely. But many people die each year at the hands of drunk drivers:

> About 45% of all traffic fatalities in 1992 involved an intoxicated or alcohol-impaired driver or nonoccupant. Of these 17,695 alcohol-related traffic fatalities, an estimated 14,125 occurred in accidents in which a driver or nonoccupant was intoxicated, and the remainder involved a driver or nonoccupant who had been drinking but was not legally intoxicated. Alcohol was also a factor in about 10% of serious injury accidents and 5% of property damage accidents. The estimated cost of all alcohol-related motor vehicle accidents in 1993 was $26.7 billion.
> [Source: *The 1995 World Almanac*]

17,000 people are a lot of people. $26.7 billion is a lot of money. In that same year about 23,000 people were murdered in the U.S., so the numbers are approximately equal. Should we, as a society, keep alcohol legal for the sake of the millions of people who use it properly or make it illegal to avoid risk to innocent bystanders? What about other drugs, which are currently illegal? What about cigarettes, which kill roughly 400,000 people per year?

> Cigarette smoking is responsible for 90% of lung cancer cases among men, 79% among women—about 87% overall. Smoking accounts for about 30% of all cancer deaths. Those who smoke two or more packs of cigarettes a day have lung cancer mortality rates 12-25 times greater than nonsmokers.
> [Source: *The 1995 World Almanac*]

Should people have the right to choose to smoke cigarettes, or should we make them illegal because of the health problems?

These are all interesting points of discussion. You get to form your own opinions on all of them. One of things you will notice once you form your opinions is that half of the people around you will agree, while the other half will disagree. You think you are right, and they think they are just as right. You have taken information from the environment to form your opinion, and they have taken the same information to form a different one. This is how our society works.

CHAPTER 39

People are People

Y ou are a person. You will spend a good portion of your time dealing with other people. These are both facts of life. Because of these facts of life, it is important that you understand something about *human nature*. By understanding what makes people tick, you can work with them rather than against them and accomplish your goals much more quickly.

PEOPLE RESPOND POSITIVELY TO COMPLEMENTS AND GIFTS

If a person were to come up to you and give you a really nice compliment or hand you a nice gift for no apparent reason, what would you think about this person? You would be flattered and think that this person is really nice! Say you are at school one day and a teacher comes up and for no reason says, "You know, you did a really superb job on the last paper you turned in, and I just want you to know how impressed I was." You are going to feel amazingly good, and you are going to have a good feeling about that teacher. This is so obvious that it seems ridiculous to point it out; of *course* people like other people who give them compliments and gifts!

So a good question to ask yourself is, "When was the last time I spontaneously gave someone a nice compliment or a gift?"

PEOPLE RESPOND NEGATIVELY TO PAIN, PUNISHMENT, THREATS AND CRITICISM

How do you feel about people who are constantly criticizing you, threatening you, punishing you and so on? You probably do not like these people very much. Neither does anyone else. Constant criticism simply is no fun for the receiver. Criticism is OK, but it must be constructive rather than destructive, and it must be balanced by compliments as well. Constant destructive criticism is debilitating and people tend to hate people who deliver it.

A good question to ask yourself is, "Am I constantly criticizing anyone, and if so, is there a way to change that pattern." Another good question is, "Is there anyone constantly criticizing me, and if so, is there a way I can speak to this person at a higher level (see Chapter 22) to try to change that behavior?"

PEOPLE LIKE THINGS TO BE "FAIR"

Ever since you were three- or four-years old you have worried about things being "fair." If you have a brother or sister (or if you go watch two five-year olds who are brother and sister), you will find that they are tremendously preoccupied with "fairness." If one person gets a cookie, the other should get a cookie. If one person gets to ride in the front seat one day, the other person should get to ride in the front seat the next day. And so on. This tendency continues into adulthood. We want people to treat us and other people fairly.

A good question to ask yourself is, "Do I treat other people fairly?"

PEOPLE LIKE PEOPLE TO OBEY THE RULES

Most people carry inside themselves an understanding that there are "rules" that need to be "followed," and when everyone follows the rules society benefits. For example, everyone understands that a red light means stop. We know it is important that everyone understand and obey that rule, so when we see someone run a red light we are disturbed by it. It is the same way when people "cut in line" in front of us. We all understand that lines represent a "first come, first served" rule, and we do not like it when people break that rule. We feel that same way about players obeying the rules in sports, family members obeying the rules of a family and so on.

We obey rules, and we like other people to obey rules because we understand that rules are fair and useful when everyone abides by them.

Having said that, you can now see why people get mad at you when you break the rules (see also Chapter 35).

PEOPLE DO NOT LIKE TO BE TOLD THEY CANNOT DO SOMETHING

If you go all the way back to the story of Adam and Eve and the apple tree, you can see that people do not like to be told not to do things. In many cases, telling someone *not* to do something virtually guarantees that they will do it. So when God told Adam and Eve not to eat from the apple tree, He virtually guaranteed that they would. That's human nature. You may have noticed this behavior in yourself: When someone tells you not to do something, you tend to want to do it. This particular part of human nature is so strong that we often use it backwards in a practice called *reverse psychology*. The fact that reverse psychology sometimes works tells you a lot about human nature.

There are several important things that you can learn from this particular piece of human nature. For example, you generally should not *tell* someone not to do something. You should instead explain the problem and *ask* for cooperation. Almost always this approach will work better.

In some situations a good question to ask yourself is, "Am I wanting to do this strictly because someone told me *not* to do it?"

People Do Not Like to Be Told What to Do, and People Hate Being Nagged

In the same way that people do not like being told what they cannot do, people generally hate to be told that they *must* do something. In particular they hate being constantly nagged about something. Ultimatums are always received negatively because of this particular trait of human nature.

As a teenager you are especially sensitive to this part of human nature. It is likely that you receive ultimatums and threats constantly. One reason you look forward to adulthood is that you believe that the ultimatums and rigid rules will end. One way to gain better control of the ultimatums now is to talk with your parents and teachers *as an adult* and start a dialog that shows you should no longer be treated as a child (see in particular Chapters 22, 39 and 43). By consistently acting like an adult and by understanding the reasoning behind the rules, you can have valuable discussions that cause the ultimatums to end.

People Like Having a Choice

People like to be given a choice. That is why restaurants have menus. It is why grocery stores are stocked with thousands of different items. It is why you can get the same basic car in 25 different colors and with 20 different option packages. It is why there are electives in college. It is the basis of democracy. And so on.

If I tell you that you must do something, the reason you do not like it is because you have no choice. If I forbid you from doing something, the reason you dislike it is because you have no choice. Therefore, the previous two traits are offshoots of the "choice" trait of human nature.

There is an interesting psychology experiment that shows the power that choice has on human beings. Imagine that a person is placed alone in a small room and asked to complete a multiple choice test. As soon as the person starts taking the test, an extremely loud and annoying cacophony of noise starts pouring out of a set of speakers in the room. Imagine that you ask 100 people to take the test in that room, and you average together their scores.

Now you take another 100 people, and you do the same thing to them with just one difference. With the second batch of 100 people you place a button in the room and you say to each person, "When you start taking the test, a loud noise will start playing through the speakers. We would like for you to take the test with the noise blaring. However, if at any time it gets to be too much for you, you can push this button and the noise will stop. There will be no penalty for pushing the button." It turns out that the second group of people will do significantly better on the test, *even though none of them will push the button.* Same test. Same noise. The *only* difference that makes the second group perform better is the fact that the people in the second group have the *choice* of turning off the noise, even though they never exercise that option. That says a lot about the way human nature works.

One of the simplest ways you can take advantage of the "choice" trait of human nature is to *ask* other people to do things instead of *telling* them to do things. That simple difference between asking and telling can make a huge difference in how people respond to you. Whenever you tell someone to do something you put up a wall because you are violating a fundamental rule of human nature (see also Chapter 24).

PEOPLE ARE DIFFERENT

Look around at the people you know. You will notice:

- Some people are morning people, some people are night people.
- Some people are neat, some people are messy.
- Some people like to keep track of little details, while other people can't stand details.
- Some people are artistic, some are very technical.
- Some are optimistic, some are pessimistic.
- Some people are good with words, some are good with numbers.
- Some people are very rational and logical, while others are very emotional and rely on their "feelings."
- Some people are confident, some are shy.
- Some people are extroverted and outgoing while some are introverted and quiet.
- Some people like elegant restaurants, some like fast food.

- Some people do everything quickly, some people are slow and relaxed.
- Some people get angry at the slightest thing, while other people never get angry.
- And so on.

In other words, people are different! Just because you might be a neat, morning person who likes details, is artistic, shy and who never gets angry, that does not mean the rest of the world is like that. In fact, the rest of the world is completely different. And that is OK. The question to ask yourself is, "Am I willing to accept the fact that all people are different, and that I am too?"

PEOPLE DO NOT LIKE SUDDEN CHANGE

Once people are familiar with something, they tend to like for it to stay that way. People generally do not like sudden changes. For example, if your parents come home one day and tell you that your family is moving to a new city, it would likely be uncomfortable because it is a change.

One way to soften the blow of change is to warn people. If you warn people that a change is coming, they will take it much better than if they are surprised unexpectedly. The classic human response to sudden, unexpected change is to get "defensive" about it.

PEOPLE PREFER TO BE WITH PEOPLE WHO ARE HAPPY

Given a choice between spending time with someone who is happy and someone who is miserable, people will almost unanimously choose to spend time with someone who is happy (see Chapter 15 for further details).

If you like being around people and want people to enjoy being around you, try being happy.

PEOPLE REMEMBER FIRST IMPRESSIONS

It is well known but easy to forget that a person's first impression of you is the impression that lasts. To understand this phenomena, imagine that you meet a new person and the very first thing you see this person do is scream at and kick a dog. At that moment, you have a blank slate for this person in your mind. The very first thing drawn on the slate is this image of screaming and kicking. That image will be with you always because it is the first, and it will be very difficult for you to see the person without recalling the image. That is why first impressions are important.

To apply this rule in your own life, be sure that the first impression you make on others is a good one (see also Chapter 17).

PEOPLE MAKE MISTAKES

People are human beings, and as human beings they make mistakes. That is a fact of life. People make mistakes in judgment, mistakes of omission, mistakes in memory, mistakes in calculations and so on. In many cases, a person does not realize that he or she is making a mistake until much later.

Another thing human beings have is the ability to forgive.

PEOPLE LIKE TO BE THANKED AND APPRECIATED

Let's say you go out of your way to do something nice for a person or a group of people. Maybe you spend two days setting up a party, making a gift for someone or whatever. It is nice to have your work appreciated and have someone say, "Thank you." This is why your parents might make you write thank you cards at Christmas. Even though you don't understand why it is important as a six-year-old kid, your parents know that it is important to the person who sent the gift.

Since you like to be thanked and appreciated, the obvious question to ask is, "When was the last time I thanked someone for something they did for me?"

PEOPLE BEHAVE DIFFERENTLY IN GROUPS

Human beings are social animals. Therefore, they behave differently alone than they do in groups. This sort of thing is common among all living things that have social programming. If you put an ant in an ant farm alone it will do nothing, but if you put 30 ants in with it they will start digging tunnels. Fish act differently alone than in schools. A dog alone acts much differently than it does in a group of other dogs. It is the same with people. When you go out with someone on a date he or she might behave completely differently than at school.

Social animals want to be accepted by their group. If you are with a group and the group is doing something you don't like, you might do it anyway simply to go along with everyone else and "fit in." If you were alone you would behave completely differently.

A good question to ask yourself when you are in a group is, "If I were alone would I be doing this?"

CONCLUSION

As you go through life you will notice hundreds of other facts about people and the way they operate. You will also notice hundreds of facts about yourself. By understanding human nature you understand why you react the way you do in certain situations, and you also understand how other people will react to things that you and others do to them. A clear understanding of human nature gives you the ability to predict the future, and this ability can be extremely important to success.

CHAPTER 40

You Are Not Alone

When something happens to you it can sometimes seem like you alone are suffering. This is a natural feeling. For example, if a close friend dies or you get rejected by the college of your choice, it can seem like you have been singled out for punishment. You feel like you are alone and the world is against you.

The key thing to realize is that you are not alone. First, there are people all around you who will listen and help if they can. Second, *anything* that is happening to you has already happened to thousands or millions of other people. You can gain strength and perspective by talking to these people or by reading books that discuss the problems you face. Since thousands or millions of people have faced what you are facing and have learned to cope with it in some way, you can gain strength in your struggle to cope with it yourself. Bad things happen to everyone. You are not alone.

REJECTION AND FAILURE

Rejection is a fact of life. It is a constant throughout life, because in every attempt to succeed you face the possibility of failure. You may have experienced one or more of the following situations:

- Colleges and scholarship organizations reject you and tell you to go away.
- Job applications are returned or never processed, or you get rejection letters.
- Members of the opposite sex say no when you ask them out.
- You try out for a team and are told you don't have what it takes.
- You submit art work or articles to contests or publishers and they are rejected.
- People laugh at you because of something you have done.
- People, both peers and adults, tell you that you are stupid.

285

- And so on.

Rejection happens quite frequently to teenagers because teenagers are trying a lot of new things. For example, as a senior in high school you are applying for college, scholarships and summer jobs. All three of these efforts will generate rejections at a very high rate.

Rejections are never easy to take. They all hurt. They can be bewildering. They make you feel like you are worthless. It is especially hard when you work for months on a project only to have it rejected. There is not a lot of fun in rejections.

The thing to realize in a rejection—*any* rejection—is that it is not the end of the world. I can remember, at age 17, being rejected by the college that I wanted to attend. I *really* wanted to attend this college. I had worked extremely hard on the application. I had visited and toured the campus (which was 2,000 miles from home) for a weekend. I had gone for personal interviews with alumni in my home town. I had excellent grades, SAT scores and recommendations. And yet I was rejected. At that moment it seemed like the absolute end of the world. And yet it wasn't. A year later I was attending a different college, just as good if not better, and doing well. Looking at it now, 20 years later, it seems absolutely and totally irrelevant. In the grand scheme of things it just did not matter.

The point is that from a perspective of three months later, or a year later, a lot of the sting will have gone away and you will have gained something important: You will be stronger for the next rejection, so it will be easier to take and understand. There are a lot of professions where rejection is a constant fact of life: acting, writing and sales all fall into this category. In major league baseball the typical batter fails two thirds of the times he steps up to the plate. To be in these professions you must learn how to accept and deal with rejection on a regular basis. The rejections you cope with as a teenager help you to get ready for the many rejections you will receive throughout the rest of your life. Look on them as learning experiences and understand that everyone around you gets rejected constantly in exactly the same way.

CRISES

As a teenager there are a number of crises that can pop up to "ruin your life" for a period of time:

- An unexpected pregnancy
- A life-threatening disease
- A car wreck or other life-threatening accident
- A split or divorce between your parents
- A crisis with your girlfriend or boyfriend
- And so on.

When these kinds of things happen it can seem like the end of the world. Learning to cope with situations like these is a mark of maturity. All through life each of us is tested by circumstances beyond our control and beyond our normal sphere of activity. The way you "pass" the test is to rise above it and make it to the other side. A person is respected most for his or her way of handling adversity.

When you face adversity, take the time to talk to someone who can offer perspective. This person might be one of your parents, a trusted relative or a teacher or counselor at school. What you want to do is come to the point where you can think about and deal with the problem rationally so that you can rise above it. By talking with someone, you can clarify things in your own mind and understand your options (see Chapter 24). You will also learn that you are not alone, and despite whatever problem you face people still love and care about you.

DEATH

Death is a fact of life. Like love, it is so central to human existence that it defines what it means to be human. There are three fundamental facts of life that surround death:

1. You will die.
2. Many of the important people around you will die in your lifetime.
3. The death of anyone close to you is extremely painful, and that pain can last for years.

I had a fair amount of experience with death as a teenager. All of my grandparents were dead before I graduated from college. My aunt and cousin died in a car accident when I was 12. My father died when I was 15, also in an accident. My next door neighbor, who was something of a surrogate father for me after my father died, died of lung cancer several years later.

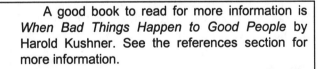 A good book to read for more information is *When Bad Things Happen to Good People* by Harold Kushner. See the references section for more information.

It was the death of my father that affected me the most. It affected me for years. There is nothing easy about death. The thing that is so painful about it is that it is so permanent. It is the end of contact and conversation. It is the end of hugs and smiles. It is the end of touching and being with someone you know and love. The emptiness caused by the permanence of death is a yawning dark cavern. There is not a thing you can do about it.

I remember when my father died I took it personally. Very personally. I felt as though I had been singled out in some way, and I felt the "unfairness" of it very strongly. I learned several important lessons in the process, however. One thing I learned as I worked through the pain is that death is painful. That is a fact of life. It doesn't make it any easier, but understanding that death is fundamentally painful for everyone tells you where you stand. A 60-year-old adult feels the same tremendous pain when a friend or loved one dies that you feel as a teenager. The difference between a 60-year-old person and most teenagers is that the 60-year old knows that the pain of death is normal and it is OK. The pain of death is a part of life. The 60-year old has felt that pain before and knows that it will diminish over time. A teenager who feels the pain of death for the first time does not know or understand that it will end one day. That makes it a lot harder for the teenager to gain perspective. A teenager feels the intense pain, and it appears to be endless.

Another thing I learned is that on any given day thousands of people die and thousands of people are experiencing the pain of death. No one is alone in the pain of death—we all feel it throughout our lives. When someone is in the middle of the pain of death, there is nothing anyone else can do but stand quietly or hug the person and understand and listen.

The most important thing I learned is that no one is singled out by death. The fact that my father died did not mean anything. It was not a punishment for anything I had done. It did not indicate that God or my father had abandoned me. Its timing was not symbolic. It simply happened. People die. That is a fact of life. You feel the incredible pain of it and you endure that pain. Then you move on. Over time the pain eases.

When someone important to you dies, you will feel pain. That pain is normal. You will feel empty. That emptiness is normal. You will feel incredibly alone. That loneliness is normal. However, it is not permanent. You can ride it out and things will get better in time. You will have to trust me on that.

SUICIDE

I once had a discussion with a friend of mine as we were driving over the Golden Gate Bridge in San Francisco. The bridge is a frequently used site for people who want to commit suicide. If you have ever walked across the bridge you can see why—all you have to do is hop over a hand rail and you can plummet to your death in the water hundreds of feet below.

There has been a long debate about erecting some kind of fence, wall or barrier along the bridge to make suicide attempts more difficult. My friend and I were discussing the options. He felt that the barriers were a good idea. I thought they would look ugly on such a beautiful bridge. I made the following point, "If someone wants to commit suicide, they are going to commit suicide—there is nothing you can do to stop them." He made an even better point, "If someone is thinking about suicide, all you have to do is delay him by an hour or two and he will get past it." That is not always true, but it is true in the vast majority of cases. The desire to commit suicide is often caused by an event or set of events that make the world look hopeless. If you can get past that event by a few hours or a day or a week, you can get the perspective you need to understand that suicide is not a good option. *Nothing* is so bad that you need to commit suicide to get away from it.

A letter to Ann Landers that appeared in her December 22, 1996 column provides an excellent example of teenage suicide:

> I could not hold back the tears when I read the news story in the *Fort Lauderdale Sun-Sentinel* about a local 12-year-old boy who hanged himself in his parent's back yard.
>
> It seems the boy was overweight and didn't want to go to school because his classmates continually teased him about being fat. He just couldn't take it anymore. He got up in the middle of the night, found a rope, went to the back yard and ended his life. When his younger brothers, 8 and 10, were getting ready for school in the morning, they looked outside and saw their brother hanging from the limb of a tree. There was a step stool and a flashlight beside the body.
>
> The police pronounced the boy dead at the scene. The boy's mother collapsed. His father immediately chopped down the tree.
>
> Ann, it is hard to imagine a worse nightmare. The boy was 5-feet-4 and weighed 174 pounds. His parents had taken him to physicians and counselors hoping to build his self-esteem.
>
> Most parents try to teach their children right from wrong, good manners and respect, but they overlook teaching compassion. I always told my kids to put themselves in the other person's shoes and stand up for the underdog.
>
> I am asking you to please print this letter, Ann. Children need to know that ridicule can be a cruel weapon. This young boy's life was cut short because of it.—So Sorry in Florida

Obviously, the boy was being teased mercilessly. However, it is important to recognize that the solution he chose to his problem probably was not the best one available. There are three things to consider if you are in a situation like this one and you are considering suicide:

- It was his peers who were doing the teasing, and their opinions are irrelevant (see Chapter 4). He listened to a group whose opinions do not matter in the grand scheme of things.

- In committing suicide the boy inflicted incredible damage on his mother, father and two brothers (see Chapter 18).
- The boy, by committing suicide, lost all chance of ever contributing anything to the world. If nothing else, he could have started a foundation that would try to help people who must endure what he did. Having committed suicide that is impossible.

Committing suicide is one option he had (see Chapter 24), but it certainly was not the best option.

If you are in a situation and are thinking that suicide is looking like a good option, talk about it with an adult you trust. Explain your line of reasoning to this person and see what he or she says. Whenever you find yourself thinking about suicide, it means you are in a tunnel and you simply are not seeing the world clearly. By talking to someone you can find another way to solve the problem. Look at your options (see Chapter 24) and choose another one. The pain you are going to inflict on yourself and those around you is not of any value.

WHAT TO DO WHEN YOU FEEL ALONE

When you experience a tragedy such as the death of a close friend, or when you find yourself in a place where things seem to be coming unglued (for example, you feel that the only way out of a situation is suicide), there are a number of things you can do to get past that point. Here are some ideas:

- Talk—First and foremost, talk with someone you trust. Tell them exactly what you are thinking and feeling and ask them to help you search for options.
- Write—Writing is different from talking. It uses a different part of your brain and involves only yourself. It can be therapeutic, and it can help you organize and understand what is happening to you. Try writing down how you feel. Simply use a stream of consciousness approach at first, then come back and organize it if that helps.
- Pray—Prayer is talking to God. Tell God how you feel and ask for His help. Also, thank God for the things you do have.
- Walk—Your brain is housed inside your body, and the brain and body interact. Walking is a way of using that interaction beneficially. Pick a point two or three miles away and force yourself to walk there. Then you will have to walk back and you will almost always feel better in some way.
- Work—I can remember the day my father died. It was such an incredibly hard, sad day for all of us. I can clearly remember a scene from that day. I walked into the bathroom downstairs and

there was my mother, on her knees, crying profusely as she scrubbed the toilet. I cry now as I think of that scene, because it was so like my mother to turn to work in a time of utmost sadness. What else is there to do? You cannot simply stand still and let the pain bludgeon you. You have to do something. That is why walking can help. Working is the same—it can distract you in some small way from the pain. My first book was written very much as a distraction from pain. I could work on it 16 hours a day and then go to sleep, and for periods of time I could get so wrapped up in the book that I would forget.

- Think—Stop and think and gain a rational perspective on your problem. Writing and talking both help the process.
- Cry—There is nothing wrong with crying. It is a way to grieve.
- Wait—It is almost impossible to convince yourself of this while you are in the pain of death or rejection, but the pain will lessen and then pass if you simply wait long enough. Be patient.
- Help—In many cases there is no better medicine for pain than helping others. In helping others you are able to focus on their problems rather than your own. In that way you gain both release and perspective.
- Join a new club or group—Sometimes getting involved in a new activity can help take your mind off things. You might join a group at church, sign up for something unusual like rock-climbing lessons, join a volunteer organization or work on a political campaign. Look for something different that will take your mind off of the problem at hand.

CHAPTER 41

Material Things Do
Not Bring
Happiness

Material things do not necessarily bring you happiness. That is a fact of life. It is a hard fact to understand sometimes, especially in a society that tries very hard to teach you otherwise.

It is very common to get into a mode where you think, "If only I had object X my life would be perfect and I would be happy." You REALLY want something: a new TV, a new car, a special pair of shoes, whatever. Then you buy it and you LOVE having it for a few days. But over time you get bored or it wears out. You can see this pattern repeated constantly in your own life. For example, your parents and grandparents likely spent thousands and thousands of dollars on toys for you as you were growing up: Dump trucks and Barbie dolls and video games and electric cars and on and on and on. All of those toys got boring or broken or outgrown eventually. They brought happiness for a moment or a week, but over time they became worthless and your desire turned to a new object.

This pattern begs the following question: "If material things bring just a temporary and short-term happiness, then what does that mean?" It might mean that you have to buy material objects at a rate of perhaps one per day to sustain the temporary and short-term high of getting something new. The problem is, that begins to sound a lot like a drug habit. This train of thinking can get you into some very deep areas. Things like:

- What is happiness?
- What does it mean to be happy?
- What do I want to do in my life?
- Does life have meaning?
- And so on.

Very deep.

There is a difference between *material happiness*, which implies having all the basic (or extravagant) comforts necessary to live life, and *spiritual happiness*, which implies something else altogether. I had a friend whose philosophy was this:

> No matter how much money you make, you always want more. So if you make $25,000 (1997) you believe that if you just made $50,000 you would be happy. But then you begin to make $50,000. At that point you believe that if you just made $100,000 you would be happy, and so on through life. This pattern is true whether you make $25,000 or $10,000,000 a year, because as you earn more money you acquire more expensive tastes. It seems to me that you might as well learn to be happy on $25,000 a year, figure out an easy way to earn it and then have the rest of your time free to do what you want.

This sort of philosophy implies that you can find something other than material happiness to give meaning to your life.

The thing about "wealth" is that there is more than one way to measure it. Traditionally it is measured in dollars, but there are many other scales. You can be "rich" in ways that have nothing to do with money. For example:

- Rich in friends—A person who cultivates friendships and who is a joy to be around can have hundreds of good friends and can be rich beyond the wildest dreams of others.
- Rich in health—A person who spends time eating right, exercising and relaxing from stress can be extremely healthy, and this health can be far more valuable than any amount of money.
- Rich in strength—A person who works out with weights every day, runs, swims, etc. can be rich in strength and will have an attractive body.
- Rich in family—A person who devotes time to his or her spouse and children will have a strong and happy family that is rewarding throughout life.
- Rich in knowledge—A person who reads and studies will become rich in knowledge.
- Rich in skill—A person who practices anything daily (a skill, a sport, prayer, whatever) will become excellent in that skill area. Excellence has its own rewards.
- Rich in character— A person who works hard at being honest and truthful in all situations will become rich in character and will be trusted by everyone.

One funny thing about all of these different areas is that none of them are taxed. You are taxed on the money you earn, and that is it. There is no knowledge tax, for example. You can learn freely throughout life and acquire a huge "bank account" of knowledge. No one can steal it

Enjoying Your Job

Enjoying your job is particularly important
to your overall well-being and happiness.
As mentioned in Chapter 1, you must
have a job to live life. At the very
minimum, you have to make enough
money to cover food, shelter, clothing and
health care. You will therefore spend a
significant part of your time "on the job."
So why not find a job you *truly* enjoy—
something you are excited about each
day when you wake up. That is one key to
happiness. See Chapter 6 for details.

or diminish it in any way.
Presumably, knowledge is
the one thing you might be
able to take with you to
Heaven.

All of these
alternative types of wealth
are different from
financial wealth, and yet
all of them can be equally
rewarding in their own
ways. The point is that the
act of buying things by
itself, despite what
television tells you, may not be what will bring you maximum happiness
in life. Things like good friends, a loving spouse, well-raised children, a
home built on love, a good relationship with God, a clear conscience, a
worthy goal and a job you truly enjoy bring you contentment that lasts
and has meaning. These things are often very hard for some teenagers to
understand, but as you mature they become more important.

As you look at the world around you and come to understand what is
important to you, keep these things in mind. Think about what it is that
you enjoy and what makes

*"Man does not live by
bread alone."*

-The Bible: Matthew 4:4

you truly happy. See what
you find. In thinking about it
consciously, you might be
surprised by what you
discover. Money is incredibly
important—you need it to survive. But it is not the *only* thing you need,
and money itself will not bring lasting happiness to most people. Man
does not live by bread alone.

THE MEANING OF LIFE

As you ponder things like the importance of money and the role of
happiness, you often end up at the question, "What is the meaning of
life?" For most teenagers, this question is both important and
confounding. Like its partner, "Who am I?" it is unique to you. Only you
can provide the answer.

There are as many answers to the question, "What is the meaning of
life?" as there are people. However, the answers often break into broad
categories. By looking at some of the categories (as well as creating
categories of your own) you can often come to understand how you want

to answer the question. The following three sections look at three different ways that you can think about the question. This list is not exhaustive, and I am not advocating any of them. They simply offer you some examples.

Life Has No Meaning

What is the meaning of life for a rabbit? A rabbit is born. It eats and sleeps. It reaches sexual maturity and has children of its own. It is either eaten or dies of natural causes. When it dies there is no "heaven." It simply dies and that is the end of it. In such a scenario it is possible to conclude that life for a rabbit has no meaning. Rabbits exist to produce other rabbits and thus keep the species alive, but even that has little or no meaning in the grand scheme of things.

The "life has no meaning" school of thought applies that same line of reasoning to human beings. Humans, so the logic goes, have no soul and no afterlife, and therefore are no different from rabbits. When we die we die, and that is the end of it. This thought process can lead to one of several behavior patterns:

- Because life has no meaning, there is no point to living. I should wallow in self-pity and a private misery for years at a time.
- Because life has no meaning, I might as well be as obnoxious as possible—This is the "juvenile delinquent" and "career criminal" school of thought. Since life is meaningless, you might as well make as many people miserable as possible by killing people, robbing them, vandalizing things and so on. It is unclear how the connection from "my life has no meaning" to "therefore everyone else should be miserable" is made, but these people make it nonetheless.
- Because life has no meaning, I might as well enjoy it while I am alive—A corollary is "I may die tomorrow, so I had better live it up today." Another somewhat more positive corollary is, "Life is a journey; enjoy the ride." In either case, life is seen as a terminating state of being, so the more you enjoy it now the better.
- Life may have no meaning, but I choose to make other lives better during my time here—This is the opposite and positive side of the "juvenile delinquent" school of thought.

Life Has Meaning Through Human Society

Assume that there is no God and no afterlife. Even so, it is possible for life to have meaning through the larger and ongoing society we live in. By looking at your life as a part of a whole rather than as an individual life, it can have meaning when you ask a question like, "Where is humanity, as a whole, headed?"

Think of it this way: Human beings have progressed from the point where we were strictly animals to the point where we are thinking, knowing beings who have just started to harness space travel, computers and communication. In just 100 years we have gone from an agricultural society to a technical society. This transformation has not occurred because of one person, but instead because of the contributions of billions of people. Each of us does one small thing that moves society forward. For example, many people worked to develop the telephone and build the switching infrastructure that makes up the telephone network. Many other people invented the Internet and built the systems on top of the phone system that make the Internet possible. Many more people worked to get a phone wire to your house. Still more people invented, refined and popularized computer hardware and software. Many more worked on modems and web sites. As a result of all of this effort you can now easily dial in to the Internet and retrieve billions of bytes of data from around the world using the World Wide Web.

Given our rate of technical progress, imagine what you will be able to do 100 years from now in terms of communication, calculations, travel, and so on. One day we will be able to colonize other planets. One day we will be able to travel to other solar systems and galaxies. One day we will be able to move huge amounts of matter to create new planets. One day we will, in theory, be able to design our own universes. When that happens, humanity will have become something else entirely. If we become immortal and can redesign or create universes, then we will be entirely unlike what we are today. Perhaps at that point we will find a completely different way to look at the universe and understand its significance.

In such a context, you are one part of the process that gets us there. Choose a worthwhile goal that moves humanity forward and work toward it.

Life Has Meaning Through God

Most religions contain a concept of Heaven or an afterlife. Christians, for example, believe in an eternal life through belief in Jesus Christ:

> For God so loved the world that He gave His one and only Son, that whoever believes in Him shall not perish but have eternal life. [Source: *The Bible: John 3:16*]

By believing in God, Heaven and an afterlife, life has meaning because it is not an end in itself. Instead, life is part of an ongoing and eternal process. The life we have on earth is just one small step.

If you believe in God and Heaven the questions then shift:

- If there is a Heaven and Hell, how can I get into the former and avoid the latter?
- What do I take with me to Heaven? What can I do to prepare?

Many teenagers rebel against the idea of God and Heaven in much the way that they rebel against Santa Claus as pre-teens. There is, after all, no direct proof that God exists. For example, He has never taken over all the TV stations and spoken to all of humanity to prove His existence.

And yet there is more subtle evidence. There is the universe itself, for example. Where did it come from? There are thousands of consistent and reputable stories about near-death experiences. There is growing scientific evidence of the power of prayer (see, for example, the April 1996 issue of McCall's magazine, page 86 for an overview). These things combine together in such a way that you must wonder: Is there more to life than what we can see? And if so, how does it affect us when we die? These questions often lead adults to God. God gives their lives meaning because death is not the end—it is the beginning.

Good Books

A good book to read for more information is *A Simple Path* by Mother Teresa. See the references section for more information.

CHAPTER 42
You Can Avoid Scams

Tthere are a million enterprises on this planet that depend on ignorance for their livelihood. That is a fact of life. Some of these activities are outright scams (for example, a shell game in New York City), while others are legitimate businesses that use rather odd practices or situations that cause you to do things you would not normally do (for example, time shares). Adults understand how these enterprises work and avoid them because they have already learned about them. Unfortunately, "There is a sucker born every minute." What that expression means is that when you are born you are naïve. You can be sucked into a scam because of your inexperience. Each year the millions of naïve teenagers who turn into new adults (suckers) keep these enterprises going because they can each be scammed once. That is all it takes.

This chapter introduces you to some of the familiar scams that most adults already know about so that you can avoid them. The sections below discuss six of the most common.

THREE CARD MONTE AND THE SHELL GAME

"Three Card Monte" and "the Shell Game" are classic street games you will find in tourist areas of New York and other large cities. You will normally see a person (the dealer) who has set up a couple of boxes or a small table. Five to 20 people will be gathered around watching. If you catch the scam near the beginning the dealer will be doing his thing and a person "from the audience" will be playing. If it is the shell game, for example, the dealer will be moving shells around and the player will be trying to watch the shells (cups, cans, whatever) to keep track of the one containing a ball. The player will have bet perhaps $20 that he can keep track of the ball. When the dealer stops the player will point to one of the shells. And he will win $20 because he is right! And he will play again and he will win! And he will play again, and you will be watching intently and he will win again and you will say to yourself, "Hey! This is easy! I can make an easy $20 here!" and you will step up to play.

You might win the first time. But the second time you will certainly lose and you will continue losing until you run out of money or stop. You will not understand, because it looked so easy when the first guy was playing.

The first person you were watching is a shill. He won because he and the dealer are partners. The idea is to find a sucker who does not know that (hence the preponderance of these games in tourist areas) and make him or her think it is easy.

If you are in New York sometime and see one of these games, simply walk past. If you can't stand the suspense, go ahead and watch. But do not play. It is pointless.

CON MEN

I can tell you a number of funny personal stories about the scams "con men" pull. Let me tell you two of them here so you can see how they work.

The first one occurred in college. I went to New York one day when I was a freshman. One thing I discovered, having never been to a large city, is that there are a *lot* of homeless people in New York. I had what is probably a pretty normal outlook on life for a teenager—I felt sorry for homeless people and wanted to help. But there were so many of them! There was one particular homeless person who caught my attention, however. He was an old man, a native American, and he held a sign that told a sad tale. He was living on the street and all he wanted was money to get back to Arizona to be with his people. I spoke with him for several minutes, asking him how he had gotten trapped in New York and where he had come from and how long he thought it would be before he went home. He said just a few more days and he would have the money. I gave him $5 and felt very good about it.

A year later I happened to be in New York again. I happened by the same place and there was the same man! Same sign. Same shtick. I was amazed! "Why haven't you gone back to Arizona?!" I asked, incredulously. He obviously did not remember me, but I kept questioning him. Finally he took my arm and said, "Look, kid, this is an act. Lots of tourists come by here and they think the story is true. This is how I make money. Now get out of here!" If you walk around any city you will see the same thing. The same people sitting on the same corners using the same lines over and over again for months or years at a time. With a good story and a good stream of tourists they can make a decent amount of money. These are "passive con men."

There is another variety of con men who are much more active, and it seems like I am approached by one of them about once a year. I travel a lot, so maybe I see more of it than the average person. Today (December 10, 1996) I was approached by such a person in San Francisco. I let the thing play out naturally so I could write it down. Here is how the con works. I step out of the hotel at 5:00 A.M. for a walk. It is raining. A man, obviously flustered, walks up and says, "Look, I know this is going to sound stupid, but I work as a janitor across the street and I have locked my keys and my wallet in my car. I live near a BART (the local train system in San Francisco) station, and I need $7.60 to go home and get a spare set of keys from my wife and come back. If you could just loan me the money, I will be back in an hour and I will repay you. I can have the concierge ring your room. You would really be helping me out. This is really embarrassing to me. I have only been here two months, it's raining and I have gotten my new suede jacket wet. This just isn't my day! Please, if you can just help me, I will buy your breakfast when I get back." In every way this man came across as completely honest, completely normal and completely sincere.

There are several responses to this sort of thing. Your response depends on where you are, how sure you are of yourself and whether you feel safe or not. Let me show you a range of options:

- "I cannot help you. I am sorry." Honest. Frank. Closes the door. If pestered further simply say, "I cannot help you." And walk away. This is probably the best response.
- "I'm sorry, I have no money with me." This is an easy way to get out of it, but it is dishonest if you actually have money on you.
- "Show me the car." I have had enough people come up to me with stories like this— "car broke down and I need money, but I WILL

New York Scams

New York is full of scams. One of the more amusing scams you will see there is the "going out of business" scam. A business will plaster its windows with signs that say, "Going out of business! Huge Savings!" You will go inside and find trash on the floor and prices on the display cases. There will be, "Going out of business sale prices!" on everything. But something is not quite right... It will feel funny. Then a year later you go back and the business is still there, still going out of business and apparently doing very well. This is another trap for tourists. Since tourists will not see the business again, they think that they are getting a "deal." What's more, the business can say "All sales final—no returns" and people will accept that because the business is apparently going out of business. It's a pretty effective scam all around!

repay you," "Missed my flight and I need money, but I WILL repay you," "Can't get home and I need money, but I WILL repay you" and so on—that I know this is a con. Asking to see the car calls his bluff. You would only want to do this if you are in a well-lit and well-populated area.

- "Don't lie to me." Since it is obviously a scam this is a direct confrontation of the scammer and calls the bluff in a direct manner. The scammer will claim innocence, but it is fairly easy to eliminate that innocence with a few simple questions. The problem with this approach, like the previous one, is that you are wasting your time on a person who does not deserve it. Life is too short.
- "I understand. Here is $10." If for any reason you fear for your safety, this might be the best way out of the situation.

With my goal of playing it out to show that it is a scam, I said the following, "Here is $10 and my business card. When you get back leave the money with the person at the front desk, or call my office to arrange for mailing the money to me. But don't let me down here—I am going to write about you in a book if you are lying to me." He said, "I will definitely bring the money back. Bless you for this. Bless you!" And he made some presumably religious sign on his face with his hand and turned away. I turned the other way, and he called to me, "Here! Take my umbrella! I am already soaked." I told him I was fine and we parted.

I never saw the money or him again. He never came to the hotel. He never called. Now, you are asking, "How could a person who seems that sincere be lying like that?" Because he is a con man. This is how he makes his money. If I had not seen it about once a year for 15 years, I would probably feel differently about it. But I have *never* had someone who frantically asked me for money on the street repay it like they promised they would. That is a fact of life. After the second or third time you simply start to say "No." I gave him money and a business card in this case specifically to prove the point, and it turned out exactly as expected. The umbrella was a nice and unexpected touch of extra sincerity and shows he understands human nature *very* well. He offered the umbrella knowing I would not take it.

MULTI-LEVEL MARKETING

At some point you are going to get a call from someone who is involved in multi-level marketing (MLM). The call will come either from a friend or a friend of a friend, and it will start something like this, "I got your name from your friend Bill. I am wondering, if I told you about a way to make some extra money in your spare time, would you be interested? Could you use some spare money in your budget right now?" You will probably say, "Yes." Why wouldn't you be interested? And you and this person will have a long conversation about this "opportunity." There will be two things that you notice about this conversation. First, the name of a company will never be mentioned. Even if you ask, "What is the name of the company?" your question will be deflected. Second, you will be asked to attend a "presentation." You will go and it will inevitably be a presentation for a MLM company.

Multi-level marketing works like this. Someone signs you up, and you are supposed to sell something: home care products, jewelry, alarm systems, long-distance time, whatever. However, selling the product is really secondary to what you can do to make BIG money, which is to sign up other people to sell the product. They in turn are supposed to sign up other people, and so on. The idea is that for each person you sign up,

MLM Zealots

I have seen several acquaintances converted into religious zealots by MLM companies. You go to see them one day or they call and they are like zombies chanting their little sales pitch. They tell you how stupid you are for not signing up and describe in vivid detail how they will soon be making $100,000 a year lying in bed doing nothing. And you will think to yourself, "Good Lord, not another one!" Several months later they snap out of it and they apologize and return to normalcy.

There are two things they gain from the experience: 1) A lot of the MLM shtick has to do with optimism and self-motivation, both of which are valuable, and 2) It gets them thinking about setting up businesses of their own—they see that it might be possible. They often take those concepts and apply them to other places in life with great benefit.

you get a cut of their sales. So if you sign up 20 people as sales associates you get 10% of their sales. Then if those 20 people each sign up 20 *more* people, you get a 5% cut of their sales, and so on. At this rate you will soon be making $100,000 a year doing nothing! That is the way all MLM companies work. And that is the pitch all of them use—you will make incredible money for doing nothing.

This sounds extremely good. You will be told about all of the people who are making $100,000 a year without lifting a finger. And I am sure that somewhere there are people for whom this is true. However, if you think about it no one makes anything unless someone sells something. *Someone* has to do some real work. That part is often neglected.

If you are susceptible to this sort of sales pitch you will sign up, you will get the MLM religion and you will start calling and bugging your friends and relatives with your product. Of course, you will be trying to sign them up as well, which means you will be having little presentations at your house. The problem is, this sort of behavior is *incredibly* annoying. It feels something like "Invasion of the Body Snatchers" to your friends.

These organizations are not scams. MLM is a legitimate approach to marketing products. The problem is that MLM is incredibly annoying. If you ever get a call from a friend who is trying to give you a new way to make lots of money but will *not* tell you what the name of the company is, rest assured it is an MLM company. You might want to go to one of the presentations because it is an interesting concept. Unfortunately, the concept is offensive to many people.

LIFE INSURANCE

Life insurance is not a scam. It is a legitimate, worthwhile product. However, the way it is often sold and the pressure tactics that are used to sell it often make it a scam. See Chapter 33 for more details.

TIME SHARES

Time shares, like life insurance, are not scams. A *time share* is a legitimate piece of real estate. A time share differs from normal real estate in that it is both time- and location-based. Most real estate that people buy does not have a time component. For example, if you buy a piece of land you own that land every minute of every day until you sell it. Time shares are different. With a time share you own a particular piece of real estate for only a particular period of time each year. Usually it is a specific week each year, such as the 42nd week of the year. Quite a bit of vacation real estate is sold this way. Who is going to use a vacation condo more than a week or two each year? The fact that you are buying only $1/52^{nd}$ of the property means that the cost of the property is much lower than it would be if you bought the full year's use of the property. Since vacation property is often quite expensive, time shares open up vacation real estate to people who could not otherwise afford it.

The problem with time shares is that they are often sold in extremely odd ways and at incredibly inflated prices. You will be invited to a presentation, and usually you will be lured with "free prizes" or a "free trip." These prizes and trips are normally legitimate, although they are never as good as they sound in the brochure. When you arrive at the presentation, you will be given a three-hour sales pitch and you will find that it is fairly high pressure. At the end of the presentation you will be told to make a decision then and there. If you do not act immediately the offer will disappear. This is the part that is a scam.

A time share week normally costs $10,000 to $20,000 (1997) if you buy it this way. No normal human being would spend $20,000 without a tremendous amount of consideration and study. However, because the presentation is crafted in such a way, because you are receiving the free gifts, because the deal is made to sound so good, because the financing is so easy, because you don't want to miss this great opportunity and because you are made to feel like a total loser if you pass up this amazing offer, millions of people sign up right on the spot. It is truly amazing.

Here is an important fact to carry in your head when you are looking at time shares. Good time shares are legitimate deeded real estate. That means that people can sell them just like any other piece of real estate. There is an incredible secondary market for used time share weeks, and you can buy them on this market for far less money than you can from a marketing company. The price often falls by half on the secondary market because the price you are charged by the marketing company has to cover all of the free trips and prizes as well as the advertising and commissions.

If you are interested in buying a time share, go in with both eyes open. Investigate the secondary market first. Then listen to the presentation. Then ask if you can think about it for a day and leave. Of course, if you call back the next day they will take your $20,000! But if you hunt you can probably buy the same thing for much, much less on the resale market.

DIET PROGRAMS

Let's say you are overweight. Lots of people are. If you would like to lose weight there is a simple rule:

TO LOSE WEIGHT, EAT LESS AND EXERCISE MORE

In America there is a multi-billion dollar diet industry that "helps" people lose weight. However, there is no way to get around this simple fact of life: You cannot lose weight unless you eat less and exercise more.

The funny thing you will notice about all of the diet gadgets and diet foods and diet pills you see is that they all have testimonials from people who "lost 30, 50, even 100 pounds using this product!" And those claims are true. Here is why: If you take 10,000 people and put them on *any* diet program, a few of them will lose weight because at about the same time they start the program they will make a conscious decision to *really* lose weight this time. These people eat less and exercise more through their own will power and actually lose weight. The fact that they started the diet program at the same time is a coincidence, in other words. Nonetheless, these people can be carted out as victorious users of that particular diet program.

For example, I could take 10,000 people and start them on "The Marshall Brain Stand on Your Head Weight Loss Program." In this program you will stand on your head for just 10 minutes each day. Now, if I provide people with a booklet that suggests it is essential to eat less each day "to avoid stomach upset while inverted" and that also suggests some vigorous walking each day to "improve circulation while inverted," then I am set. My diet program is going to work for some people by causing them to eat less and exercise more. The standing-on-your-head part is a red herring. At least 1% of the 10,000 people will actually lose weight by coincidence. Then I can display their stories in my ads and get on talk shows and make a fortune.

What diet companies do is take a known solution to a common problem, repackage it, market it and reap the reward. Not a bad way to make a living, actually. The point is that you can do the same thing yourself, just as easily and at no cost whatsoever, simply by eating less and exercising more.

PSYCHICS

One of the hottest recent scams involves television "psychics." Their ads claim that they can predict your future, cure disease, lead you to love and so on. Psychics are scams. There is no such thing as a psychic who can predict the future or "read your thoughts." If there were, they would be able to do all sorts of things. For example, why would you have to call a psychic? Why wouldn't several psychics call you at exactly the moment you need them? If they can predict the future, why don't psychics call the police and prevent all murders and other mayhem? Why don't psychics go to a casino, win every game and then retire?

Into this category falls other scams like Ouija boards. If you ever want to see if an Ouija board works, have someone who is a "believer" try to do it blindfolded.

GENERAL NOTES ABOUT SCAMS

Here are some simple guidelines to help you avoid scams:
- You cannot get something for nothing.
- If it sounds too good to be true, it probably is.
- If you "must act now," you normally should not.
- Remember that things often are not what they seem. Take time to investigate comparable offers. If it is a legitimate deal the seller will have no problem with that. Then actually do it. If people did

this for time shares, for example, they could get them for much less money.

- If you are asked for your credit card number in an unsolicited phone call, there is a problem. Do not give out any personal or financial information unless you place the call.

If you apply these simple rules you will be largely scam-proof.

Chapter 43
Your Parents are Human Beings

One of the things you might notice after reading this book is that a lot of the things your parents do make more sense now. You may still not *like* what your parents do, but their actions make more sense. This chapter will help you to consolidate your understanding of your parents.

WHY WON'T MY PARENTS LET ME BUY A $400 PROM DRESS?

As discussed in Chapter 1, money is important. Your parents make a finite amount of money, and they likely have a budget that is constrained by normal monthly bills and expenses. When you ask for something like a prom dress, your parents must give up something else. As an alternative to asking your parents to buy the dress, think about getting a job and earning the money yourself. You will learn a lot about the value of things, and about independence, in the process.

WHY DO MY PARENTS CARE ABOUT "THE ECONOMY" AND "TAXES" AND "THE STOCK MARKET" SO MUCH? WHY DO THEY TALK ABOUT THIS STUFF ALL THE TIME?

Say you are at a gathering that includes a large number of adults. A wedding, for example. All the adults are standing around and they are talking about things that make absolutely no sense to you; things like money, the stock market, taxes and house prices. You can say to yourself one of two things:

- "What a bunch of stupid and boring people." Or...
- "Wow, I don't have the slightest idea what they are talking about, or why they care. But I am making minimum wage and these

people are making 10 times as much. Maybe I should learn about what they are talking about."

I can remember as a teenager thinking adults were stupid. But why? Why would I think that people who are capable of earning 10 times more than me are stupid? That was my Teenage Illusion Module talking (see Chapter 2). I should have instead tried to learn their language.

If you ask adults why they are so interested in money, taxes and stocks and then listen to their answers, here are some of the things you will learn:

- Adults are interested in money and jobs because they realize that without money they (and their children) become homeless. See Chapter 1.

- Adults are worried about taxes because they probably lose at least a third of what they make to taxes each year. A family earning $60,000 a year might lose $20,000 or more of it to taxes. As mentioned in Chapter 1, anytime you have someone taking $20,000 a year away from you, you are going to be concerned.

- Because taxes are controlled by politicians, and because we live in a democracy where adults elect the politicians, adults are

Contempt and Respect

Watch yourself as you live your life and you will notice a funny thing. For example:

- You are watching an Olympic athlete on TV. When he makes a mistake you think, "I can't believe how uncoordinated he is!"

- You are watching a movie starring an actress that you don't particularly care for and you think, "I can't believe she is in this movie! She doesn't know how to act!"

- You look at people like Charles Schwab, Bill Gates or Lee Iacocca (all multi-millionaires or billionaires) and you think, "I can't believe this guy is making any money. He is such an idiot!"

All of these people are wildly successful. The Olympic athlete has trained for years to get to a point where a billion people are watching him on TV. The movie star has worked for years honing her interpersonal and acting skills to get to the point where she can command millions of dollars per movie. The businessmen have taken their ideas and built empires, encouraging millions of people to follow their dream and buy their products. Where, exactly, does the contempt and lack of respect come from given their position compared to yours?

Keep this phenomena in mind when you find yourself looking at your parents and other adults with contempt.

interested in politicians.

- Your parents are at a point in their lives where they are half way to retiring. Retirement becomes "real" at this point. They start actively saving for retirement because the prospect of being poor retirees scares them. Their retirement money, along with other parts of their savings, is probably invested in the stock market. Therefore, they are very interested in what the stock market is doing. Many, many adults have half a million or a million dollars saved up toward retirement and much of it is in stocks. That level of investment makes the stock market a major concern (see Chapter 30).

- Another part of your parent's wealth, perhaps $100,000 or more, is tied up in the house you live in. Therefore, your parents are concerned about house prices, land values, new construction in the area (which affects prices and values) and so on (see Chapter 32).

In moving from a teenager to an adult, you will notice a very odd transformation: What the adults are talking about actually starts to make sense! And in fact, it is all important stuff. What you will also recognize is that the reason it is so boring and impenetrable to you as a teenager is because you are inexperienced. The adults are talking, essentially, in a foreign language. If you take the time to learn that language as a teenager and then to learn and understand the important concepts and techniques that adults use on a daily basis to live their lives, you can speed up your development by about 10 years. You will be much further along. This, by the way, is a common lament among all adults: "If I had only known all of this was so important when I was a teenager, I could have learned a tremendous amount from my parents and their friends."

Let me give you an example of what I am talking about. On the next page there is a definition of a mutual fund that is likely to seem impenetrable and boring to you. Take a minute and try to make your way through it.

Look at this definition. It may seem totally dry, meaningless and boring to you. Any successful adult, however, would read it, understand it completely and say, "Yes, this is true. I own shares in several different mutual funds. They are an integral part of my retirement plan." Why is it boring and meaningless to you? Because you don't have any of the vocabulary, experiences or money, for that matter, to understand what it is saying. Does that make adults boring and stupid? No. It is extremely interesting to go from age 15 to age 35 knowing that you thought you "knew it all" at age 15. You were sure that adults were some of the most ridiculous people on the planet, and then you realize that you felt that way at age 15 because you didn't know how the world works. As a teenager now, you can learn quite a bit from the adults around you.

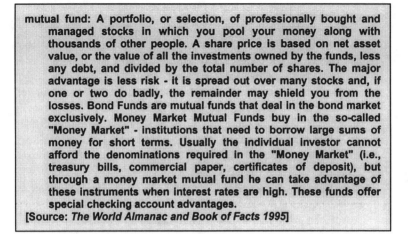

mutual fund: A portfolio, or selection, of professionally bought and managed stocks in which you pool your money along with thousands of other people. A share price is based on net asset value, or the value of all the investments owned by the funds, less any debt, and divided by the total number of shares. The major advantage is less risk - it is spread out over many stocks and, if one or two do badly, the remainder may shield you from the losses. Bond Funds are mutual funds that deal in the bond market exclusively. Money Market Mutual Funds buy in the so-called "Money Market" - institutions that need to borrow large sums of money for short terms. Usually the individual investor cannot afford the denominations required in the "Money Market" (i.e., treasury bills, commercial paper, certificates of deposit), but through a money market mutual fund he can take advantage of these instruments when interest rates are high. These funds offer special checking account advantages.
[Source: *The World Almanac and Book of Facts 1995*]

One path to enlightenment on mutual funds: Dismantle the definition into all its concepts and start to understand them. Another path: Get out on the Internet, or get a book on financial management, and start learning about mutual funds. Another path: Invest some amount of your own money in a mutual fund. All of a sudden stock prices and "the market" will become important to you. Best path: The next time you hear adults talking about this stuff, tell them you are interested in learning about it and ask them to start explaining it to you. Tell them you realize that it is complicated and will take time, but that you also realize it is important and you want to start learning.

WHY DO MY PARENTS MAKE ME CLEAN MY ROOM?

I was a total slob as a teenager and it drove my mother crazy. I could never understand why, but now I do. Let me try to explain it.

Your parents take good care of their house because they know it is valuable and they know how much work it took to get it. They spent tens of thousands of dollars to make the down payment, and they spend quite a bit of money every month on the mortgage payment. They spend additional money fixing it, redecorating it, buying furniture and appliances for it and so on. They treat their house with respect because it means a tremendous amount to them. Without the house they are homeless.

Now you come along and move into a room and what do you care? You didn't make any sacrifices to buy this house. You aren't making payments. You didn't redecorate it. So you take it for granted. You truly do not care. However, they do, and therein lies the conflict. They want *their* house to look nice. All of it. Sure they love you, but they want you to take care of what they have worked so hard to provide.

WHY DO MY PARENTS MAKE ME PUT THINGS AWAY?

Imagine the following scenario. Imagine your parents at age 26. They have just bought their first home, and they have decided to plant some bushes in the front yard to spruce it up. Just about every cent they had went into the down payment on the house, so they feel pretty poor. In order to plant the shrubs, however, they need a shovel. So they go down to the hardware store and find a shovel that costs $20 (1997).

The shovel turns out to be useful for lots of yard tasks. One day your father uses it for something, and before he gets done and can put it away the phone rings and distracts him. As a result the shovel does not get put away. The next day is Monday, so it is left outside another day. And so on. One of two things happens. Either one day he gets home and it has been stolen, or several months later he finally gets around to putting it away and it has gotten all rusty and the handle has started to rot from being in the rain. In either case, your father now has to buy *another* shovel for $20. That sort of thing really makes you angry with yourself because there are many other things the money could be spent on besides a *second* shovel.

After that same sort of scene repeats itself in your life 50 or 100 times, and after you have spent money on 50 or 100 things twice instead of once, you eventually get in the habit of putting things away. The economics of life have taught you that it is important.

By the time your kids come along and start leaving expensive toys in the yard and all over the house (where they get stepped on and broken), you cannot stand it. You don't want to buy these expensive toys *twice*. It drives you crazy. So you constantly bug your kids about it, and it drives your kids crazy until one day they grow up and go buy a shovel, and then accidentally leave it outside... This cycle has been repeating itself for thousands of years.

As soon as you are paying for things yourself, you will understand exactly why your parents want you to put things away and take care of the things you own.

WHY DO MY PARENTS LISTEN TO SUCH STUPID MUSIC?

If you are a normal teenager, music is probably important to you and you enjoy listening to whatever music is popular at the moment. This is "pop" music, and it is a part of "pop" culture. There are two strange phenomena at work making pop music "sound good" to you:

- Strange phenomena #1: All across the United States millions of teenagers in thousands of communities all seem to love the same songs at the same time. Why is that? The whole idea that there can be "top-40" music is impossible really. Why would teenagers in California like exactly the same music at the same time as teenagers in Iowa, New York and Miami? That makes no sense. Nonetheless that is exactly what happens. Is there a weird force field causing all teenagers to simultaneously wear the same clothes, watch the same shows and listen to the same music? It's hard to say.
- Strange phenomena #2: During your teen years music seems incredibly important to you and your friends, but by the time you reach 30 or 40 you likely won't care about it one bit. However, you will still like hearing the songs you heard as a teenager because they bring back lots of good memories.

These two strange phenomena cause something odd to happen. As a teenager you and millions of teenagers like you are all exposed to a set of songs. You hold these songs in common memory with all other teenagers your same age. Then at some point in your life music becomes much less important to you. It's like a part of your brain turns on and tunes in to music around the time of puberty and then 10 years later it turns off again. Whatever songs you absorb during those 10 years are "your songs." They are also "your generation's" songs. Throughout the rest of your life the songs you absorbed during that 10-year window "sound good" to you, and all other music "sounds stupid."

You, as a teenager, are absorbing songs right now as part of your 10 year window. Your parents, on the other hand, closed their window many years ago and like the songs they heard as teenagers. You think their music sounds stupid, and they think your music sounds stupid. You will do exactly the same thing when you are older.

WHY DO MY PARENTS CARE WHAT I WEAR TO SCHOOL? WHY ARE MY PARENTS ALWAYS BUGGING ME TO SIT UP STRAIGHT?

Your clothes and your posture are two of the most obvious things that people use to form their first impression of you (see Chapter 17). Your parents want you to be successful and they know that first impressions are important to success, so they want you to look good.

WHY DO MY PARENTS CARE IF I HAVE SEX AS A TEENAGER?

If you reread Chapter 9 about sex and babies, you can understand why you and your parents differ on whether or not you should have sex as a teenager. It's because you are looking at it from one perspective and they are looking at it from another. From your perspective sex "feels good." Therefore you want to have sex. From your parents perspective sex "creates a baby." They then extrapolate from that: a baby needs two loving and committed parents who are married, stable and able to support themselves and the baby. Therefore you should not have sex. You are looking at the short-term pleasure of sex. They are looking at the long-term consequences of having a baby. As a teenager you are able to provide nothing that a baby needs, so sex is irresponsible. That is where your parents are coming from. See also Chapter 13.

WHY WON'T MY PARENTS LET ME WATCH TV ALL DAY?

TV is an absolute wasteland. Your parents simply hate to see you waste your life in that way. Life is short, and life is much more valuable to your parents than it is to you because your parents are older and have less life left. Read Chapter 37. Try turning off the TV and doing something different. See Chapter 6 for some activities that can change your life. Successful people do not sit around on the couch all day watching TV.

WHY DO MY PARENTS TREAT ME LIKE A CHILD?

Let's talk about how you came to be born. Your parents, perhaps as teenagers, fell in love. You know what it is like to be in love, and they were *exactly* the same way. They were ecstatic. They got married. They went on the honeymoon. They lived together as a married couple for a period of time and fell more deeply in love. They dreamed about having a baby and saved up money for that day. Then they started trying to have a baby. Perhaps they had to try for six months, each month getting more worried that maybe they might not be able to have a baby. Finally they found out they were pregnant and they were incredibly happy. They told everyone joyously. For nine months they waited and watched and anticipated the moment of your birth. The day you were born was the happiest day of their life together. Their whole life centered around you, the baby. You cannot imagine how important you were to your parents and your grandparents when you were born, or how important to them you are now. They spend every waking moment thinking about you.

They watched you grow. They watched you learn to eat solid food. They watched you learn to walk. They watched you learn to talk. They watched you start school. Each event like this brought them great pride.

During this time of development, however, they knew you as a child. They changed your diapers. They kissed your skinned knees. They washed your drawings off the walls. They tied your shoes.

When you go through puberty a Teenage Illusion Module (see Chapter 2) forms in your brain. It makes you think you are the smartest person in the world. You want your independence! However, your parents know exactly how young you are. They are thinking, "Just a couple of years ago your brain did not possess the structures to allow abstract reasoning, and now you want total independence? Are you kidding???" They are also struggling with the problem every parent faces: They love you so much, but now they must begin to release you so you can go out and become your own person. That is incredibly hard. Add to that the fact that they approach most situations from a long-term standpoint while you approach them with a short-term view and there will be even more disagreement.

All of these things mix together to make the relationship you have with your parents turbulent at times. For your entire life they have known you as a child, and it is hard to shake that knowledge. Therefore, if you want your parents to treat you like an adult, what you can do is act like an adult *all the time*. If you slip back and forth between childish behavior and adult behavior, then they have to continue treating you like a child. If you become a mature adult and display adult behaviors consistently, you will be treated like an adult. By reading this book you have learned many of the facts of life that will allow you to act in a mature manner. In particular, pay attention to chapters like the chapter on anger (Chapter 26) and the chapter on working at a high level (Chapter 22). By acting like an adult *consistently,* your parents will be able to treat you like an adult.

WHY DO MY PARENTS MAKE ME DO MY HOMEWORK? WHY DO MY PARENTS MAKE ME DO CHORES?

Your parents make you do your homework because of a fairly short reasoning chain. The chain goes something like this:

- You have to pay the rent or you become homeless.
- You have to have a job to pay the rent.
- Working 60 hours a week in a dead-end minimum wage job really stinks. Therefore...
- You need to get a good job.

- In order to get a good job you have to go to college or enter some other sort of training program and actually learn something while you are there.
- In order to get into college or a training program you need discipline, good grades and good SAT scores.
- To get good grades you have to do your homework.

Both chores and homework will teach you how to work consistently, even when you don't want to work. Working at a job eight hours a day takes discipline. It will take your brain a while to learn and accept this discipline. Homework and chores help you to get there more quickly and prepare you for the working world. You *must* have a job (see Chapter 1). Your parents are simply getting you ready for it.

WHY DO MY PARENTS AND I FIGHT CONSTANTLY?

If you want to stop fighting with your parents, there are two possible approaches:

- Try unilateral kindness and see what happens. *Unilateral* means *one-sided*. You cannot control them, so try to control yourself. Try for one full month to be a mature, caring, high-level individual. Do not throw tantrums. Do not disobey. When your parents ask you to do something, do it. If you want something ask for it and if they say no say, "I understand." See what happens. You might be surprised.
- Call a truce. Say, "I would like to have a different relationship with you. I understand that in our relationship now there is a great deal of anger and distrust between us. I would like to find a way to solve our problems so that we can have a relationship that is open and loving and trusting. How can we move to that point?" Try it once in your own words and see what happens. If that goes badly, try again and read it from this book. If that goes badly, ask them to read this book and see what they think. Perhaps you and your parents can work on things as a team rather than constantly opposing one another.

CONCLUSION

Your parents are human beings, just like you. They see the world differently because they have had a much broader set of experiences than you have. They have made mistakes, or seen lots of other people make mistakes, and would rather you did not repeat them. One approach would be to listen to your parents. If what they say and do makes no sense ask them to explain it, in detail. Ask them to describe their complete reasoning chain. You might be surprised by what you learn.

CHAPTER 44

America is Designed
for Business

The American Economy is designed for business. That is a fact of life. The entire economic environment of this country favors people who start and operate businesses. By starting a business you have the potential to tap into this economic engine. In this chapter you will learn how you can start a small business in America. In the process you will learn a great deal about how the world works.

Before we start, let's talk for a minute about *The American Dream*. What is the American Dream, and what do people mean when they talk about it? Probably one of the best ways to understand the American Dream would be to go to a poverty-stricken third world country. For example, go to the poorest sections of Mexico, the slums in India or many parts of Africa. What you will find is people living in shacks with dirt floors. There is no running water, no sewer system and no electricity. At any given time it is unclear where the next meal will come from. The adults are thin and stunted from lack of food. The children are dirty and constantly hungry. There is no medical care available, so when someone gets sick they often die. No one is educated, so they cannot read or write. It is not a pleasant way to live life.

For the individual people and families involved, the fundamental problem with these conditions is the fact that there is nothing they can do to change things. They cannot go to school, learn a trade, get a job and start buying food, clothing and shelter. They cannot move somewhere else. They cannot protest against the government for better conditions. They can do nothing.

The American Dream is the opposite of this condition, and it is the reason that people all over the world fantasize about coming to this country. In America there is a huge, vibrant economy. Anyone who lives in this country—even someone living on welfare—has access to running water, food, clothing, shelter and medical care. But there is something else available that is far more important: hope. If you are poor, there is the real possibility that you can completely change your situation in America. You can go to school, learn how to do something, get a job, work hard, earn money and take yourself wherever you would like to go. For every person in this country there is the opportunity to save money and buy a house. What's more, there is no limit to your potential success. In America it is completely possible to go from welfare to millionaire. That is the American Dream. There is no other country on earth where you have the freedom to completely control your life in this way.

It is important to recognize that with freedom goes responsibility. In few other countries on this planet do you have the freedom to go from welfare to riches. At the same time, in few other developed countries do you have the ability to fall as low as you can in America. If you sit around and do nothing in America, you will become homeless. That is a fact of life. The freedom that we have in America means that everyone has the responsibility to use it wisely and make the most of it. It also means you have the freedom to fail.

Given an environment where there is a huge potential reward for trying and succeeding, it makes sense to take a shot. Let's say that you are a normal, average teenager. You are 16 years old. You live in a suburban neighborhood. You do not want to flip hamburgers. You also don't particularly like the idea of working for someone else. But you are willing to work hard and risk failure. If that is your situation then you are a perfect candidate for starting a business. Starting you own business is one of the best ways to tap into the economic engine of this country and achieve the American Dream. It is also a great way to learn about business, people, our government and the economy. A business that you start as a teenager may not be one that you stick with for more than a year or two. However, what you learn in the process will be very valuable to you in your career or in other businesses that you start later.

BUSINESS OPPORTUNITIES

As a 16-year-old teenager there are several different things that are going to determine what sort of business you can start. First of all, you probably do not have access to a tremendous pool of start-up capital (money). Therefore, you are not going to be starting a car company or a steel foundry. You do not have a tremendous amount of experience, so you will want to start something fairly simple. You are still in school, so your business needs to be part-time and you do not want "emergency situations" with your customers conflicting with your school time. Therefore, you might want to create a summer or weekend business. Depending on your personality, you might want your business to be the kind that you can run all by yourself or one that you start with a friend. Given these constraints, what sorts of businesses might your consider? Here are seven suggestions:

- Lawn or yard care—During the summer you mow lawns, trim hedges and so on. In the fall you rake leaves. In the winter you shovel snow.

- House painting, indoor or outdoor—You advertise your ability to paint individual rooms in a customer's house. If you have some experience and are working with a friend, you might want to consider painting exteriors. Exteriors present a much bigger challenge and risk, however, so do not try it unless you have experience or an adult advisor.

- Baked goods (cookies, cakes etc.)—Many families are too busy to bake their own cookies and cakes these days. However, having fresh-baked goods around the house is nice. Also, a family might need a home-baked cake for a school bake sale or a party. You could provide baked goods for special occasions like these or sell baked goods at local craft or farmers markets.

- Baby-sitting—Any community that has families with small children needs baby-sitters. However, it is extremely hard to find reasonably-priced, trustworthy and reliable baby-sitters who are available on a regular basis. Your business would provide in-home baby-sitting services.

- Cleaning—If you enjoy cleaning and do it well, then house cleaning for others is straightforward and easy. Find busy people in your neighborhood and clean for them once every week or two. The same could be done washing cars.

- Dog walking or vacation pet care—Most people who have pets want to give them the best care possible. Your business would help pet owners to do that by walking their pets daily or by providing in-home pet care when owners are on vacation.

- Errand-running for busy people—Busy people often do not have time today to stand in line to get their license plates renewed, to buy groceries or to run other errands. Your business would handle these tasks for them.

All of these businesses could be started with a low initial investment. In the future they could turn into legitimate, full-scale businesses if you are so inclined (see Chapter 22 for an idea on how to turn your business into something much larger). You should be able to think of other business ideas as well. Look around you, look at your neighborhood and ask your parents. What goods or services do people need that they would be willing to pay for on a regular basis?

BUSINESS SUCCESS FACTORS

To create and run a successful business, you have to do just four simple things:

- You must attract clients to your business so that you are able to sell your goods and services to them.
- You must make a profit each time you sell something.
- You must do a good job so that existing clients come back and recommend you to others.
- You must avoid critical mistakes that destroy your business.

Each of these rules is important. Let's examine them one at a time to understand why each is important.

The first rule talks about the importance of clients. Without clients you certainly cannot make any money. It turns out that finding clients is often the hardest part of being in business. It is also important that you sell a product that someone would want to buy. It might be impossible to find clients if you are selling snow shovels in Los Angeles, for example.

The second rule talks about making a profit. The reason you open a business is to make money. If it does not make money it is a hobby or a charity, not a business. You have to be able to set your price and control your costs so that each sale results in a profit substantial enough to support the business. If you do not make a profit, then your business will make no money and it will fail.

The third rule talks about retaining clients. If you do a bad job for a client, the client will either not pay you (thus you lose money) or will never call you again (leaving you with one less client). Either way you lose.

The fourth rule warns against mistakes. If you make a critical mistake, the consequences can be severe. For example, you might:

- run your lawn mower over a prize-winning begonia.
- allow a child to be severely injured while baby-sitting.
- agree to take care of a pet, but never show up because you get sick, causing the pet to die.

In any of these cases your customer will have the right to sue you for negligence or non-performance, and such a lawsuit can cost you an incredible amount of time and money. Being in business is a serious thing and opens you to serious risks if you are not careful.

One of the best ways to "learn the ropes," and especially to avoid the mistakes you might make as a new business owner, is to work for someone who runs a business like the one you are planning to open. For example, if you are planning to run a lawn-care business, you might want to work on a crew for a lawn-care company for a summer and see what kind of equipment they use, what sorts of clients they cater to, how much they charge for a job and what problems they try to avoid. If you are thinking about baby-sitting, you might want to work or volunteer at a church day care center for a period of time. If you are planning to paint rooms, read a good book on painting and paint your entire house for your parents. Or go work for a painter and see how it's done. The techniques, tricks of the trade and problems you discover will be valuable to you when you attempt to start your own business.

In the examples that follow a lawn-care business is used as the primary demonstration business. It is simple and easy to understand. It will also involve spending some money for equipment. This requirement for start-up capital will make the section on business planning more interesting. The techniques that we apply to a lawn-care business are important to any sort of business that you start.

CREATING A BUSINESS PLAN

If you were to attempt to start a business the same day you thought of it, it is very likely that the business would fail. At the very least the business will not reach its full potential, and it is very likely that you will not charge enough for your products or services. There is an adage: "Failing to plan means planning to fail." This adage applies to any business venture. The goal of a *business plan* is to understand exactly how your business is going to operate ahead of time and to accurately predict your costs so that you can price your services fairly. A business is one of the few places where you can predict the future with some accuracy. By building a business plan, you increase the accuracy of your predictions and the chances of your success.

Let me give you an example of the sort of information a business plan can give you. I can remember starting my first business when I was about 6 years old. Every day an ice cream truck came around our neighborhood selling Popsicles and Nutty Buddies. I felt certain I could sell them for less than the ice cream man was charging. So I mixed up a pitcher of cherry Kool-Aid, used Dixie cups for molds and plastic straws for sticks, and I made up a batch of Popsicles that were quite good. I sold them for a nickel each and felt like I was making a fortune. After a week I got bored with it and closed the business.

Why did I feel like I was making a fortune? Because my parents never raised a stink about me using up all of their sugar and Dixie cups. I was running the business, but I was not covering my expenses. If I were to try to start a Popsicle business from scratch, I would have to buy or lease:

- A freezer
- Space for the freezer

- Power for the freezer
- Molds
- Popsicle sticks
- Sugar and flavoring
- Water
- Packaging
- Some sort of distribution system (like a truck)

All of these things cost money. They are *expenses*. After covering all of these costs in the price, I would then have to charge even more to make a profit so that I could pay myself. It is all of the equipment and other expenses, combined with the desire to make a reasonable profit, the cost of advertising, unexpected long-term costs like spoilage, insurance, health permits and so on that makes Popsicles cost so much when you buy them at the store. Many people who start a new business tend to forget these hidden costs, so they do not charge nearly enough for their services. A business plan helps you to discover the costs and plan your prices accordingly.

Here is another example to help you understand the point. Let's say

 Good Books

A good book to read for more information is *Adams Streetwise Small Business Start-up* by Bob Adams. See the references section for more information.

that you jump in and start an errand-running business. Mrs. Jones down the street calls you and asks you to go to the mall to buy her a wedding present for her niece. You hop in your mother's car, drive 20 miles to the mall and 20 miles back and get the present in 1.5 hours. You charge Ms. Jones $7.50 for your time and think you are making a lot of money. You are missing several things, however. One is the cost of gasoline and other general wear and tear on your mother's car. The IRS assumes that it costs the average driver 31 cents per mile (in 1997) to operate an automobile. If you were having to buy the car ($15,000 to $30,000), buy the gasoline (5 cents a mile), replace the tires, change the oil, pay the repair bills and so on, you would understand that. At 31 cents a mile, you should be charging Mrs. Jones $12.40 simply to cover the cost of the vehicle. You should then add payment for your time on top of that. The very minimum you should have charged her is $19.90. Other costs you failed to cover in your price include advertising, setup time, the phone line, etc. In addition, you have charged essentially a minimum-wage rate for your time, and while this is fine (and may be perfectly acceptable to you) as a teenager, it means that the business is not viable in the "real world." You might be

Understanding Business Models

If it costs $30 to pick up a wedding present for Mrs. Jones, why can Domino's deliver a pizza to your door for $10.00 to $15.00? How are they making any money? In discovering the answer to that question you can learn a great deal about how the world works. Go talk to people at Domino's. What do they pay their employees? What do they pay their drivers? What do they pay for floor space and ingredients and power and advertising? How much profit do they make on a pizza? Can you apply any of this new knowledge to an errand-running business? You can learn a tremendous amount by analyzing existing businesses to understand the business model each one uses.

willing to accept that and use your business as a part-time way to make some spending money as a teenager, or you might not. After taking all of these factors into consideration, it turns out that you may need to be charging Mrs. Jones $30 to pick up the wedding gift. Would she be willing to pay that? Perhaps not, and that tells you something about your business and its viability. It certainly tells you something about your pricing structure and the sort of clients you will be seeking.

Building a business plan takes time and effort. Your first impulse, especially as a teenager, will be to jump right in and start your business without doing any planning. Let me ask you to try to suppress that impulse here. As we have seen in the two examples above, the lack of a business plan can cause you to severely under-price your services. If you do that here you stand to lose a lot of money, or you will make a lot of people angry by making promises that are difficult to keep.

A business plan normally consists of a number of standard sections. For the lawn-care example here we will use a simplified plan consisting of the sections listed below:

- General description of the business
- Customer Profile
- Marketing Strategy
- Competition
- Start-up expenses
- Operating expenses
- Pricing model
- Billing model
- Expected revenue
- Risks

Remember that the primary goal of creating this plan is to take the time to sit down and think about things like marketing and finances ahead of time. By doing this planning up front, you will be able to meet the four requirements of a successful business.

General Description of the Business

This section should contain a straightforward description of the business. For a lawn-care business it might say:

> The XYZ lawn care company provides high quality lawn-care services, including mowing, edging and hedge trimming, during the summer months to a select group of clients.

If you are going to provide other services in other seasons, like raking and snow shoveling, then discuss those as well. Mention if you are going to provide service outside the summer months. The key thing to remember is that when you sign clients up for your services, they need to be able to clearly understand what they are getting. For example, if you sign up someone in June with every intention of terminating service in September when school starts, you and the customer should understand that. For many people that will be fine—they might want someone to mow their yard for just three weeks while they go on vacation. For others, however, that may present a problem because they expect the service to last into October when the grass stops growing. Be sure you understand the commitments you are willing to make to your customers and state them in the plan.

Customer Profile

In this section, describe the sort of customers you are seeking. You might, for example, want to precisely target people who need their lawns mowed for two weeks while they go on vacation (and you might be able to provide other services like mail and paper collection if that is your audience). You might want to provide full-time, year-round service to just four people within walking distance of your house. You might want to find 10 people and service them just for the summer and one month into the fall. Think about what you want to do, how long you are willing to do it, how many people you can reasonably service and so on, then describe your customer profile.

In preparing to start your business, it would be a good idea to go talk with some of your neighbors and potential customers and ask them what sort of service they would like to see. This is a *market survey,* and it is a technique frequently used by businesses to determine what products and services the market is willing to purchase.

For your lawn-care business this section of the business plan might state:

> The initial customers of the XYZ lawn-care service will consist of my family and four neighboring families on our street. The business will actively seek four other clients similar in needs to the existing client base.

Marketing Strategy

The marketing strategy describes how you plan to advertise your services so that you can acquire new customers. The options available to you, as a small business with finite scope, include:

- Knocking on doors and personally selling your services
- Mailing out flyers
- Word of mouth, or directly asking people you know to recommend you to others
- Signs posted on community bulletin boards (see http://www.bygpub.com/cbb)
- A small ad placed in the church bulletin or local paper

Each of these approaches has a different cost associated with it. Some are free but require lots of time (door to door). Some are expensive but take very little time (advertising in a church bulletin). Some may sound good but may in fact generate zero responses (mailed flyers may have no effect unless you do it once a week for many weeks).

This section of the business plan might state:

> The XYZ lawn-care company will use a personalized sales model that will involve visiting 100 households within walking distance of my home in the ABC subdivision. At each visit the customer will also receive a flyer describing the business and will be asked to pass the flyer along to anyone who might need lawn-care services.

Competition

Before starting any business it is important to completely understand your primary competition. Some of the things you would like to know include:

- How much does the competition charge?
- How do they determine the charge (flat rate, size of yard, number of trees, etc.)?
- What services do they provide as part of the charge?

- What services do they not provide?
- What commitments do they make to the client?
- What do they do about things like rain?
- How often do they perform their services?

All of the answers to these questions tell you something about your own business. Perhaps the local lawn-care company charges a flat rate of $30 a week for mowing and edging but not hedge trimming and requires the customer to sign a detailed contract that specifies that service will continue for the entire season. You might take that information as input but decide you want your business to work on a verbal agreement that allows the customers to discontinue service whenever they like. That flexibility might give you a competitive advantage, and that decision should appear in your business plan.

In this section, talk to at least two competitors and write down what you find. You might stop and talk to a competing service when you see one of their trucks in the neighborhood, or you can call on the phone and ask for a description of the company's rates and services. Many businesses will also mail you a brochure if you ask for it.

Start-up Expenses

You will need a certain amount of equipment to start your business. One way to obtain it, of course, is to borrow all of your parents' stuff. A better way is to actually buy your own new or used equipment so that you understand the effects of start-up capital on a business.

Let's say that your business model calls for you to service clients within a five-mile radius of your home. Your customers will typically have small yards, so you need a push-style rather than a riding mower. Assume that your parents have given you a car that you plan to use for getting around. Your start-up expenses might look like this:

Start-up Expenses	
Trailer	$400
Trailer hitch, trailer license	$150
Sears model xxx self-propelled lawn mower	$250
Grass catcher attachment for mower	$50
Sears model xxx Gas-powered string trimmer	$125
Two Gas cans	$20
Cost of advertising flyers	$10
Water cooler	$15
Total	$1,020

You need the trailer to haul the equipment around with your car. Everything else is self-explanatory.

Note that if you were in this business for real, you would have to include the cost of your vehicle in your start-up costs. Note also that if you serviced clients within walking distance of your house, you could eliminate almost half of these start-up costs. The part of your business model that causes you to service people "within a five-mile radius" has significantly changed your start-up costs by forcing you to buy a trailer.

Operating Expenses

Your operating expenses will be negligible, but you should list them. They might include:

Weekly expenses	
Gasoline for mowers	$10
Wear and tear on car (30 miles @$0.31/mile)	$10
Two-stroke oil	$3
Wear and tear on trailer (tires)	$2
Total	$25

What these two sections tell you is that every week you have to clear at least $25 to break even, plus you need to do something to pay back your loan.

Pricing Model

There are several different ways to set your price:
- Ask potential clients what they would be willing to pay.
- If your market research shows that the going rate in your neighborhood is $30 a yard, you might charge that. Or you might feel that you are willing to undercut that price by $5 because of your lower start-up costs, so you charge $25 per yard.
- You might decide how much you want to make per hour, look at the costs you need to cover during the summer, determine how long a typical yard takes and set a price from that information.

Billing Model

The billing model indicates how you will bill your customers for services. You might, for example, accept payment in person when you finish each job.

Expected Revenue

Assume that, in your neighborhood, a typical yard takes two hours when you factor in getting there, setting up, cleaning up and getting home. Say also that you are willing to work 30 hours a week for the 12 weeks of summer (a less-than-40 hour week would also give you some slack in weeks after a lot of rain). Assume that you reasonably expect to acquire 10 customers without difficulty, and you believe you can acquire 15 with extra effort. You might have two revenue projections:

Revenue model #1: 10 clients through the entire summer

Revenue projections	
INCOME	
10 customers per week @ $25 per job *12 weeks	$3,000
EXPENSES	
Start-up expenses	$1,020
Weekly expenses @ $25 per week * 12 weeks	$300
RESIDUAL VALUE	
Residual value of equipment at end of season	$400
Total Income	$2,080

In this model, the total take for the summer is projected to be $3,000. The start-up and operating expenses are subtracted from that amount. The "residual value" is then added back in. This is the amount of money that you think you could get if you sold your equipment used at the end of the season. Businesses handle this sort of depreciation in different ways. Here we have taken the simple approach. If you were to run your business a second year, obviously you would not sell the equipment. That would drop your start-up expenses the second year significantly. If not, you will be able to sell the equipment and count that money as part of the income.

What you can see from this revenue model is that you will be working 20 hours a week for 12 weeks to make $2,080. That is $8.66 per hour. What does that tell you? It tells you exactly how much money you will really be making. If you did not create this business plan, then you would never know that number. If you don't like that number, you have several options. You could raise the price or you could seek more customers in order to spread the fixed costs of doing business (the mower, trailer, etc.) across more jobs.

Revenue model #2: 15 clients through the entire summer

Revenue projections	
INCOME	
15 customers per week @ $25 per job *12 weeks	$4,500
EXPENSES	
Start-up expenses	$1,020
Weekly expenses @ $25 per week * 12 weeks	$300
RESIDUAL VALUE	
Residual value of equipment at end of season	$400
Total Income	**$3,580**

In this second model you are working 30 hours a week for 12 weeks to make $3,580. That works out to $9.94 an hour.

Risks

It is important to understand the risks your business will face. The funny thing about business is that it is very hard to completely understand the risks until you know what they are. You can learn about them by trial and error, or you can learn them by working for someone else. Here are some basic risks for a lawn-care business:

- You find no customers—If this happens, you stand the chance of making no money, which leaves you with a loan you cannot repay.
- You find an insufficient number of customers—In this case, you work all summer but do not make enough money to make a profit because of your start-up costs.
- A customer fails to pay—Your billing model should limit this to a single occurrence per customer.
- Equipment failure—If your lawn mower self-destructs you will have to buy another.

You should try to think of other risks, and write about what you plan to do for each one.

GOING TO THE LOAN OFFICER

Based on the start-up expenses detailed in your business plan, you can see that you will need a loan to get this business off the ground. To obtain this loan you have two choices. You can borrow the money from your parents or a relative, or you can go to the bank and try to get a loan. A third option would be to sell stock and use the money raised to start your company. This process is a little more involved, but it is an interesting possibility. Study the history of Ben and Jerry's Ice Cream to learn more. I am going to strongly encourage you to go to the bank and try to get a loan. It is very likely that you will be rejected at all of the banks you go to, but the amount you will learn in the process is so great that it will be well worth the effort. If you try three banks and are rejected three times, you can then consider it time to talk to your parents.

In order to approach a loan officer, you need a business plan. This plan lays out your goals and ideas for the business: what it will do, how it will do it, how you will obtain clients, how much money you might make and how much money you need to get started. With the business plan in hand, you are ready to approach a bank for a loan. The process of building a business plan as described in the previous section should yield for you an adequate plan.

You start the process of getting a loan by making an appointment with the loan officer at the bank. You do this by calling ahead of time. For many teenagers this poses a nearly insurmountable barrier already, because talking on the phone to adults is not something that comes easily. Imagine a call going something like this:

> [Phone rings]
> Adult: Good morning, XYZ Bank. How may I help you?
> Teen: Um. Well, like, is there some way, like, you know, I could ask you, like, well, about a loan??? You know?
> Adult: Excuse me?

You are going to have to come to the point where you have the confidence to call the bank and talk to the people there in a natural and adult-like way. For example, if you can get to the point where you can call the bank and say, "Hello, my name is John Smith. I would like to schedule an appointment with your loan officer to discuss a loan for a small business," you are set. You can get to that point by practicing with

"Toy" vs. "Real" Businesses

What we are talking about here is a "toy" business. You, as a teenager, have the ability under current tax law to make some amount of money without having to worry about taxes. This provision allows teenagers to baby-sit and mow lawns. Provided your business makes less than the maximum amount of money allowed under this provision, you simplify a lot of things. If you want to run a "real" business you will have to approach the world differently. You will have to register your business with the state, for example. You will have to pay taxes. You may need to obtain licenses or permits.

Understand the type of business you are creating. If you find you are extremely successful, make sure you keep track of the boundary between "toy" and "real" so that you can stay legal.

your parents or with another adult friend.

Take a minute to analyze this suggested greeting:

Hello, my name is John Smith. I would like to schedule an appointment with your loan officer to discuss a loan for a small business.

There are several important lessons packed into these two sentences:
- You state your name up front because you are confident, honest and have nothing to hide (see Chapters 14 and 18).
- You know what you want and you state it clearly.
- You call ahead of time to set an appointment. You do that for two reasons:
  1. The loan officer is a busy person. If you drop in unannounced you are making an assumption that the person is just sitting around in his or her office with nothing better to do. That is almost certainly not the case.
  2. Since you are a teenager you will have one strike against you when the loan officer first meets you. You want to delay that strike as long as possible.

The person who answers your call at the bank will probably say one of four things:
  1. "No." This is not a personal rejection, it is a blanket rejection. Perhaps the bank does not make loans to small businesses. In that case call another bank.
  2. "Can you give me more information about your business?" It is quite possible in a small bank that the loan officer will answer the phone directly. If you feel comfortable talking about your business on the phone, then do so. If you do not, you can say, "I have created a business plan. Could I send it to you now, then schedule an appointment to meet with you in person?"
  3. "Yes. How would 2:00 on Monday work for you?" If that time does not work for you, suggest another. Most banks are strictly weekday-only, 9:00 A.M. to 5:00 P.M. businesses, so plan on working into that sort of schedule.
  4. "When would be a convenient time?" Suggest a time that is convenient to you. Keep in mind the normal business hours of the bank.

At this point you should request and write down the loan officer's name: "Can you tell me the loan officer's name?" Let's say it is Sally Johnson. Then you should ask an important question, "Would it be possible for me to send my business plan to Ms. Johnson so she can read it prior to our meeting?" The answer will almost certainly be, "Yes," in which case you should ask for the mailing address. If for some reason the answer is "No," then it probably tells you that you should try another bank.

The whole conversation might go something like this:

> You: Hello, my name is John Smith. I would like to schedule an appointment with your loan officer to discuss a loan for a small business.
> Bank: That would be fine. How would 2:00 on Monday work for you?
> You: Would it be possible to get something closer to 4:00?
> Bank: Yes, on Wednesday that would work.
> You: That is fine. Who will I be meeting with?
> Bank: Sally Johnson is our loan officer.
> You: Would it be possible for me to send my business plan to Ms. Johnson so that she can read it prior to our meeting?
> Bank: Yes.
> You: Can you please give me her address?
> Bank: Our address is 123 Main Street, Peoria, IL, 11111. Send it care of the XYZ Bank.
> You: Thank you very much. I will look forward to meeting Ms. Johnson on Wednesday at 4:00.
> Bank: Goodbye.

Notice how clean and straightforward this conversation is. There is very strong evidence that you know exactly how the world works and that you know exactly what you want. Following the conversation, you should send your typed business plan to Ms. Johnson along with a brief (two- or three-sentence) cover letter. Type her name and address on the envelope.

On Wednesday at 3:55 you should arrive at the bank. You should be wearing your suit and tie. Your suit should fit. Your shoes should be polished. Your hair should be cut in a business-like manner (no pony-tails, no purple hair—see Chapter 8). You should present yourself to the receptionist in the bank by saying, "Hello, My name is John Smith. I have an appointment with Sally Johnson at 4:00 today." You will probably be asked to sit down. If so, sit and read the copy of the business proposal you have brought with you.

When Ms. Johnson comes out of her office to greet you, you should extend your hand. Shake her hand while looking her in the eye and say, "My name is John Smith. Thank you for taking the time to meet with me today" (see Chapter 8). You will be invited into her office and offered a seat.

Now, in Ms. Johnson's mind will appear one or more of the following thoughts:

- "Oh, for Heavens sake: this person is a child. This is ridiculous. Why does this always happen to me? I've got to get this kid out of here or I will be a laughing stock."

- "Oh, for Heavens sake: this person is a child. But it is good to see a young person trying to set himself apart and make a difference. That was a very well done business proposal, too. Let's see what happens."
- "Oh, for Heavens sake: this person is a child. This ought to be interesting!"

You have several things you could say at this point. If you are completely confident, you could open with confidence, just like an adult would, and present your case, "Did you receive my business plan and have a chance to review it? I am glad. As it indicates, I am seeking a loan for $1,200 to start a new lawn-care business. In my plan I have outlined the goals of the business, the predicted financials and the starting capital that I need to get this business off the ground. Are there any questions that I can answer about the business plan?" That might be how a confident adult who has started several businesses in the past would begin the conversation.

Or is it? Is that what an adult would actually say to the loan officer? Possibly, but probably not. An experienced and confident adult would have a prior relationship with Ms. Johnson that had been cultivated over several years. The relationship began when the adult started building his or her credit record with the bank (see Chapter 29) and has continued through a series of monthly greetings, get-togethers and meetings. Therefore, the conversation an experienced adult might have with Ms. Johnson might look completely different. It might look something like this:

Adult: Hey! Sally, how are you doing today?
Bank: John! Good to see you! I'm doing great. How are you liking the new house?
Adult: It's just wonderful. We couldn't be more pleased. Joan just got the living room recarpeted last week and it changed the entire feel of the place. We love it!
Bank: I'm glad. What can I do for you today?
Adult: You remember that preliminary business plan I gave you last week? Did you have a chance to look at it?
Bank: You know, I skimmed it and it looked good. Why don't you come into my office here and fill me in on the details. Or what are you planning to do for lunch tomorrow? Maybe we could get a sandwich and talk about it then.

And so on. You can see that this level of interaction might be radically different from anything you have ever experienced with an adult. The difference is that the two people in this conversation are working from a foundation of a *personal relationship* formed over the course of *several years*, as opposed to a *business relationship* that starts at ground zero. You are probably not in a personal relationship position with anyone at the bank. Unless you have taken the time to form one, or unless your parents have taken the time and effort to ease you in to their relationship with the bank by bringing you along, you know no one. Therefore, you start at a disadvantage. Is that fair? Maybe or maybe not, but it is a fact of life.

Keep this point in mind, and now look at your meeting with Sally in a new light. As a person who does not have the benefit of a personal relationship, you are walking into Sally's office cold. Therefore, one of your primary goals in this interaction should be to begin forming a relationship with Sally. This will be the first of many meetings you hope to have with her as you form that relationship. Another goal of this meeting should be to learn as much as you can about how the world works. It may be wise for you to indicate this goal by saying, "This is my first attempt at starting a business and at working with a bank. I realize I am young, so one of my goals with you today is to introduce myself and to learn more about the process. I would appreciate it if we could discuss my business proposal, and then I would be happy to listen to any comments or suggestions that you might have so that I can make it better." Then begin discussing the proposal. Simply explain each section of the proposal in perhaps a total of three to five minutes.

One of two things will happen. Either the loan officer will be totally turned off because you are so young, listen inattentively for five minutes and politely or rudely eject you from her office. If that happens, simply walk away and forget about it. There is about a 25% chance of it

Important Relationships

Have you ever noticed that rich people seem to have kids who are also rich people? It is not just by accident. One reason is simple: Rich people form a large number of high-quality business relationships, and they take the time and effort to hand those relationships down to their children. Imagine a rich father. He and his wife have cultivated in their children a respect for other adults and the skill of talking to adults comfortably. This training started very early in life. Perhaps the father begins taking his son to the bank when Junior turns 10. He introduces Junior to people, makes sure Junior is a part of certain lunch meetings and continues to do this monthly for a decade. When junior turns 20 and needs a loan, he simply walks in to the bank, sits down with the banker as an old friend and is granted one almost immediately. Fair? Certainly. What is unfair about it? There is nothing that stops *you* from forming a personal relationship with a banker, except for the fact that you have never thought about doing it.

There is a saying: "It's not what you know—it's who you know." This is true. Start meeting people.

happening, and it means absolutely nothing. Do not get mad. Do not get disappointed. Do not get anything. Ms. Johnson simply has no idea what was going on, is likely ignorant of a number of other things as well, and that's life. Simply walk away from it and try a different bank next week. If you are like most people, it will leave a bad taste in your mouth. Wait two or three days and that taste will dissipate and you can forget about the whole thing. Do not waste the time forming a grudge. You have better things to do with your life.

The other possibility is that Ms. Johnson will understand exactly what is going on. You are young, you are wanting to learn how the world works, and you are making an honest, earnest effort to do that in an adult and professional way. It is very likely that she will offer you several pieces of useful advise. For example, she might say the following: "John, I appreciate what you are trying to do. However, there are two things that prevent me from making a loan like this to you. First, you have no credit history. Second, you are still in school and that prevents you from working on this business full-time. That adds a lot of risk to the business. Also, the bank officers would have an extremely hard time making a loan of this size to you unless your parents co-sign it. However, I believe your proposal is sound. Your financial analysis is top-notch. If you would be willing to come back with your parents, I think we might be able to work something out."

As a result of the meeting, you did not get a loan. However, you picked up several useful pieces of information. You learned that your business plan is sound, and that should give you confidence that you are on the right track.

The point of going through the process of getting a loan is not to be embarrassed. It's to learn something. If it makes you feel uncomfortable that is all right—the key to success is facing your discomforts and getting past them with practice.

RUNNING YOUR BUSINESS

Whether you have gotten the money from a bank or from your parents, it is now time to start your business. You can go buy your equipment and begin executing your plan. You can start advertising and signing up customers and mowing their lawns.

One thing you should do while in business is keep careful records. Track every cent you spend and make. Write receipts for customers. You can get an "official" receipt book at an office supply store and that will work. Deposit all money in a bank account and withdraw it as you need to. Putting it in a bank account makes it easier to track.

The important thing to understand once your business is running is that you have made commitments to your customers and you need to keep them. It is very easy to think about starting a business, get it started and then get bored with it. You have to be willing to meet the commitments you make or you will not stay in business for very long.

On the other hand, if you start your business and consistently provide your customers with a quality product professionally delivered, you will find that people will appreciate what you are doing. They will tell their friends. And soon you will have a thriving business. That is the joy of being in business for yourself.

Discrimination?

Why does the fact that you are "young" require you to get your parents to co-sign? This seems like a form of discrimination, but it is not. It does not matter if you are young or old, rich or poor, single or married. Banks all work the same way: Banks loan money to people who have a very high probability of repaying the loan. Banks are not in business to lose money, and no bank wants to give out a loan unless the probability of repayment is high. Think about it: If you have $10,000 on deposit with the bank, you do not want the bank throwing your money away on risky business ventures. The bank echoes the concerns of its depositors.

Therefore a bank wants to have some sort of *security* on each loan it gives. This might be in the form of collateral. For example, when a bank makes a car loan the car acts as collateral. The bank can take the car away from you if you fail to make timely loan payments. In the case of a business loan, the bank wants you to sign a document that says, in essence, "If I fail to repay this business loan, I give the bank the right to take any or all of my personal assets to pay off the loan." When an adult signs a piece of paper like that, he or she is putting his or her house, car, jewelry, furniture, clothes and anything else of value on the line. In essence, the adult will lose *everything* before the bank loses anything. Because you are 16 you have three strikes against you in the bank's eyes:

- You have nothing of value, so the bank sees that you are an extremely poor risk for a loan.

- You have no credit history, so the bank cannot look at your past performance with loans.

- The bank has to take its generalization of the "average teenager" into account. Teenagers, for the most part, are fairly irresponsible and inexperienced. You get lumped into that category whether you like it or not. It is up to you to prove that you are worthy of different treatment, and that is a long, uphill battle.

CHAPTER 45

World Wide Web Resources

The World Wide Web is a gigantic library of material, and much of it is useful to teenagers. For example, nearly every college and university in the country offers a web site that describes the college, talks about the admissions process and lets you view the course catalog electronically. You can also find information on jobs and careers, résumés, love, teenage problems... The list is endless.

Because there is so much good information for teenagers on the web, BYG Publishing offers a companion web site for this book. This site acts as a good starting point for teenagers who want to learn more from the World Wide Web. On this site you will find a huge collection of links for teenagers, additional chapters for this book, questions and answers and many other resources. The site is completely free. Go to:

http://www.bygpub.com

Epilog

This book contains a *ton* of material. It contains stories, advice, exercises and lots of things to think about. If you have taken the time to plow through it all you have certainly loaded a lot of information into your head. You have seen the immutable facts of life and discovered how the world works. You may be asking questions like, "What is the next step? What can I do to become successful? How do I actually apply this material to my life?"

The first thing to do is realize that you *will* be successful. If you set goals for yourself, if you work hard and if you take responsibility for your life and your actions, you will succeed. You will have both good and bad days, but you will become successful and happy if that is your goal and you work toward it.

The next thing to realize is that this is going to take time. Therefore, you want to pick one or two things you feel are important and start to work on them. For example, pick one topic discussed in this book and try to apply it to your own life. If you would like to be more confident, go to the chapter on confidence and try some of the suggestions there. If you want to accomplish something, go to the chapter on goals and try setting one. If you are interested in starting a business, try starting one as described in Chapter 44. If you want to work toward a career, look at Part 2 and test some of the ideas there. Try these ideas with the knowledge that you may fail on your first attempt. Program yourself for perseverance so that you can get past the mistakes and problems you will face as you make yourself successful.

Another thing you can do is look for other books and start reading them. The references at the end of the book give you a place to start. You can pick almost anything you want to accomplish or anything that is causing you a problem, and chances are there is a book available that will help you understand things better. Go to a library or a bookstore (or the Web) and see what you can find.

337

After you sit down and think about this book for awhile, I believe that you are going to notice something interesting. You will begin to see that everything in it is interconnected. Let me give you an example. In Chapter 9 you learned about sex. You also learned that the purpose of sex is to create a baby, and that a baby needs and deserves two parents. That gets you into the subject of marriage. If you are going to have a baby you should be married. That takes you to Chapter 12, where you learned that marriage is about commitment. Commitment has to do with honesty and integrity, which you learned about in Chapter 18. If you are going to get married and have a baby, another thing you need is a home (Chapter 32) and money (Chapter 1) and a good job (Chapter 6). The funny thing is, honest and committed people make good employees (Chapter 7), so your chances of getting a good job increase. And so on.

Do you see what I mean? I can remember as a teenager looking at all these disjointed things and wondering if and how they would ever fit together. I can remember seeing no connections at all. But if you look at it now you can see that all the pieces described in this book lock together like a big jigsaw puzzle. Once you get one part of your life on the right track, other parts begin to fall into place. If you do what's right, life will repay you a hundred times over eventually, even if it doesn't always seem that way at first.

I hope that this book helps you understand the world around you. I hope that you become happier and more successful as a result of reading it. Keep in mind the concepts presented in Chapter 0: You get to design your life, and you can choose to become anything you want. As you transform yourself into an adult, keep these facts in mind so you can control where you are heading. As long as you keep yourself pointed in the right direction, you will eventually get there. That is the key to success!

References

Adams, Bob. *Adams Streetwise Small Business Start-up*. Adams Media, 1996.

The American Heritage Dictionary of the English Language, Third Edition. Houghton-Mifflin Company.

The Bible.

Boorstin, Daniel J. *The Discoverers*. New York: Random House, 1983.

Buscaglia, Leo F. *Living, Loving and Learning*. New York: Ballantine Books, 1990.

Carnegie, Dale. *How to Win Friends and Influence People*. New York, Pocket Books, 1936.

Chilton, David. *The Wealthy Barber: Everyone's Common-Sense Guide to Becoming Financially Independent*. Rocklin, California: Prima Publishing, 1991.

Csikszentmihalyi, Mihaly, Rathunde, Kevin and Whalen, Samuel. *Talented Teenagers, The Roots of Success and Failure*. Cambridge University Press, 1997.

The Columbia Dictionary of Quotations. Columbia University Press.

The Concise Columbia Encyclopedia. Columbia University Press.

de Bono, Edward. *Lateral Thinking*. New York: Harper & Row, Publishers, 1973.

Edwards, Betty. *Drawing on the Right Side of the Brain*. Los Angeles: Jeremy P. Tarcher, Inc., 1989.

Fein, Ellen and Schneider, Sherri. *The Rules: Time-Tested Secrets for Capturing the Heart of Mr. Right*. New York: Warner Books, 1997.

339

Gates, Bill. *The Road Ahead*. Penguin Highbridge Audio, 1996

Gray, John. *Men Are from Mars, Women Are from Venus: A Practical Guide for Improving Communication and Getting What You Want in Your Relationships*. New York: HarperCollins Publishers, 1996.

Herriot , James. *All Creatures Great and Small*. Bantam Books. 1990.

Hilton, Conrad. *Be My Guest*. New York: Fireside, 1994.

Hirsch, E.D. Jr. *Cultural Literacy*. Boston: Houghton Mifflin Company, 1987.

Iacocca, Lee, and Novak, William. *Iacocca, an Autobiography*. New York: Bantam Book, 1984.

Judson, Horace Freeland. *The Search for Solutions*. New York: Holt, Rinehart and Winston, 1980.

Kushner, Harold S. *When Bad Things Happen to Good People*. New York: Avon Books, 1981.

Marin, Peter and Cohen, Allan Y. *Understanding Drug Use: An Adult's Guide to Drugs and the Young*. New York: Harper & Row Publishers, 1971

McCoy, Kathy and Wibblesman, Charles. *Life Happens*. New York, The Berkley Publishing Group, 1995.

Morris, Desmond. *The Naked Ape*. New York: McGraw-Hill Book Company, 1967.

Peck, Scott M. *The Road Less Traveled: A New Psychology of Love, Traditional Values and Spiritual Growth*. New York, Simon and Schuster, 1978.

Peters, Thomas J. and Waterman, Robert H. Jr. *In Search of Excellence: Lessons from America's Best-Run Companies*. New York, Warener Books, 1984.

Ravitch, Diane, and Finn, Chester E. Jr. *What do our 17-Year-Olds Know?* New York: Harper & Row, Publishers.

Schlessinger, Dr. Laura. *How could you do that?!* New York: HarperCollins Publishers, 1996.

Smith, Thomas G. *Industrial Light & Magic*. New York: Ballentine Books, 1986.

Stone, Irving. *The Agony and the Ecstasy*. New York: Doubleday & Company, Inc., 1961.

Teutsch, Austin. *The Sam Walton Story*. New York: Berkley Books, 1992.

von Oech, Roger. *A Whack on the Side of the Head*. New York: Warner Books, 1990.

Waitley, Denis. *Seeds of Greatness*. Old Tappan, New Jersey: Fleming H. Revell Company, 1983.

The World Almanac and Book of Facts 1995. Funk & Wagnalls Corporation.

Index

**BYG** Publishing

For supplements to
The Teenager's Guide to the Real World
and other on-line information,
please see Chapter 45
and visit the
BYG Publishing Web Site at:

http://www.bygpub.com

 **BYG** Publishing

Order Form

Electronic:	sales@bygpub.com, http://www.bygpub.com
Telephone Orders:	Call Toll Free: 1-888-BYGPUB1 Have your VISA or MasterCard ready
Postal Orders:	BYG Publishing, Inc. Order Fulfillment Center P.O. Box 40492 Raleigh, NC 27629

The Teenager's Guide to the Real World
Number of copies _____ at $19.95/copy   Sub-Total: _____

Sales Tax:* _____

Shipping:** _____

Total: _____

Shipping Information:

Name: _____

Address: _____

City: _____ State: _____ Zip: _____

Telephone: (_____) _____

*Sales Tax:
Please add 6.5% for books shipped to North Carolina.

**Shipping:
Please add $3.00 for the first book and 75 cents for each additional book.

Educational Sales:
For information on quantity discounts, please call BYG Publishing at:
1-888-294-7820

Payment:
_____ Check made out to BYG Publishing, Inc.

_____ Credit Card   _____ VISA _____ MasterCard

Card Number: _____

Name on card: _____ Exp. Date: _____/_____

 **BYG**
Publishing

Web
Information

For supplements to
The Teenager's Guide to the Real World
and other on-line information,
please see Chapter 45
and visit the
BYG Publishing Web Site at:

http://www.bygpub.com

BYG Publishing

Order Form

Electronic:	sales@bygpub.com, http://www.bygpub.com
Telephone Orders:	Call Toll Free: 1-888-BYGPUB1 Have your VISA or MasterCard ready
Postal Orders:	BYG Publishing, Inc. Order Fulfillment Center P.O. Box 40492 Raleigh, NC 27629

The Teenager's Guide to the Real World

Number of copies _____ at $19.95/copy

Sub-Total: _____

Sales Tax:* _____

Shipping:** _____

Total: _____

Shipping Information:

Name: _____

Address: _____

City: _____ State: _____ Zip: _____

Telephone: (____) _____

*Sales Tax:
Please add 6.5% for books shipped to North Carolina.

**Shipping:
Please add $3.00 for the first book and 75 cents for each additional book.

Educational Sales:
For information on quantity discounts, please call BYG Publishing at:
1-888-294-7820

Payment:
_____ Check made out to BYG Publishing, Inc.

_____ Credit Card   _____ VISA _____ MasterCard

Card Number: _____

Name on card: _____ Exp. Date: ____ / ____

For supplements to
The Teenager's Guide to the Real World
and other on-line information,
please see Chapter 45
and visit the
BYG Publishing Web Site at:

http://www.bygpub.com

 **BYG** Publishing

Order Form

Electronic:	sales@bygpub.com, http://www.bygpub.com
Telephone Orders:	Call Toll Free: 1-888-BYGPUB1 Have your VISA or MasterCard ready
Postal Orders:	BYG Publishing, Inc. Order Fulfillment Center P.O. Box 40492 Raleigh, NC 27629

The Teenager's Guide to the Real World

Number of copies _____ at $19.95/copy

Sub-Total: _____

Sales Tax:* _____

Shipping:** _____

Total: _____

Shipping Information:

Name: _____

Address: _____

City: _____ State: _____ Zip: _____

Telephone: (_____) _____

*Sales Tax:
Please add 6.5% for books shipped to North Carolina.

**Shipping:
Please add $3.00 for the first book and 75 cents for each additional book.

Educational Sales:
For information on quantity discounts, please call BYG Publishing at:
1-888-294-7820

Payment:
_____ Check made out to BYG Publishing, Inc.

_____ Credit Card _____ VISA _____ MasterCard

Card Number: _____

Name on card: _____ Exp. Date: ____/____